Sacred Sites Contested Rites/Rights

Sacred Sites
Contested Rites/Rights

JENNY BLAIN AND ROBERT WALLIS

sussex
ACADEMIC
PRESS

BRIGHTON • *PORTLAND*

2 4 6 8 10 9 7 5 3 1

First published 2007 in Great Britain by
SUSSEX ACADEMIC PRESS
PO Box 139
Eastbourne BN24 9BP

and in the United States of America by
SUSSEX ACADEMIC PRESS
920 NE 58th Avenue, Suite 300
Portland, Oregon 97213–3786

British Library Cataloguing in Publication Data
A CIP catalogue record for this book is available from the British Library.

Library of Congress Cataloging-in-Publication Data
Blain, Jenny.
    Sacred sites—contested rites/rights : pagan engagements with archaeological monuments / Jenny Blain and Robert Wallis.
       p. cm.
    Includes bibliographical references and index.
    ISBN 978-1-84519-130-6 (pbk. : acid-free paper)
    1. Sacred space—England. 2. Paganism—England. 3. Cultural property—
Protection—Religious aspects—Paganism. 4. Cultural property—Protection—England.
5. England—Antiquities. I. Wallis, Robert J. II. Title.

BL980.G7B53   2007
207'.50942—dc22   2007004312

Typeset and designed by Sussex Academic Press, Brighton & Eastbourne.
Printed by TJ International, Padstow, Cornwall.
This book is printed on acid-free paper.

To all our ancestors,
and to their landscapes
in four nations of Britain
and beyond.

Contents

List of Illustrations	x
Preface	xiii
Acknowledgements	xix

Introduction: The Politics of 'Location'	1
Previous scholarship: pagans and sacred sites	3
Introducing paganisms	6
Neo-tribes, new-indigenes, animist ontologies and living landscapes	9
Discourses and practices, locations and methodologies	11
Chapter outline – sites and areas of interest	17

Chapter 1 'Sacred Sites'? Paganisms, Representation and Imaginings of the Past	21
Tradition, authenticity, enchantment	21
Tradition	24
Authenticity	25
Enchantment	26
The 'sacred' in the sites	28
The preservation ethos	33
The preservation ethos and heritage management	34
Implications of the preservation ethos for the non-specialist	36
Pagan discourses	38
Preservation ethos and 'personal-growth druids'	38
Counter-cultural Druids and festival celebrants	39
Pagans at sacred sites	40

Chapter 2 Avebury	47
The Avebury landscape	47
Avebury and the Sacred Sites project	52
Pagans and sites in Avebury	55
Performing Avebury	64
Silbury Hill and Silbury Hole	70
Archaeologists and pagans: performing ownership	74

Chapter 3   Stonehenge   77

'Stonehenges' in discourse   77
'Managed open access'   82
Media attention   91
Alternative voices   93
Eventing at the 'right time'   96
Sacred partying   97
Stone-standing and solutions   100
Widening participation and engaging diversity?   104
    The future   110
Alternative meanings   113
Animism and the landscape   121

Chapter 4   Derbyshire and Yorkshire: Stanton Moor and Thornborough Henges   124

Stanton Moor, its context and recent history   125
Stanton Moor: engagements and reactions, protestors and
    others   129
    The place   129
    The protest   133
    Representation and ritual   137
Issues and tensions   141
Thornborough henges   144
Contesting landscape   149

Chapter 5   Spirits of Moor and Glen: Pagans and Rock Art Sites in Britain   151

The Kilmartin Valley, Argyll   152
Shamanic tourism: inspiration and appropriation   157
Ilkley Moor, Yorkshire   164
Contesting polarisation   172

Chapter 6   The Rollright Stones and the Rollright Trust   173

The Rollrights: The King's Men, The Whispering Knights
    and The King Stone   174
Folklore of the Rollrights   175
The Rollright Trust   176
Plurality and multivocality: a context of inclusiveness   179
Damage and preservation   181
Facilitating engagement   184

Chapter 7   Reburial, Museums, Pagans and Respect   189
  Pagans and ancestors   189
  Druid voices   194
  Negotiating the issues   201
  Respect, reburial and repatriation   203

*Chapter 8   Towards a Conclusion: Strategies for
  Dialogic Interaction and Future Directions*   209
  'Stepping stones to common ground'   210
    Taking each other seriously, tolerantly, and
      deconstructing negative stereotypes   211
    Productive collaborative dialogues   212
    Research ethics and rights   213
    Joint stewardship programmes   213
    Informed consent protocols   214
  Future directions   215

  Notes   217
  Bibliography   225
  Index   243

List of Illustrations

0.1 Druids and others gather to make ritual in the south
circle at Avebury. 8

0.2 Offerings of cones, flowers and other items at the tiny
circle of Doll Tor, in the Peak District. 10

0.3 Chaco Canyon: a sign to remind tourists that the site is
sacred. 15

1.1 Druids make ritual at Avebury, processing around the
banks and assembling before the 'Devil's Chair' in the
southern entrance. 25

1.2 Artefacts from the past become pagan symbols of the
present. 27

1.3 Thingvellir, Iceland: beauty and history intertwined.
The site is sacred to many people today. 29

1.4 Stonehenge today – 'a dramatic ruin, devoid of people'.
Visitors are restricted to the tourist path around the
monument. 37

1.5 The ASLaN Charter, distributed at the Rollright Stones. 43

2.1 'Tourist Avebury' immediately before summer solstice,
photographed from the south bank. 51

2.2 Inside West Kennet Long Barrow, after winter solstice
2004, with offerings of mistletoe and rosemary, coins,
joss-sticks and a charred smudge-stick. 56

2.3 West Kennet Long Barrow, chalk-art showing an antlered
figure, with offerings. This orthostat displays
soot marks and cracking associated with tea lights. 57

2.4 A poster and litter-bag: pagans associated with Avebury
request that visitors 'respect this sacred site' at summer
solstice 2003. 58

2.5 Text of 'Avebury Guardians announcement, online at the
National Trust website. 60

2.6 Pagans and others begin to assemble at the Red Lion in
the centre of Avebury on solstice eve. 62

2.7 Druids make an arch of staffs at Avebury as part of a
summer solstice ritual. 65

2.8 Tourists and media crowd around the Druid solstice ritual. 66

2.9 Pagans and others at the 'Save Silbury' demonstration,
May 2004. 71

3.1 The impression of 'splendid isolation' is maintained by a
rope which separates tourists from monument. 78

3.2 Images of Stonehenge are reproduced on tea towels and
     many other items, for sale in the Visitor Centre shop.   80
3.3 Prior to the summer solstice 2006 managed open access
     event, English Heritage released this statement as well
     as a comprehensive list stipulating 'Conditions of
     Entry'. Similar conditions were made available in
     previous years.   85
3.4 A Stonehenge of alternative lifestyles (2001). Memories
     of the Battle of the Beanfield and the years of the
     exclusion zone.   86
3.5 Nora Morris, celebrated and loved by all who knew her:
     a veteran of Greenham Common and a stalwart
     campaigner for Stonehenge to be open to those who
     would celebrate there.   87
3.6 In the growing light, people wait for sunrise at
     Stonehenge on summer solstice.   94
3.7 The fenced monument as seen from the A344 today
     (2006).   98
3.8 A vague and simplistic reason embedded in heritage
     'preservation ethos' discourse for why the stones are
     inaccessible during usual daylight opening hours,
     from the 'Frequently Asked Questions' of the English
     Heritage website devoted to Stonehenge.   104
3.9 Tourists, confined to the path, may 'experience'
     Stonehenge through an audio-tour.   109
3.10 Stonehenge 'improvement options' current in 2006.   112
4.1 By the Nine Ladies circle, an outcrop shows new
     'rock art'.   131
4.2 Arbor Low Henge, immediately after Samhain, looking
     across the flattened stones to the entrance to the henge
     and the landscape beyond.   132
4.3 The Nine Ladies circle shows many moods through
     the seasons.   139
4.4 A banner above the path to the Nine Ladies shows
     protestors' opposition to the idea that 'it's OK'.   139
5.1 Temple Wood, in the Kilmartin Glen, is the site of two
     circles including one of the oldest stone circles in the
     British Isles.   153
5.2 Achnabreck, south of the glen and approaching
     Dunnadd, has the largest expanse of rock art in
     Scotland.   161
5.3 The landscape of Kilmartin Glen showing the Glebe
     Cairn, part of Kilmartin's linear cemetery.   162
5.4 Contemporary rock art on Ilkley Moor: A 'Pictish'
     style deer.   167

5.5 Contemporary rock art on Ilkley Moor: a carved Gorgon's
     head is accompanied by a triangle, both coloured red,
     with a Capricorn symbol in silver fixed into the rock
     inside the triangle.   168
5.6 Runic graffiti at the Willy Hall's Wood Stone,
     Ilkley Moor.   168
6.1 Visitors to the King's Men stone circle try their hand
     at dowsing.   185
6.2 The Whispering Knights, a dolmen, with project
     members Robert Wallis and Andy Letcher.   186
6.3 The stones are reflected in the sculpture by Kapoor.   186
7.1 An imaginative reconstruction of the original
     Woodford burial, by Philip Shallcrass, 2003.   200
7.2 The chambered cairn at Nether Largie South is the
     oldest in the Kilmartin 'linear cemetery'.   207

Preface

'Is Stonehenge worth it?' was a question we were all asked. . . .
At one level, the answer has to be 'No'; but, at another, and more
strongly, it has to be 'Yes', if only because the Stonehenge issue
was not only about Stonehenge. For decades now, events at
Stonehenge have continued to reflect in miniature the changing
spirit of the larger society in which it stands. What we see in this
mirror for our times is about ourselves, all of us, including you –
our past and our present and, some would say, our future too.
(*Who Owns Stonehenge?* Chippindale et al. 1990: 8)

At the outset of the twenty-first century, Britain is one of the mostly
densely populated areas of Europe and the world. In its four nations,
most people are urban-dwellers. Art and creativity appear less valued
than science and technology, communication is instant through
broadband and mobile technology, and the consumer, if not king, at
least seems to have power. Amongst what is consumed is 'heritage'.
Ideas of heritage as ancient and enduring appear of persistent interest, and indeed attract tourists from all parts of the world. People
come to Britain in search of roots or in search of 'ancientness'. People
from all over Britain consume 'television archaeology' and heritage
'restoration' programmes, and on a more local scale endeavour to
defend aspects of 'heritage' which have meaning for them. The
tourist gaze encompasses built environment and local people alike.
Heritage tourism is a major industry in today's Britain, and icons of
heritage symbolise variously 'Britishness' or its component national
parts on a global scale. Everyone has heard of Stonehenge or seen
images of this world-famous site on an almost daily basis – on television, on bill-boards, in magazines and in other visual media. The
prehistoric monuments of Britain, particularly the World Heritage
Sites of Stonehenge and Avebury in England, or the stone circle of
Callanish in Scotland, or in Wales the dolmen named Pentre Ifan, are
icons of Britishness (as well as Englishness, Scottishness and
Welshness, respectively), signatures of great and enduring antiquity,
and images of this heritage surround us.

These visual cultures are, of course, mediated re-presentations, not
neutral, objective or impartial interpretations (e.g. Smiles and Moser
2005) and representations resonate with stories, narratives and identities of the present. At the most basic levels, places and representations
are contested. Callanish becomes an icon of Lewis, of the Hebrides, of

Scottishness or of Britishness, or of all of these at once, to different people. Through various disseminations of these re-presentations of the past in the present, people may associate themselves in diverse ways with episodes, times, places and perceived 'ancestors'. Stonehenge especially is represented as timeless, enduring, unique and mysterious, both in heritage literature and in popular culture, and especially the media. This air of mystery is not new: the romantic paintings of John Constable and J. M. W. Turner depict a ruined monument isolated in a mist-laden, pastoral, landscape idyll. More recently, English Heritage has mobilised the romance of Stonehenge in its visitor information, and the Stonehenge Project aims to remove the modern roads and visitor centre in order to return the site to a perceived 'original' state, or at least one free of the intrusions of the modern world (major roads, car park, inadequate visitor centre, etc.).

The mystery of Stonehenge (and other archaeological sites often eclipsed by this magisterial site that are no less significant) is a quality also embraced by an increasingly prominent interest group – contemporary pagans – as well as other 'alternative' visitors. Paganism as a generic term encompasses several recognised and coherent sets of beliefs and practices – perhaps more accurately discussed as *paganisms*, with a variety of allied or associated 'paths' or 'traditions' including Wicca, Druidry, Heathenry, and Goddess Spirituality,[1] which focus on direct engagements with 'nature' as deified, sacred or otherwise animated by 'spirit' or forming a living community of 'spirits'. Pagans associate themselves with particular times or cultures and with historic landscapes, constructing spiritual identity by recovering and reclaiming ideas, stories, sites and artefacts. Pagans engage with pagan pasts and the pasts associated with ancient sites, and pagans themselves are a source of interest to others. Many people, in Britain, Europe and beyond to North America and elsewhere, are familiar with the televised annual fiasco over access to Stonehenge at the summer solstice, for instance. Indeed pagans and heritage-seekers from the US, Canada, Australia and all areas of Europe make the pilgrimage to Stonehenge for this and other festivals; some to celebrate the sacredness of landscape and the mystery of the stones, some to see others celebrate, and to feel they are part of an occasion that links cultures of the present with antiquity. Issues of solstice and access have been foregrounded in National Geographic online (Mayell 2002) and in the magazine of the Archaeological Institute of America (Powell 2003) in addition to British magazines and newspapers. Contemporary pagans and others with an interest in 'sacred sites' are increasingly drawn to the past, to these special monuments, to the landscapes they are situated in, and to the beliefs and ways of life of the ancestors who built and used them. Pagan claims to the past, with their rites at sites, as well as claims for rights, alongside those of 'new travellers', earth mystics and other alternative communities, are celebrated as typically, eccentrically British by some people, and resisted by those who see a threat to sacred sites. As perhaps they always have been, sacred sites are contested sites.

During the summer solstice in 2006 (21–22 June), English Heritage facilitated 'managed open access' for 17 hours (8 p.m. on Tuesday to 1 p.m. on Wednesday), allowing an estimated 21,000 people into the Stonehenge environs – including within 'the Stones' – to celebrate the auspicious occasion. This was the seventh consecutive year such an event had been organised, agreed by most to have been largely successful, and something of an achievement after the difficult years since the Stonehenge Festival which had culminated in the infamous 'battle of the beanfield' between new travellers, pagans and others, and the police in 1985. Stonehenge may quite obviously capture the imagination of popular culture, but many of the other prehistoric sites in Britain are increasingly a focus of pagan attentions as well. At Avebury, the World Heritage Site twin to Stonehenge, 16 per cent of people expressed 'spiritual motivation' and 11 per cent said 'personal meditation' was the purpose of their visit (Calver 1998). Indeed, at Avebury in recent years, local pagans have worked in an unofficial capacity with the National Trust to establish a Guardianship Scheme to protect the monuments from such human impact as chalk graffiti and votive offerings of coins wedged into the cracks of megaliths. Across the country, people are attending to the needs of their local 'sacred sites'.

Such attention has been vital over the last decade or so. Around the spring equinox of 1993 at the stone circle of Doll Tor in Derbyshire, 'persons unknown "restored" it prior to holding rituals there' (Barnatt 1997: 81). In 1996 and 1999, stones of the West Kennet Avenue at Avebury were covered with painted graffiti, some of it claimed by the academic archaeology journal *Antiquity* to be the work of 'new age crazies'. Also in 1999, on 'the sacred night' of the fifth of November, a group calling itself 'Friends of the Stone' vandalised the famous Cornish site of Men-an-Tol, by setting fire to an ersatz napalm-like substance. In April 2004, yellow paint was splattered over the Rollright stones in Oxfordshire, apparently as an April Fool 'joke'. Soon after this vandalism, the cup-and-ring engraved Willy Hall's Wood stone on Ilkley Moor was daubed with rune-staves in red paint. More recently, in March 2005 one of the stones of the Twelve Apostles stone circle on Ilkley Moor was split in two, probably by a single heavy blow with an instrument which caused the stone to crack. Just as 'sacred sites' in Britain are receiving increasing attentions from those who respect them for spiritual reasons, so bizarre instances of vandalism begging the term 'ritualistic' seem to be in the ascendant also.

The sheer diversity of alternative interests makes it impossible to hold a single group responsible for negative impacts on archaeological sites. These are serious instances of vandalism, but they cannot all be linked reliably to pagans and in our collating of them here we do not suggest a cohesive link; at the very least, the decentralised and heterogeneous nature of paganisms signals these are isolated and rare events. It is also misleading to polarise 'heritage-friendly pagans' from 'heritage-abusing pagans', or even associating all such activity with a singular, homogenised 'paganism' at all – the more accurate but cumbersome 'paganisms' might be preferable. At the summer solstice at Stonehenge, some people climb the trilithons in contravention of English Heritage's 'conditions of access', while others persuade them to come down, sometimes physically dragging them; a case of community self-policing. Meanwhile, parents help their children to climb fallen stones in a megalithic 'playground' and people inevitably walk over fallen stones when so many people are cramped into such a confined space, risking damage to rare lichens. Issues of access to sacred sites, what sort of 'damage' is reasonably acceptable and what people should do and should not do at them are complex and are not focused on one specific interest group or the clash of one group with another.

The variety of alternative interests in these special places, motivations for visiting them and doing whatever it is that people do at them – from hand-fasting (pagan marriage) and child blessing to ritual graffiti – and the impact this has on sites, indicates that a sustained academic study is begging. This book, attending to these complex and timely issues, is the result of a cross-disciplinary collaboration. The *Sacred Sites, Contested Rights/Rites* project (<http://www.sacredsites.org.uk>), co-directed by an archaeologist of visual culture, Dr Robert J. Wallis (Richmond University), and an anthropologist, Dr Jenny Blain (Sheffield Hallam University), has spent the past six years exploring theoretical and pragmatic on-site issues of how British archaeological sites have been renamed 'sacred sites' by the pagans and other alternative interest groups who engage with them 'spiritually', and indeed by heritage management itself which has had to negotiate these issues. The Sacred Sites project has examined the renewed currency of 'sacredness' in archaeology and pagan discourse, and the interface between them. In so doing, we have explored practical and theoretical issues of paganisms and identities in today's society, as well as meanings of 'sacredness', beliefs and practices.

Our exploration of the discursive construction of 'sacred sites' by pagans and heritage management arose from research based in perceptions of changing and problematic inscriptions of meaning and 'rights', within a context of the growth of paganisms, particularly in Britain and the US, as expressions of (often counter-cultural) 'spirituality'; of emerging (increasingly reflexive) research on paganisms in various parts of the world (e.g. Blain, Ezzy and Harvey 2004); and of increasing interest in 'the past' (especially via 'television archaeology') as contributor to the shaping of British identities in the present. Initial work on *Sacred Sites, Contested Rights*, later funded by Sheffield Hallam Human Rights Centre (in 2001-2002), confirmed the importance of this area for detailed investigation, as validated by an ESRC research award (ESRC RES-000-22-0074) in 2002–2003 which enabled the funding of a post-doctoral researcher, Dr Andy Letcher. Wallis and Blain, meanwhile, have conducted ongoing site visits, interviews with the interest groups, participant-observation in pagan rituals and round table meetings, and photographic recording at pagan festival times over the six years of the project.

The project's output has included co-authored journal articles (e.g. Blain and Wallis 2004a, 2004b, 2006d; Wallis and Blain 2003) and chapters in edited volumes (e.g. Letcher, Blain and Wallis forthcoming; Blain and Wallis 2006b). In an effort to reach both academic and pagan audiences, this includes papers in popular magazines (e.g. Wallis and Blain 2004; Wallis 2002a) including those read by pagans (e.g. Blain and Wallis 2002, 2006c; Wallis 2002b). More immediately, we have given papers from the project at a range of venues, internationally, including the Association of Social Anthropologists conference, ASANAS (Alternative Sprualities and New Age Studies) events, the British Sociology Association Study Group on Religion, Cambridge Heritage Seminars, ESRC seminars on European Ethnology, conferences of the Centre for Tourism and Cultural Change, and others including practitioner events such as Pagan Federation conferences and the Association of Polytheist Traditions event in 2006, and prepared and made available discussion documents via the project website. In addition, we have offered submissions to such official bodies as APPAG (All Party Parliamentary Archaeology Group, January 2002; see: <http://www.sacredsites. org.uk/reports/APPAG.shtml>), English Heritage (July 2001, see: <http://www.sacredsites.org.uk/reports/StonehengeJune2001.html>), and the Peak District National Park Authority (March 2004: see <http://www.sacredsites.org.uk/reports/pdnpacomments.html>).

The issues raised by the *Sacred Sites* project have implications for, most obviously, archaeologists who excavate and interpret sacred sites, and heritage managers who curate (re-present, manage and conserve) them. The implications extend to anthropologists interested in constructions of identity in contemporary Britain and the contribution of prehistoric 'sacred' heritage to identity formation among those – such as tourists from the US – with ancestry in Britain. Local communities and the hospitality industry are also implicated – as, of course, are pagans and associated alternative communities themselves. This book represents a bringing together of many different encounters of pagan and management perspectives of sites and landscapes. In it, we attempt to delineate varied and diverse understandings and approaches, and indicate ways in which hostilities may be tempered and alliances forged, very differently in the specific places and areas which we detail here. But such events are not isolated to Britain: elsewhere in the world 'sacred sites' are a focus of increasing attention and tension, from Angkor Watt in Cambodia to Chaco Canyon in New Mexico, and from Uluru (formerly Ayer's Rock) in Australia to Machu Piccu in South America. We have focused our attentions on England with a wider eye on Britain generally, and in contact with colleagues working in other parts of the world. We are active participants in the increasingly prominent cross-disciplinary study of 'sacred sites'. And we are seeing an emerging sub-discipline of 'sacred sites studies'. These trends indicate that, within the scope of this study, interest in archaeological sites and the past from Britain's contemporary pagans and other alternative communities demands serious attention. This volume attends to these demands academically, while cognisant of the fact that attention, discussion and debate beyond the academy is also essential.

Acknowledgements

This book would not have been possible without the assistance and co-operation of many people in the pagan and alternative communities who consented to our interviews, photographs and other intrusions into their activities at sacred sites across the country, as well as those on a variety of email discussion lists whose perspectives on the past contributed to the development of the project. Thank you. In particular, we would like to honour the memory of Nora Morris, a long-standing peace campaigner, negotiator for solstice access to Stonehenge and major contributor to the 'peace process', who died on 8 January 2006. Valuable feedback was gratefully received at a number of conferences over the duration of the project, including the Association of Social Anthropologists, TAG (Theoretical Archaeology Group), ESRC Research Seminars in European Ethnology, Cambridge Heritage Seminars, The Open University Religious Studies Research Group, British Sociological Association Study Group on Religion, Celtic-Nordic-Baltic Folklore Symposium, Pagan Federation, ASLaN (Ancient Sacred Landscape Network), Folklore Society and Megalithomania: Celebrating 5000 Years at the Monuments. The *Sacred Sites, Contested Rites/Rights* six-month pilot project was initially funded by *Sheffield Hallam Human Rights Fund* and was supported by the School of Social Science and Law, Sheffield Hallam University and the Department of Archaeology, University of Southampton. An Economic and Social Research Council grant (ESRC RES-000-22-0074) facilitated important aspects of the project's development, including the post-doctoral work of Dr Andy Letcher.

The bulk of the project was conducted while Wallis was in post as Associate Professor of Visual Culture and Associate Director of the MA in Art History at Richmond University in London, and the university has been supportive by way of an extremely collegial environment and grants for conference attendance from the Faculty Research and Development Committee. A special thank you to Alex Seago, Chair of the Department of Humanities and Social Sciences, for his enthusiasm, especially for our bi-annual 'Pagan Sacred Sites' trips – and to all those students who attended, and Martin Winter; another to Elizabeth Lawrence and Rob Sykes, previously heads of Sociology and of Social Policy at Sheffield Hallam University, and to Peter Arnold, current head of Sociology and Social Policy, whose support has enabled conference trips and greatly facilitated theoretical dimensions of the project; to Phil Rumney and Mark O'Brien, whose

Human Rights Fund gave a start to the work, and all the students on the 'Belief, Consciousness and Taboo' undergraduate module and on the MA Social Science Research Methods, again at Hallam, who have put up with various accounts of its construction.

Last but not least, we thank our friends and colleagues in paganisms, archaeology, heritage management, campaigning organisations, anthropology and religious and tourism studies, and apologise to those neglected by this list: Karin Attwood, John Barnatt, Marion Bowman, Tim Champion, George Chaplin, Simon Crook, Paul Devereux and the Dragon Project Trust, Thomas Dowson, Alexa Duir, Clews Everard, Doug Ezzy, the late George Firsoff, Nick and Carol Ford and all at Grey Mare, Christopher Gingell, Pete Glastonbury, Darren Glazier, Graham Harvey, Liath Hollins, Jon Humble, Ronald Hutton, Nathan Johnson, Katy Jordan, George Lambrick, Andy Letcher, Kenneth Lymer, Kevin Luce, Gordon MacLellan, David Miles, Andy Norfolk, Diana Paxson, King Arthur Pendragon, David Picard, Mark Pilkington, Melanie Pomeroy, Tim Previtt and the 'Megalithic Meets', Emma Restall Orr, David Picard, Mike Pitts, Dave Raven, Mike Robinson, Kathryn Rountree, Ian Russell, Tim Sebastion, Philip Shallcrass, Clare Slaney, Donald Sutton, Andy Tickle, Chris Tweed and 'Stones', Jez Uppadine, Brian Viziondanz, Rowan of White Dragon fame, and those who have sung with us in long barrows and processed with us over moorlands, talked with us, played music and sung at sacred places, or given us your feedback or your ideas. You do not all know each other, and you do not all 'get along' with each other, but to all we say 'Thank You' as this project and this book are in part due to you.

The Politics of 'Location'

That 'heritage matters to people' might seem obvious. Who, though, are those people to whom it matters? They are not a generic 'public', nor can they all be described simply as 'tourists' and many of them do not see themselves as merely 'visitors' to sites, locations, museums or galleries demarcated by officials as 'heritage'. The condition of heritage, including prehistoric monuments, is centrally a matter of ongoing concern to archaeologists and heritage managers (e.g. Cleere 1989). It is such also to increasing numbers of 'alternative' interest groups, most notably contemporary pagans. Yet where the impact of tourists, unscrupulous land owners and developers, and farmers is often addressed by archaeologists (e.g. Morris 1998), the actions and agency of alternative interest groups have only recently been seen as worthy of note. Heritage management in the UK seems to be adopting – or co-opting – a new term: the 'sacred site'. This advent begs analysis: what range of meaning is encompassed by this term 'sacred', to whom, and what implications does it have for the future of heritage management?

Heritage bodies such as English Heritage, the National Trust, Historic Scotland, and CADW (Welsh National Heritage) appear increasingly aware of the 'sacred site', since this nomenclature is finding its way into heritage discourse – not only in the discourse of indigenous archaeology on the global stage, but in the heritage discourse of Britain. The English Heritage World Heritage Site Management Plan for Avebury argues: 'Paganism may well be the fastest growing religion in Britain and this is linked with the increasing interest in the mystical significance of Avebury as a "sacred" place' (Pomeroy 1998: 27). Commenting on his negotiations with Pagans, David Miles (Chief Archaeologist, English Heritage) used the term 'sacred site' when referring to 'Seahenge', stating: 'the experience of working and discussing with [Pagans] was extremely fruitful' (Wallis and Lymer 2001: 107). Similarly, during his involvement at Seahenge, archaeologist Francis Prior, commenting on the *Time Team* special on Seahenge, stated that: 'I think that what I've learnt, largely due to our pagan friends, is that as an archaeologist I'm too analytical and I'm too removed from [Seahenge] . . . I've learnt to get back to treating it as a religious site, as a religious thing'. And Clews Everard, former manager of Stonehenge, agreed that the term 'sacred site' enabled round table dialogue over open access negotiations (pc). The Conservation and Management Plan for the Rollright Stones (Lambrick 2001), meanwhile, explicitly addresses pagan engagements with the site and how these can be managed.

This book is the outcome of over six years of research exploring contemporary pagan engagements with the past, principally at prehistoric monuments in England. While we have been involved in the monitoring of sites elsewhere in Britain (for example the Kilmartin Valley in Argyll, to which we make a brief incursion here) and abroad (for instance, Carnac and associated monuments in Brittany), the project focuses on monuments in England at this time in order to offer a detailed analysis of a selection of sites and their political and social locations rather than a generalist overview of many. The project has been collaborative, with the authors being an archaeologist of visual culture (Wallis) and an anthropologist (Blain). Our approach has been qualitative, examining the ways in which pagans engage with sites, why they do this, when, and with what implications; rather than that of quantitatively or 'scientifically' measuring erosion rates, etc. There is no single way in which pagans engage with sites. Indeed, analysis of the diversity of engagement, understanding, interpretation and perception are key components of this study.

On the one hand, the concept of pagan uses of sacred sites conjures 'harmless' images of romantic Druids, either in sacred groves or in stone circles. On another, it appears problematic: Pagans create 'ritual litter' and demand open access policies. In this light pagans are perceived as a monolithic group, as people who engage in 'strange' practices and leave 'offerings' such as flowers or tea-lights, and who may cause graffiti, fire or other damage to ancient 'monuments'. Within existing reports, the preservation ethos appears in binary opposition to the 'visits' of pagans, new travellers, and others who seek to use sacred sites for spiritual/community purposes; and likewise to those of most earth mysteries adherents (or 'earth mystics'), who might poke things into the ground in pursuit of ascientific 'research'. We show, here, rather different practices, and indicate ways in which these constituencies, far from being a threat to 'heritage', contribute to understandings of place, landscape and identity, and further may constitute the greatest support where other threats emerge. There exist a number of areas in which a climate of misunderstanding and mistrust has emerged between heritage managers/archaeologists and pagans/alternative interest groups, though with some attempts to challenge this by individuals or groups. These sustained and serious attempts might, in our view, be supported by analysis of the discursive and political frameworks in which contestations occur. The (still) ongoing negotiations around

Stonehenge open access are a case in point: during negotiations around this hotly contested site, it often becomes hard for those actively working to promote harmony to see where the discursive boundaries of other (official, political, or alternative) framings lie, and the implications of phrasing and emphasis in creating trust or mistrust. While the monument itself is central to many interpretations, contingencies of politics and history create distrust and factionalism. Official discourses enable different questions from those of pagans and other alternative interest groups, and these differences require exploration to facilitate transparency of intention.

Previous scholarship: pagans and sacred sites

There is an extensive literature on heritage and tourism pertaining to sacred sites (for incisive discussions of tourism and heritage see e.g. Urry 1990; Boniface and Fowler 1993), and on indigenous archaeologies and anthropologies regarding site-specific issues (e.g. Layton 1989a; Carmichael et al. 1994; Swidler et al. 1997; Smith 1999; Watkins 2000), yet little attention has been paid to pagan and alternative understandings of 'sacred sites' or similarities between indigenous understandings and inscription of sacredness elsewhere (Hubert 1994) and these pagan interventions. We take note of how tourism research is extending into areas of how people are changed by place and landscape, in addition to how landscape is narrativised, 'packaged' and commodified for a tourist gaze which is itself not a unitary approach or experience. Work of the *Centre for Tourism and Cultural Change* has formed a focus for analysis of place and people that, because not 'contained' with any single discipline area, can inform critical ethnography and comment that connects anthropological theory with social and heritage policy implications. Thus, in this volume, we attempt to relate understandings from Pagan Studies and anthropology to the specific situations relating pagans and heritage 'monuments', in order to provide understandings and insights that may inform both policy and practice.

While the scholarship on paganisms has become a sub-discipline in itself over the last decade or so (e.g. Harvey and Hardman 1995; Harvey 1997; Hutton 1999; Blain 2002; Greenwood 2000, 2005; Pearson 2003; Wallis 2003; Blain, Ezzy and Harvey 2004; Clifton and Harvey 2004), there has been little academic comment on pagan engagements with archaeological and other sacred sites. The most even-handed treatment outside 'Pagan Studies' appears in work by Chippindale and Bender (e.g. Bender 1993, 1998; Chippindale 1986; Chippindale et al. 1990). A multiplicity of views is presented in this important if now dated work, yet it focuses on Stonehenge and there is clearly a need to look beyond this monument to other locations. Furthermore, there is no direct engagement with the approaches of heritage managers in Bender's volume (in fact the voice of English Heritage is invented in her 1998 discussion).[2] Interestingly, the National Trust Avebury Management Plan (1997) and English Heritage Avebury World Heritage Site Management Plan (Pomeroy 1998) raise concerns about pagan engagements with sites, but these documents homogenise the diversity of pagan practices and offer no strategies for addressing the situation. Pagans are simply 'there', and we address this neglect of diversity in later chapters. More cognisant of the significance of pagan interests and in contrast to other site management plans, the plan for the Rollright Stones goes some way to assuming that active engagement with the site is negotiable, and indeed desirable (Lambrick 2001). In terms of gauging perspectives on sacred sites, the Avebury Visitor Research 1996–1998 (Calver 1998) conducted by Bournemouth University for the National Trust is an important contribution, but once again is site-specific and in not moving beyond general comment it fails to establish specific Pagan engagements with sites and their implications. More generally in archaeology, important if sporadic efforts have been made to establish the study of 'alternative archaeology', principally Denning's pioneering work (Denning 1999a, 1999b), as well as Meskell's criticial analysis of the use of ancient 'evidence' by Goddess Spirituality (Meskell 1995, 1998, 1999), and Finn's (1997) paper on New Age activity at Chaco Canyon in New Mexico (developed in Wallis 2003).

More recently, Ivakhiv (2001) has theorised engagements with sacred sites in his examination of various forms of pilgrimage, including pagan, to the sites of Glastonbury (Somerset, UK) and Sedona (Arizona, USA). Ivakhiv agues that as spaces where meaning is created, contested and negotiated by a variety of agencies (only some of whom are held to be human), sacred spaces are – drawing on Foucault – heterotopic. This theorising is important to our own discussion but Ivakhiv's case studies are specific to two examples only, both of which implicate many non-pagan interests. Hetherington (2000) also deploys the concept of heterotopias in his study of new travellers, including traveller interests in Stonehenge, with travellers occupying 'a place of alternative order, an as-yet-uncertain order' (Hetherington 2000: 175), or 'an unrepresentable "place of otherness" ambivalence, paradox and shifting representations' (Hetherington 2000: 28). Accordingly, '[s]uch spaces do not exist in themselves but are instead the revelation of ordering processes attached to space' (Hetherington 2000: 28. See also discussions of 'third space' by Bhabha [1994] and Soja [1996]). Again,

Hetherington's theoretically engaged discussion informs our approach here, but his volume concentrates on new travellers, without discussion of pagans – perhaps the most significant interest group engaging with sacred sites at the present time. Outside Britain, at the 'goddess' site of Çatalhöyük in Turkey, the ongoing interest of Goddess followers has behoved archaeologist Ian Hodder (1997) and his team to engage reflexively with alternative interest groups: Hassan (1997), however, argues that where Hodder claims multivocality (e.g. Hodder 2000), it is still the white, male academic whose more 'legitimate' interpretations prevail over and above Goddess Spirituality. More recently, Rountree (2003a) has discussed issues of conflicts which may preclude reflexivity and personal insights – academic competitiveness may make people unwilling to discuss these freely. Increasingly, none the less, community and other archaeologists are reflexively brokering their knowledge beyond academe (e.g. Lucas 2001; the Community Archaeology Project at Quseir al-Qadim in Egypt <http://www.arch.soton.ac.uk/Projects/projects.asp?ProjectID=20>, and various articles by UCL's Leskernick project <http://www.ucl.ac.uk/leskernick/articles.html>). Furthermore, Rountree's (e.g. 2002, 2003b, 2006) work on Goddess followers in Malta interrogates their relationship with place and monument; she, like Ivakhiv, deals with spiritual tourists who make pilgrimage to specific, sacred, places and she examines the constructions of Goddess tourism as an economic and social phenomenon, though particularly emphasising the spiritual transformations of worshipper and place, and the contradictions that may arise in claiming identity in sacred sites.

Research and theory, then, as regard pagan approaches to sacred spaces, while now developing have clearly been quite limited and this is particularly so with respect to the landscapes of Britain. No academic study has attempted to address the range of responses and effects, the potential magnitude of implications (e.g. for heritage and tourism), and the phenomenon of 'indigenous' pagan adoption of 'sacred sites', in Britain, as a part of relations between people and 'the land' or 'landscape'. In a 'post-processual' climate in which archaeologists, heritage managers and others must be reflexive, transparent, and open up their research/data to external scrutiny, examination of the diversity of pagan engagements with 'archaeological sites' is begging. This is especially the case since pagans and alternative interest groups are themselves very active in self-publicity, self-publishing and networking on the internet and in a variety of private and public forums such as conferences and pub moots. Pagan views of sacredness are therefore receiving increasing amounts of attention in the public gaze – outside academia and policy circles.

The *Sacred Sites, Contested Rites/Rights Project* emerged from Wallis' earlier PhD on queer/alternative pagan/neo-Shamanic archaeologies and thereafter postdoctoral work as a Research Fellow in the Department of Archaeology at Southampton University (e.g. 1999b, 2000, 2003; also Wallis and Lymer 2001), and Blain's investigations of paganisms, identity and meaning, discourse, and auto-ethnography (1998, 2001, 2002), initially with a grant from the Social Sciences and Humanities Research Council of Canada. A pilot study, funded by Sheffield Hallam University Human Rights Fund, enabled an overview of contemporary pagan engagements with sacred sites (Wallis and Blain 2001: available online at <http://www.sacredsites. org.uk>). The current project has provided to date the most significant body of research and literature pertaining to the issues of pagan engagements with sacred sites in Britain (e.g. Wallis and Blain 2003; 2005; Blain and Wallis 2004a, 2004b, 2006b, 2006d, 2007; Blain, Letcher and Wallis 2004). Before embarking on detailed and sustained discussion of how pagans engage with sites, in this volume, it is incumbent upon us to offer orientation on what our understanding of paganism is, and clarify our theoretical and methodological considerations.

Introducing paganisms

The term 'pagan' still arouses concern or embarrassment in some quarters, and it is only now that, as numbers of those identifying as 'pagan' steadily increase, serious, sensitive academic interest in 'paganism' as a substantial cultural and spiritual strand within the UK population, and elsewhere, is burgeoning. Indeed there are pagans across the Western world and beyond (Western, Central and Eastern Europe, North America, Australia and New Zealand, and in some former Soviet and Eastern countries), and in some instances where there are consistencies in practices, there is dialogue with indigenous communities. Paganism might appear to be associated with 'new age' in some respects (a personalised approach to religion, for instance), but where new agers 'honour spirit above matter' (Harvey 1997: 122), pagan spirituality is consistently earth-orientated. Indeed, pagans often use 'new age' as a derogatory term, denoting an apparently superficial and tacky approach to spirituality (see also Pearson 1998; Shallcrass 1998: 168), with numerous suggestions in at least the past 15 years that 'newage' be pronounced, 'rather unkindly, as in "sewage"' (Fleming n.d.b).[3]

Paganism as a generic term – the 'small p' paganism to which we mostly refer in this volume – encompasses several recognised and coherent sets of beliefs and practices, along with those which are looser, less defined, and more intuitive. It encompasses those creating or engaging with pagan doctrines, theologies, worldview, liturgies and practices – all of whom would agree only with part of the terminology of this description. Pagans engage with past polytheist, pre-Christian and indigenous religions, and with very new religions possibly based on these, in order to reconstruct spiritualities relevant in today's society. Paganisms today comprise a variety of more-or-less allied or associated 'paths' or 'traditions' which focus, in some way, on engagements with environment and 'nature', variously theorised or theologised, through deities, 'spirits of place', or a more direct animist engagement with spirits or 'wights' in the landscape.

It is difficult to talk about 'paganism' without giving a sense of organisation and coherency. The four most well known pagan 'paths' or 'traditions' are Wicca, Druidry, Heathenry, and Goddess Spirituality, but while some pagans identify as 'Druid' or 'Heathen', often Druids can be as different from one another as Heathen from Wiccan. And at the same time, some Wiccans might borrow from Goddess Spirituality or Heathenry, and so on. Others who resist labels might arguably be seen as pagan, such as some new travellers. Adrian Harris's (pc) PhD work among road protesters indicates pagans who have a more 'intuitive' approach and may never have read a book on paganism or even heard of the term in contemporary usage, but who, again because of their intimate and reverential engagement with the natural world, might be viewed as pagan by scholars. This leaves a dissonance and heterogeneity which is difficult to grasp, yet there are consistencies.

Popular conceptions of pagans may suggest a tendency towards romanticism, liberalism and the middle classes: yet studies in Britain and the US indicate that pagans are frequently from all walks of life (Lewis 1996; Hutton 1999). Estimated adherents in the late 1990s in Britain numbered 110–120,000 (Weller 1997), although the Pagan Federation more recently gave estimates in the region of 200,000. The 2001 census for England and Wales, allowing people to indicate a religion, resulted in 30,000 writing in 'pagan', with smaller numbers specifying Wicca, Druidry or Heathenry: but the question was not compulsory, many pagans are known to have not answered it, and the category 'pagan' can cover a wide range of religions or spiritualities. Pagans were active immediately after the census in requesting greater provision for specifying their 'religion' in future censuses, but the sheer diversity of paganisms, including those pagans who do not conceive of their paganism as 'religious', or who may keep their paganism entirely private (including from family and friends), presents a messy problem to the authorities who require more manageable and quantifiable data.

Pagans construct their spirituality by reclaiming and re-interpreting ideas, stories and artefacts, from academic reports of archaeological assemblages to alternative readings of the Mabinogi or the Norse myths and sagas – and, of course, prehistoric sites per se. This spirituality is expressed visually and publicly in a number of ways, such as the display of reproduced artefacts (for example, Thor's hammer as a pendant for a Heathen), pilgrimages to sacred sites (and votive offerings left there) and 'visits' to museum collection displays of artefacts which offer direct visual (and other resonant) links to ancient religions. There are also less public though no less visual manifestations, from personal, internalised mythologies (such as an understanding of Odin as a patron shaman-god) to ritual equipment for private use (for instance, a Wiccan's athame [ritual knife] based on a reproduction of a Bronze Age blade).

Not all pagans concern themselves with sacred sites: some Wiccans, particularly, tend to conduct their rites in private, often indoors, or otherwise away from the public eye; Druids, on the other hand, are stereotyped as classic 'Stonehenge worshippers' with many orders purposefully conducting rituals in the full gaze of the media. Further, not all people engaging with archaeological sites as 'sacred' places are pagan. Various adherents of the 'new age', Earth Mysteries researchers (earth mystics) and many new travellers, along with a variety of local people, members of other religions and more conven-

0.1   Druids and others gather to make ritual in the south circle at Avebury.

tional 'tourists' take unconventional interests in archaeology and sites. They may attend pagan gatherings at such sites, hold their own rituals, or of course visit for entirely different reasons, including the spiritual tourism of 'new-age' and Goddess tours (regularly at Avebury, for instance). Along with tourist impact, pagan activities are now having a noticeable impact on sacred sites. This requires academic scrutiny and ongoing responses from heritage management – one only has to 'visit' Stonehenge or Avebury at one of the eight most common pagan festivals to witness how many people may perceive such places as sacred (with an approximated average of 20,000 at the Stonehenge summer solstice managed open access event at the last three such events, though not all of these necessarily approached the monument as sacred). Finds of 'offerings' of flowers and similar items at smaller and more remote sites, such as the Derbyshire stone circles at Froggatt Edge or the Nine Ladies circle on Stanton Moor, provide evidence of recent pagan 'visits'. The phenomenon of such offerings appears to have arisen chiefly within the last twenty years.

Neo-tribes, new-indigenes, animist ontologies and living landscapes

Various new traveller and pagan informants have referred to those gathered at Stonehenge and Avebury as 'the tribes' and this usage is common in some, if not all, pagan cultural contexts, as a description of present or of past (paganisms, as already made plain, are diverse). Postmodernity has been theorised by Michel Maffesoli as 'the Time of the Tribes' (1996), referring to the shifting and fluid fragmentary associations of individuals and groups within today's societies. Andy Letcher, in a doctoral thesis (2001a) at King Alfred's College, Winchester (now the University of Winchester), has commented on this usage of 'neo-tribes' and extended Maffesoli's analysis to those people who indeed call themselves 'tribes' (see also Letcher 2001b); the 'new tribes' can be understood as flexible, shifting groupings, adopting or appropriating ideas of kinship and even the term 'tribe' as a complex construction of identity *vis-à-vis* perceptions of dominant 'conventional' class-based society. Yet even in adoption of the term 'new-tribes' there is an implied claim to permanence – whereas Maffesoli's analysis deals in shifting groups within post-modernity. Today's new traveller, pagan and other 'neotribe' groups may embody both ways; drawing identity from a perceived stability of land, yet expressing this through a fluidity of movement – physically as the tribes come together and then part ('the Stones' at Stonehenge and other sacred sites are important to traveller identities as meeting

0.2   Offerings of cones, flowers and other items at the tiny circle of Doll Tor, in the Peak District.

places for 'the tribes'), and ontologically in terms of alternative archaeological ideas picked up and dropped in the establishment of identity; and perceived links to the ancient past reify conventional understandings of the term 'tribe'.

Concepts of neotribes connect to ideas of reenchantment of nature, human life and individual worldviews in an increasingly secular, mechanised and globalised world (explored in Chapter 1), inherent in connections with 'the past' and with sacred sites. The Sacred Sites project has proposed the term 'new-indigenes' to describe those pagans whose re-enchantment practices involve perceiving nature as animate – alive with spirits, 'wights', multiple deities and otherworldly beings, and who identify with pagan Iron Age and Early Mediaeval ancestors' from ancient Europe, finding resonance with earlier prehistoric cultures and indigenous 'tribal' societies elsewhere, particularly those whose 'religion' is animist and/or 'shamanistic'.[4] The term *new-indigenes* therefore acts as an extension, specific to paganisms, of Maffesoli's 'new-tribes'.

Non-pagan perceptions of pagans range from the respectful (usually from those who have had encounters with pagans and are sensitive to their views, but who are not pagans themselves), to discriminatory or mocking (fair game for television broadcasts such as Graham Norton's *Bigger Picture* [BBC1, 30 October 2006]) – despite having little connection with devil worship or ritual abuse.[5] The revising of stereotypes is a long-term process. Some reactions to our project, at conferences for example, question the 'authenticity' of pagans and this is a theme often repeated in the media. Certainly in the 1950s and since then, when paganism began to establish itself, recourse was made to an unbroken tradition of witchcraft in Britain. Debates are ongoing over the 'authenticity' of Wicca (see Hutton 1999; Heselton 2001, 2003), though most scholars of paganism treat it as a product of the mid-twentieth century, while Druidry today appears as a construct of twentieth-century engagements with (eighteenth and nineteenth century) antiquarian imagination on 'druids' rather more than as based in the evidence of the 'Celtic' Iron Age. But at which point does a 'tradition' become 'authentic' and when does it become 'valid'? Tim Sebastion (2001), Chosen Chief of the Secular Order of Druids, points out that contemporary Druidry, with a lineage dating back at least to the antiquarian William Stukeley, is at least as authentic and valid as modern archaeology which hails from the same time. And increasingly pagans are interested in how their practices are relevant in the contemporary world; as such, lineage and authenticity *vis-à-vis* the ancient pagan past (in 'Celtic' Ireland or Anglo-Saxon Wessex) is less of an issue. We argue that the interface between past and present in this instance offers a rich, dynamic field of discourse which is deeply personal and meaningful for practitioners and important to scholarly analyses of the represented past.

Discourses and practices, locations and methodologies

Discourse analysis is crucial to our theoretical and epistemological approach to pagan, management, and other involved engagements with the past. Critical discourse or textual analysis is not simply about what words are used or how they are positioned within talk or documents, but how use of specific, traceable modes of speech or writing ('discourses') enables points to be discussed, questions to be asked or concealed, and topics to be aired or avoided. Further, what background assumptions and narratives are indexed within discourse – implicitly or explicitly? How does discourse relate to power? Who can set the terms of discourse within given situations? Discourses of sites and sacredness are contextualised by historical and political processes, not only spiritual or indeed archaeological ones: but they also constitute these processes within present-day parameters. Specific questions addressed in our project that are illustrated in this book include:

1   How are spiritual engagements with 'sacred sites' and concepts of
    landscape configured and displayed – made visible or invisible – in
    (a) existing heritage literature and policy and (b) specific responses
    to increasing pressure on sites from the pagan/alternative communi-
    ties?
2   How does ongoing pagan/alternative discourse and negotiation
    accommodate or resist 'official' constructions?
3   Where do major conflicts and misunderstandings lie and how there-
    fore are political (as well as spiritual) processes being constituted
    within this area of 'sacred sites'? What groups are discursively
    marginalised within negotiation or debate? Whose 'knowledge', and
    what kind of 'knowledge' about sites and sacredness are validated or
    obscured? (For instance, in the Stonehenge management plan, while
    'research' is identified as a specific goal, no reference is made to
    constructions of meaning within the site today. What assumptions
    underlie this discourse on 'research'?).

    One may argue that people do not only describe or represent their
objects and ideas by discourses (discourse is an ordering system), but
constitute action and meaning through discourse (discourse as
agency). From theorists such as Smith (e.g. 1987, 1990, 1993), or
Fairclough et al. (2004) drawing on Foucault (e.g. 1972), our research
takes a notion of agency and experience as discursively constituted;
also that power exists in the convergence or divergence of discursive
constructions (see also chapters in Wodak and Meyer 2001). In one
sense, Foucault thought that 'discourse constitutes the real' (Cohen
2004): this is not to say that discourse is all that there is, that
discourse is the only ultimate 'reality', but it is to look at the
complex interweaving of ideas that shape perception/experience/
knowledge and hence possibilities of action (see also Blain 1993,
1994, applying such concepts to a very different topic). Examples in
later chapters of this volume include how, for instance, discourses of
'preservation ethos' or – particularly at summer solstice at
Stonehenge – 'health and safety' not only describe 'sides' in conflict
but shape the possibilities that emerge, including possibilities for
negotiation and intervention. In this sense, discourse and power
jointly shape each other. This analysis is 'critical' because it does not
seek only to describe a dialogue of discourses, but to explore areas of
power and possibility demarcated by them and by their conflict: in
short, to use discourse theory to problematise constructions of
reality that may otherwise seem 'commonsense', and so to (we hope)
produce useful knowledge. Maingueneau (2006) suggests that a
'strong' version of discourse analysis is always critical, because of
what it reveals, moving beyond the bounds of the text or the immediate speaker, saying that:

> To analyse religious or scientific discourse, for example, one must take into account not only their contents but also the institutions that make the production and the management of these texts possible . . . to achieve its purpose, discourse analysis cannot ignore the specific interests of the groups working in the field.
>
> (Maingueneau, 2006: 230)

In offering a discourse analysis of issues arising from pagan engagements with the past, the theoretical approach offered here is embedded in a postmodern shift which has impacted humanities and social sciences research (and indeed other research communities) since at least the 1980s. We embrace the idea that research cannot be 'objective' in the older sense of value-free, but that all research is situated and that researchers are themselves active participants in the process, leading to a greater or lesser degree of subjectivity. Only by discussing, unpacking and analysing subjectivity and location can a different kind of 'objectivity', that attained through juxtaposing of discourses, images and knowledges, be achieved (Haraway 1988). This is not a standpoint of 'anything goes' and we are not uncritical of all that postmodernist theory has to offer; it can be construed as an honest admission as to the limits of researchers' objectivity in an increasingly globalised world or as a reflection on the diversity of worlds that are created within spiritual and heritage practices today. In either case, it is incumbent upon us to make clear our own positions with regard to the subject and to make clear the methodology adopted. The knowledge we create, or co-create, is 'situated' by our own positions and questioning, just as it is by the techniques of analysis we adopt and by the material that we have at our disposal. In this book, then, we as its authors speak both in an authorial first person, and in a descriptive third person, as the exigencies of description and analysis require. Currently, reflexive trends within the social sciences necessitate that we – as researchers and authors – make plain our own attachment to the concepts and our part in their generation (see e.g. Alvesson and Sköldberg 2000) in creating the situated knowledges of this work.

Marcus (1998: 196) following Myers (1988) speaks of 'reflexivity as a politics of location'. Our location in this work is not simply that of abstract academics, but relates to the particular universities at which we teach, to our students, to funding restrictions (which in turn have largely restricted our work to date to better-known English sites) and the orientations of our particular departments, faculties or divisions, just as it does to the politics and intricacies of negotiating what appears as 'insider' research and our own relationships to paganisms. Issues of negotiating insider/outsider status require consideration. In a sense the researcher is never fully 'at home' in any of the cultures in which s/he stands, but moves between participant and academic or policy positions, brokering one to another (Blain 1998), sometimes occupying what Harvey has termed a 'third position' (2004: 252), related to that of 'guesting' among the Maori (and other communities) he studies, wherein respectful engagements are crucial to relations between 'researcher' and 'subject' in establishing friends or making enemies. Blain's work has dealt in discourse and critical ethnography, specifically constructions of identity within Western paganisms and neo-shamanisms, gender and sexuality, spirituality and marginalised groups. Her book *Nine Worlds of Seid-magic: Ecstasy and Neo-Shamanism in North European Paganism* (2002) examined today's re-establishment of seidr-shamanism in Heathen communities, with a strong autoethnographic and reflexive component. It included not only attempted exploration of current practices in communities in North America and Britain and tracing of politics and practices through mediaeval literature in the readership of today's Heathens, but a detailing of her own experiences and participation in this 'altered consciousness' work. She here and elsewhere has explored multiple locations of researchers of paganisms who not only speak from within the community they study (and the issues of 'irrationality' that may be raised, e.g. in Blain 2000) but are themselves part of the construction of community practice and understanding (2004). These and other issues are explored by collaborators in the edited volume *Researching Paganisms* (Blain et al. 2004). Wallis has raised the issue of the researcher negotiating 'insider' status (e.g. 2004) and offered an 'autoarchaeological' approach to neo-shamanism (Wallis 2001, 2003), in which he related his standpoint specificity as in 'insider' to both archaeology and neo-shamanism (specifically heathen shamanism) and to the theory and practice of auto-ethnography and experiential anthropology, as well as reflexive practice in archaeology. This research, particularly the volume *Shamans/neo-Shamans: Ecstasy, Alternative Archaeologies and Contemporary Pagans* (2003; see also Wallis 2000; 2002b), focused on contemporary pagan interfaces with the past, specifically neo-shamanic interpretations of Celtic and Northern sources, and engagements with archaeological monuments in Britain and the US as sacred – thus laying the groundwork for the current project. An engagement with theory and practice of auto-ethnographic work (Reed-Danahay 1997) therefore runs through the research, to which we attempt to bring issues of the multiple situation of the researcher. Our experiences are not 'typical' and while we can attempt to examine process and perception through rigorous analysis and critique, such understandings always remain specifically located: autoethnography is therefore only part of what we do.

0.3 Chaco Canyon: a sign to remind tourists that the site is sacred.

For this project, research at and associated with sites has involved following pagan, tourist, and management discourses and practices through visitor engagement, pagan ceremony, and site 'welfare'. We have participated in 'tourist visiting' and archaeological fieldtrips, in pagan ceremonies, in song and meditation, in meetings and protests. We have spoken with pagans, tourists, site managers, local people, and others in the world of heritage and archaeology. Certain interviews were formal, one-to-one, recorded on disk and in notes; others were informal, casual and conversational, facilitating recovery of other sorts of 'data'. The project has followed debates and discussions on internet forums and email discussion lists to which we subscribe, identifying ourselves and seeking permission to include key points in the work of the project. We have amassed a large bank of images which record our research visually. Having stated that researchers are embedded in their research exercise, subject to certain biases and always a part of the time and place in which they are researching, it is important that we 'upfront' our own standpoint specificities. Blain is Scottish, though now living in the Peak District, and she has lived in Canada, while Wallis is English and lives in Hampshire; both are academics, the former an anthropologist, the latter an archaeologist. As previously indicated, both of us are also pagans; specifically, we are Heathens, (on which see Blain 2005, 2006b; and chapters in Wallis 2003) meaning that our interests in 'heritage' and 'the past', and these in the present, are guided by a deep fascination beyond the purely academic, for the ancient peoples of the British Isles, including but not restricted to those who (may have) arrived during the migration age of the second half of the first millennium CE, and for the ways that they may have related to the landscapes that we now study. Both of us work, though differently, with issues of altered consciousness in our spiritual as well as academic lives, relating this to indigenous or new-indigenous understandings (see e.g. Blain 2005; Johnson and Wallis 2005). We do not claim to 'know' pagans better simply because we are pagans, nor do we claim to speak for all pagans or even to encompass all pagan engagements with sites and meanings of 'sacredness' in this one book. At the same time we do not feel that our pagan-ness compromises our scholarly ability; rather the one brings a different nuance to the other. Certainly a study of pagans and sites of a similar order, conducted by other researchers (pagan or not, anthropologist or not, archaeologist or not) would have something different and perhaps quite contradictory to say. That is as it should be, and sits well with a reflexive approach to our subject.

Our rationale for selection of sites is based partly on the level of pagan interests in specific sites and partly on our own locations in Britain, one in Hampshire and one on the Derbyshire/Yorkshire border. So, the honeypot sites of Stonehenge and Avebury have been a major focus, but we have also attended to smaller sites in southern England where pagan interests are evident, such as the Rollright Stones in Oxfordshire, little-known sites in Hampshire, and a variety of monuments in the southwest, particularly Cornwall. Further north, we have focused on monuments in the Peak District, especially around Stanton Moor, and on Ilkley Moor in Yorkshire. Thornborough Henges became crucially important during the course of this research, and were close enough (to Blain) to be included. This selection of sacred sites as research sites provides a set of focused arenas which may be seen as a series of 'case studies' enabling the conduct of detailed, sustained research rather than generalities, although our methodology is that of multi-sited ethnography rather than formal 'case study research'. Yet, we have also been cognisant of what is happening in pagan engagements with sites across Britain, and have made sporadic visits to such sites as Castlerigg stone circle in the Lake District of Cumbria and the circles, tombs and rock-art in the Kilmartin Valley in Scotland. With pagan interests in sites expanding beyond the British Isles – Julian Cope's recent publication *The Megalithic European* (2004) evinces this – we have also embarked on visits to parts of Scandinavia, and to Brittany, and our eyes are turned towards the events at Tara in Ireland. Furthermore, in an increasingly globalised world, we have been in contact with colleagues conducting similar research across the world.

This introduction concludes with a chapter outline which is based on the locations forming the focus of study.

Chapter outline – sites and areas of interest

Chapter 1 attends to theoretical issues arising from the engagement between paganisms and sacred sites. It examines the emergence of the nomenclature 'sacred site' in both pagan and heritage discourses and how these discourses deal with preservation and conservation, theorising 'what is sacredness?' when pertaining to archaeological sites and discussing paganisms in more detail.

Chapter 2 explores ongoing debates and tensions at Avebury stone circles and the wider Avebury 'complex' of monuments. Issues here concern how pagan interests are expressed in an open landscape and how heritage managers have dealt with these interests. During the late 1990s, for instance, initial confrontations were softened by a successful guardianship scheme in which pagans volunteered to collect litter and stop (witting or unwitting) damage. Pagans were also involved in protests over Silbury 'hole', after the vertical shaft in Silbury Hill collapsed and it seemed that English Heritage wavered for too long over how to repair the site. During this period, pagans volunteered to act as wardens requesting that pagan visitors avoid using the hill for rituals, in the interests of the long-term future of the site. Unofficial camping was tolerated at Avebury at this time, but a change in management since the turn of the new century has seen a hardening of attitudes over issues of parking and crowds, especially since summer solstice fallout from Stonehenge led to a large influx of alternative visitors requiring parking space in a 'sleepy' village. Tensions between pagan visitors, local pagans, non-pagan locals and the National Trust are discussed, as is theoretical analysis of the 'performance' of paganisms on this open stage, and analysis explores the diversity of views and makes suggestions for future negotiations.

Stonehenge and its environs provide the case study for Chapter 3. Access has been problematic, the centre of an on-going struggle between new travellers, pagans, other members of the 'alternative' community, English Heritage, landowners and the police. Negotiations here spotlight differences between heritage hands-off 'preservation for future generations' and pagan/alternative tactile 'open access', and Stonehenge as 'home' and 'for all people'. The chapter describes work based on sustained attendance at official and unofficial pagan events at 'the Stones' and elsewhere in the local landscape, monitoring official press releases and accounts of Stonehenge Roundtable meetings, and following pagan/alternative discussions via the StonehengePeace e-list and various websites where tensions between involved groups appear greatest, with debates drawing on accounts of past actions. Those accommodations reached for solstices and equinoxes remain contentious: distrust is rife, and examination of discourses adopted by heritage personnel, 'personal-growth' druids and pagan federation spokespersons, versus new travellers and 'counter-cultural' druids, indicates the need for awareness within all factions interested in this area. These issues also pertain to plans for the Stonehenge-area redevelopments. Boundaries are differently drawn here, with considerable alliances formed around questions of a tunnel to take the A303, and the siting of a proposed new visitor centre (see e.g. articles linked from the Stonehenge Alliance website).

Controversy over a proposal to reactivate dormant quarrying operations on Stanton Moor, within striking distance of the Nine Ladies stone circle, the focus of Chapter 4, has caused some alliance between heritage management, pagans, new travellers, and local people. Other strands such as site erosion – by pagan protests as well as 'raves', parties, and ramblers' activities – have periodically featured likewise. Local heritage managers have deliberately involved protestors, local people, and pagans in consultation, particularly about erosion and excavation. The planning decision is currently against the proposed quarrying but the process is protracted and a final decision is yet to be made. This chapter also discusses the campaign to Save Thornborough Henges, where pagans have been active with other Friends of Thornborough in protesting against proposed quarrying by the company Tarmac. This gravel extraction would reduce what has been described by English Heritage as the most important ancient site between Stonehenge and the Orkneys to just one percent of its original size.

The situation in the Peak District is compared and contrasted with that in the Kilmartin Valley in Argyll, Scotland and on Ilkley Moor in Yorkshire, in Chapter 5. The Kilmartin Valley example (the only Scottish example in this volume), with its important juxtaposition of prehistoric monuments and rock art[6] (on natural outcrops and on monuments) has figured in the construction of pagan identity and also relates back to the issue of quarry threats. At Ilkley, another area profusely rich in rock art, serious damage to the archaeology (such as the deliberate destruction of a megalith from the Twelve Apostles stone circle), as well as threats to the profuse rock art from 'graffiti', seems to be linked to alternative interests in the site, if not necessarily pagans. Differences and problems notwithstanding, where dialogue with pagans has resulted in some positive results for all the interest groups at Avebury, Stonehenge, the Peak District and Thornborough, the examples of Kilmartin and Ilkley demonstrate that engagement with pagans is lacking yet might have proved beneficial to the heritage bodies in various ways.

Chapter 6 takes this observation – collaboration – forward with the final site of study, the Rollright Stones in Oxfordshire. The Rollrights have a specific relation to pagan use, facilitated by the Rollright Trust, as site owners and managers. In contrast to other site management plans, the Rollright plan goes some way to assuming that active engagement with the site is negotiable, indeed desirable. Management discourse blends some components of pagan and heritage narratives, and this example is used to offer positive guidance for heritage-pagan engagement in the future.

Chapter 7 addresses an issue which serves to tie together the various strands addressed in this study. Where the reburial of human remains and excavated artefacts has been a major issue for archaeologists and anthropologists, especially in North America and Australia, their colleagues in Britain might be surprised to be informed that reburial is now on the agenda in Britain. British professionals dealing with human remains from indigenous contexts outside Europe have been involved in negotiations over reburial with host communities for some time; now, there is a pagan-initiated call for reburial of prehistoric 'ancestral' remains in Britain. Far from being sensationalist, dialogue on reburial in Britain, and even the reburial of remains itself, is already in action, with recent legislation requiring that museums and universities holding human remains justify why they should not rebury. This issue clearly has major implications for heritage-pagan engagements in years to come and provides a suitable means to demonstrate further issues of pagan relationships with landscape and site. A concluding chapter indexes these discussions, pointing to implications for policy and offering some suggestions for future research.

We begin, therefore, in Chapter 1, by introducing the concept of 'sacred sites' and pagan engagements with these places, as well as examining pagan and heritage discourse on sacred sites and theorising what is sacredness.

CHAPTER 1

'Sacred Sites'? Paganisms, Representation and Imaginings of the Past

Insofar as archaeology enhances people's lives and society in general, its major impact might be said to lie in popular culture rather than any noble vision of improving self-awareness.
(Lucas 2004: 119)

Tradition, authenticity, enchantment

Interest in 'the past' is currently booming, with the audience for television archaeology suggesting an interest that is not merely intellectual or academic. Channel 4's successful archaeological programme, *Time Team*, first broadcast in 1994 and now preparing its 2007 season, commands a regular audience of around three million, whilst the unexpected popularity of his *History of Britain* propelled Simon Schama to the status of celebrity academic. Schedulers have responded to this audience-led demand with a plethora of documentaries covering all periods: history and archaeology are the surprise successes of recent broadcasting. The past, and particularly the distant past, clearly *matters* to people, and does so in ways that relate to identity forged in connection with place and time.

There have been many theories, and much discussion, about how and why people seek identities in echoes of the past. Among these are that the people distant in time or space, as a 'periphery', provide an 'other' upon which contemporary hopes and fears of those at the 'centre' can be projected (Piggott 1968; Said 1978). During times of confidence and faith in the 'progress' of mainstream culture, the other is represented as exotic and primitive. At times when people become disillusioned with the mainstream, the exotic other becomes desirable, 'primitives' becoming 'noble savages' (Bowman 1995). Furthermore, during times of rapid social change, the past may represent a point or points of continuity and stability: hence 'traditions', implying continuity, may be resurrected or invented (Hobsbawm and Ranger 1983). That we are moving through a time of both rapid social change and disillusionment with traditional sources of authority is generally agreed by scholars (see Heelas et al. 1996; Sardar 2002), and consequently 'the past' has become increasingly important as a stable reference of identity and meaning. It seems to us that this is particularly so for those defining themselves by the many varieties of paganism emerging and flourishing in today's Western world, and so the complexities of pagan understandings of pasts, and their implication for heritage and for the construction of today's cultures, form the subject matter of this book.

The appeal of 'the past' is made manifest by growing numbers of 'visitors' to archaeological sites. People visit for a variety of reasons and there is considerable scholarship on this issue (see e.g. Boniface and Fowler 1993; Cleere 1989; Urry 1990). Engaging with the past, for many people, including many pagans, may give a sense of stability or continuity: the notion of the prehistoric past may be the equivalent in today's society of the stories from before, the local legends or grandmother's tales in a simpler time – if there was ever really a 'simpler time' – and the materiality of archaeology, the perception of 'fact' or reconstruction, may serve to replace local geographies and familiar landscapes; or reasons may be far more convoluted. Possibly, for many in the post-modern world, including pagans, 'the past' represents a resource which addresses a perceived lack in (post or late)modern life. For many contemporary pagans that lack is one of enchantment; the past is romantic and it re-enchants. Paganism seems united in its diverse forms by a commonality of looking to the past for sources of belief, practice and identity. It is quite common for earth mystics and alternative archaeologists to seek patterns of meaning in the past which they claim are 'overlooked' or 'ignored' by mainstream archaeology. A typical, widely held, belief by pagans and earth mystics alike is that 'ancient peoples were sensitive to aspects of the physical world that are not appreciated in modern day society' (Lambrick 2001: 20). Sites such as Avebury and Stonehenge are not simply for them places of archaeological interest. For many they are sacred places which appear to hold answers to important questions of meaning and ontology, and to meet the need for re-enchantment; they are places where they feel they belong, where they are at home.

Pagan responses to pasts, places and landscapes are as varied as paganisms themselves, but some generalisations may be made. Pagans form an important audience for presentations of archaeology and history. It is our contention that they may be better seen more often as allies of conservationists than as opponents. Indeed, some pagans have come to their spirituality through direct engagements with 'the past', whether these be history rambles or participation in archaeological digs. Conversely, it is not unknown for pagans to find themselves increasingly interested in prehistory and indeed to become prehistorians. We begin, then, with paganisms, rationalism, and the imaginings of past and landscape that constitute identities, and in particular with three concepts that will appear throughout this work – tradition, authenticity and re-enchantment.

For pagans, various periods or histories may become sources of inspiration or of knowledge, culture and artistic expressions to which they may feel drawn. This attraction of the past takes many forms. At an extreme, the past might represent a 'golden age' standard against which contemporary life can be critiqued. Such pagans may explicitly describe themselves as 'pre-modern' in their seeking identity in such pasts. See, for instance, the practitioner journal *Tyr*, for which the preamble to the first issue reads:

What does it mean to be a radical traditionalist?

> It means to reject the modern, materialist reign of quantity over quality, the absence of any meaningful spiritual values, environmental devastation, the mechanization and over-specialization of urban life, and the imperialism of corporate mono-culture, with its vulgar values of progress and efficiency. It means to yearn for the small, homogeneous tribal societies that flourished before Christianity – societies in which every aspect of life was integrated into a holistic system.

What we represent:

> Resacralization of the world versus materialism; folk/traditional culture versus mass culture; natural social order versus an artificial hierarchy based on wealth; the tribal community versus the nation-state; stewardship of the earth versus the maximization of resources; a harmonious relationship between men and women versus the war between the sexes; handicrafts and artisanship versus industrial mass-production.
> (Preface available online: <http://tyrjournal.tripod.com/about_the_journal.htm>)

Not all or perhaps even many of the contributors to the journal *Tyr*, or their readers, would go so far, and some (even among its authors) would critique severely the imagining of apparently all pre-Christian societies as small, tribal, and with people living in a gender-balanced harmony with nature; but the statements of this journal's founders may be seen as encapsulating concepts that are found in varying degrees in many of today's works by pagan authors, and in many of the comments that our informants – whether they adhere to generic Pagan, Druid, Wiccan, neo-Shaman, or Heathen or other 'reconstructionist' philosophies or spiritualities –

make to us. Particularly, these do include ideas about harmony with nature, gender equality and a feeling of belonging with other identifiable people who share in these concepts and who observe the same ritual practices, and past examples are pointed to as sources of inspiration. The intention here is not to classify pagan groups or 'traditions' as examples of pre-modern, modern, late-modern or post-modern orientations. We do not see a focus on 'tradition' as equated with a rejection of current ideologies (though we have indeed met pagans who say they would rather have lived in fifth century BCE Athens, first century CE Wales, or eighth century CE Sweden – along with some who say, of course, that they did live then in other incarnations). Rather, strands of remembering or creation, invention and appropriation, emerge within today's society, and reflexive practitioners making use of these, often deliberately, position themselves as spiritual people and construct complex cultural identities.

Tradition

The concept of *tradition* here needs some unpacking. As an example of current debates within the sociology of paganisms, Green (2003) examines paganism as a construct (or perhaps better 'constructs') of modernity, producing a critique of theorists of late modernity (notably Giddens [e.g. 1991, 1994]) for their apparent rejection of 'tradition' as a concept with current meaning. Green also engages with Hobsbawm (1983) and Gross (1992) over the framing of 'tradition' as something that *should be* relatively fixed (for Gross spanning and linking at least three generations). We are in general agreement with Green in seeing 'traditions' rather differently from these authors, as fluid strands of cultural process that are constantly in construction and under modification; that is, always in flux, in a process of invention or reinvention. Further, we do not see this as a development peculiar to advanced industrial societies: work such as that of Greene (1998) emphasises the fluidity of shamanic practice and the incorporation of ideas, and Taussig (e.g. 1987) theorises tensions between contestation and creative uses of 'traditional' practices, by spiritual leaders, workers of magic, shamans and/or artists within changing colonial and post-/neo-colonial contexts. With respect to paganisms and other alternative practices, Green debates concepts of de-traditionalisation with those of re-traditionalisation (following Heelas 1996), concluding that traditions – or their constant re-creations and emergings – have a central place within today's world. What these *traditions* are, though, and how they are invented/re-invented, we hope to display, in part, in this book. For us, items of pagan practice stem from, and themselves construct, worldviews that act to link or connect self and other, agency and

1.1 Druids make ritual at Avebury, processing around the banks and assembling before the 'Devil's Chair' in the southern entrance.

structure, and these we can see as 'traditions'; but many pagans will describe their faith or that of another pagan path as a 'tradition' – the Druid tradition, the Northern tradition – which may be problematic on a number of grounds, not least those of lack of specificity. Nevertheless, the word is part of many pagan discourses.

Authenticity

A concept closely related to that of 'tradition' is *authenticity*. For pagans, again, this links back to concepts of the past: how did *they* do spirituality *then* (whom or whatever 'they' and 'then' may be) (Blain, 2004). Authenticity presents a challenge to pagans, not only to their own development of practices but to their apparent rights to practice, when they are faced with outsiders claiming that what they do, their rituals, their sacred items, the details of their understandings, is 'not how it was done'. Pagans adopt a variety of strategies in dealing with the concept – from attempted strict adherence to ritual forms, to appropriation of spirituality seen as more authentic (notably 'Native American' practices, with associated charges of cultural theft – see Smith 1994; Rose 1992) to a shrugged 'so – I do what *I* do, I do *what works*' – or to avid readership of archaeological journals or following of current 'experts' in the field. Thus, Ronald Hutton, Professor of History at Bristol University, states in his Introduction to the volume *The Druid Renaissance: The Voice of Druidry Today*:

> It is a . . . situation in which the experts are feeding the public
> with information while leaving it free to make such imagina-
> tive reconstructions as it wishes . . . Druids [for example] are
> well placed to take advantage of it . . . indeed, it is almost a
> duty on their part to do so, for the more people who are
> involved in the work, and the broader the range of plausible
> pictures imagined, the healthier the situation.
>
> (Hutton 1996: 23)

Pagans are bricoleurs, borrowing practices, incorporating concepts,
but will defend their borrowings in different ways. Throughout, we
see pagans, ourselves included, as choosers, who whether they are
newcomers to their practices or whether they have grown up with
pagan understandings and worldviews, appear to exemplify the fluidity and change discussed by Bauman (2000) as *liquid modernity*.

Enchantment

The third concept is a favourite one for pagan authors and for
researchers of paganism (e.g. Griffin 1995, 2000; Ivahkiv 2001; Green
2001, 2003; Greenwood 2005, Ruickbie 2006), to explain the emergence and attraction of paganisms today. If today's society as a
product of modernity is categorised by Weber's description of disenchantment and bureaucratic rationalism, paganisms offer *reenchantment*. Both disenchantment and reenchantment are problematic:
Ruickbie follows other 'insider' researchers – ourselves included – in
pointing out that reenchantment implies a necessary disenchantment, thus setting pagan reenchantment at one, irrationalist, side of
a value-laden dualism (our phrase, not his). Cultural patterns are far
more permeable and permeated, far more messy, than any such neat-
ness. But 're-enchantment' is, for many pagans, what their attempts
to create new, different views of the world(s) are about.

So, here we return to imaginings and representations of the past
and to the perceived 'lacks' within today's world. For many of today's
people, pagan or otherwise, that lack is one of enchantment: the
enchanted past re-enchants. Paganism, in its diverse forms, is united
by the commonality of looking to the past – or occasionally to
perceived Sci-Fi 'futures' – for sources of belief, practice and identity.
Place and landscape become key components of many pagans' identity. Specific places which are considered to hold links to times and
people become central to understandings of belief or identity. Pagans
are not of course alone in this. From gravestones of our grandmoth-
ers to battlefields, from houses we once dwelt in to castles, crofts or
cottages presented as worthy of 'restoration' television, such places,
buildings or ruins and rural or urban scenes are indexed in family
stories, tourism narratives, popular culture and folklore, literature and

1.2   Artefacts from the past become pagan symbols of the present.

art. The emotional attachment to place, or *topophilia* (Tuan 1974) is well known as a constituent of national or ethnic identity. The place is claimed by the participant as one where they are at home or one where they seek to be, one which holds intense meaning for them. Topophilia associated with historic or prehistoric sites is described for pagan practitioners by Bowman (2000) and others, indicating that ancient sites are not for them places merely of archaeological interest. For many they are sacred places, even living temples, which appear to hold answers to important questions of meaning and ontology, and to meet the need for re-enchantment. Pagans may view themselves as the inheritors of the 'wisdom' of ancient cultures, particularly those of the British and wider European Neolithic, Bronze and Iron Ages which provide sources for this inspiration and re-enchantment. Images of sites and representations of place adorn book covers or house walls, and the geometry and symbolism of past and present paganisms finds its way into domestic design, tourist mementoes and personal decoration (North-Bates 2006; Blain and Wallis 2006b).

Practitioners feel themselves drawn to such sacred sites in Britain as Avebury, Stonehenge and the Rollright Stones for a variety of reasons. They may engage with 'nature' (and/or supernature or otherworlds) in the form of spirits, wights, gods and goddesses at such power places' where the presence of these beings are felt most strongly, considering this manifestation to be marked by the monuments erected by ancient peoples; alternatively, a sacred site may be seen as similar to a modern church, a place deliberately consecrated to deities or a generalised 'divine' presence; or a location, a hill, a copse, a river may be a particularly beautiful 'natural' site to which both deities and people are drawn (cf. Bradley 2000) or indeed a living entity in itself. At sacred sites, pagans perform seasonal rituals and rites of passage such as hand-fasting (marriage), child blessing and honouring of the recently deceased. They may conduct calendrical and astronomical celebrations or festivals which are public, also (re)forming temporary communities to celebrate pagan identity and values. Yet often, pagan rites are private, even secret, and they may involve perceived direct communication with spirits of the land via altered consciousness. Although not all pagans regularly 'visit' sacred sites, increasingly these places are forming an essential part of pagan lives. Before proceeding to examine pagan engagements with sacred sites in detail, then, it is incumbent upon us as the authors of a book on 'sacred sites', using the term throughout, to critically unpack the discursive use of 'sacred site' in reference to representations or imaginings of pasts – the purpose of this chapter.

The 'sacred' in the sites

The term *sacred site* most likely entered pagan discourse via comments on and publications by indigenous spokespersons (see e.g. Layton 1989a, 1989b; Carmichael et al. 1994). Given that pagans look directly or indirectly to some indigenous communities for inspiration for their own claims to indigeneity, many pagans are familiar with the perspectives of indigenous groups who have been vocal on such issues as the repatriation of artefacts and reburial of human remains kept in non-indigenous museums and collections (e.g. Messenger 1989; Merrill et al. 1993; Murray 1996; Mihesuah 2000; Kreps 2003; Peers and Brown 2003). Indigenous articulations of 'sacred site' have been used, in the United States for example, to contest archaeologists', anthropologists' and National Parks Services' understandings as these are related to issues of access, ownership, and management (e.g. Biolsi and Zimmerman 1997; Swidler et al. 1997). Pagans, in turn, have deployed 'sacred site' as preferred nomenclature for 'archaeological site' or 'monument' or 'remains': 'sacred' lends a reverential and spiritual element to what is otherwise perceived as only an academic resource, a dead past, or a destination on a tourist checklist. Since the mid-twentieth century, the archaeology and anthro-

1.3   Thingvellir, Iceland: beauty and history intertwined. The site is sacred to many people today.

pology of indigenous groups and cultures have undergone or created 'decolonizing methodologies' in order to revise racist and discriminatory practices of the past (e.g. Smith 1999; Watkins 2000), but Britain, and to a large extent Europe, is perceived to have no 'indigenous peoples'. Locals, people who live close to the 'site', are not deemed to be able to interpret it. Pagans as new-indigenes alongside other alternative interest groups with interests in sacred sites have seen their perspectives on the past written off as fringe, eccentric and *inauthentic*, and this largely persists: Hubert points out that:

> [Prehistoric stone circles] are not treated as sacred sites by the majority of the population today, though religious significance is claimed for some sites – Stonehenge for example – by a minority. As in many other parts of the world, the beliefs of this minority are dismissed, and the practices in the neighbourhood of the monument disallowed, even to the extant of persecution by the law of the land.
>
> (Hubert, 1994: 12)

There has been some change for Stonehenge since Hubert was writing her chapter on 'sacred beliefs', though the interpretations and folklores that flow from these changing and emergent beliefs may be still regarded with great suspicion or with laughter. And, more reflexive local histories engage with and represent contemporary local voices. Our point is not to make a straightforward, crass or neo-colonial comparison between indigenous communities and new-indigenous pagans, or to act as 'pagan apologists' (as we have been termed in the past), but rather to assert that sensitivity and mutual respect are basic starting points for productive relationships. Press reports which have a knock-on effect for public opinion are all-too-often dismissive of pagans and their perspectives on sacred sites, and some archaeologists and heritage managers take a similarly dismissive attitude (which may even extend to hostility, when pagans are perceived to obstruct excavation and investigation, and obscure interpretation – or even produce 'pseudo' explanations). Some processes of reconciliation are already underway, however, though with fluctuating results. The Stonehenge 'peace process' and round table meetings have reaped the reward of summer solstice managed open access, for instance. But considerable tensions exist between and within communities, as we shall show, and negotiations and guardianship arrangements elsewhere are subject to communication problems and changes in personnel.

Within such processes, heritage managers themselves, once viewed (and often still) as conservative, atheistic civil servants, are now also deploying the term 'sacred site': The 1998 Avebury *English Heritage Management Plan* asserted, 'Paganism may well be the fastest growing religion in Britain and this is linked with the increasing interest in the mystical significance of Avebury as a "sacred" place' (Pomeroy 1998: 27). And it is worth repeating (see Introduction) here that in commenting on their negotiations with pagans, David Miles (Chief Archaeologist, English Heritage; Wallis and Lymer 2001: 107) and Clews Everard (when Site Director, Stonehenge, pc) used the term. 'Sacred sites' are in vogue. Within this new folklore of the 'sacred site', however, the meaning of sacredness seems remarkably diverse – and lack of appreciation of this diversity as well as the political implications of the nomenclature, forms a barrier to communication. 'Sacredness', however it is contrived, is value-laden, not given, specific to particular realms of discourse which foreground one interpretation of these places over others. 'Archaeological', 'monument', 'site' and other variations in terminology are themselves discursively constituted, and archaeologists might label these places 'archaeological sites' or 'prehistoric monuments', while most pagans might prefer 'sacred site'. General acceptance or at least wide use of the term 'sacred site' should not obscure the contentious and fluid nature of such a term. 'Sacred' means different things to a wide variety of people and it is not hard to find examples of how pagans, Goddess worshippers, Christians and heritage managers will contrive a 'sacred' site in very different ways: Druids or Heathens may promote direct (tactile) engagement with sites, Wiccans make use of them as temples to approach their 'goddess', Goddess worshipers may contest the disregard for sacredness inherent in some masculist archaeologies,[1] some Christians might propose the erection of a 'monument' at a prehistoric site to celebrate Christ's second millennium while others (including pagans) oppose this (e.g. The Eden Millennium Project monument adjacent to Mayburgh henge, see <http://www.stonehenge.ukf.net/edenarts.htm>), and heritage managers, meanwhile, use 'sacred' in terms of a perceived need for 'conservation' or 'preservation'.

This implication of the 'sacred' in political contestations of site marginalisation behoves all parties using the term 'sacred site' to be explicit about what they mean, or risk appearing to support ideas or dismiss others, that they do not intend. Over time, documentary analysis shows some archaeologists and heritage managers apparently coming to both theorise the term in their discourse, and recognise diversities of 'pagan' use of both term and site. Similarly, while pagans tend to have a vague or perhaps fluid understanding of sacredness, some others are debating and problematising the term. Hubert (1994) has drawn attention to discrepancies between Christian and indigenous concepts of 'sacredness' as applied to place: peculiarly, a church can be 'deconsecrated', whereas in many indigenous understandings 'sacredness' is *inherent* in place or in non-human manifestations there. Much heritage discourse in Britain seems to us consonant with the former view, derived from a constructed dichotomy between what is 'sacred' and what is 'profane' in Christian thinking, in line with other dualisms or binary oppositions emerging from Cartesian philosophy, and migrating from religion to sociology through Durkeim's *The Elementary Forms of Religious Life* ([1912] 1964). Many theorists have critiqued dualism, with Bakhtin particularly (1968) addressing the sacred/profane opposition, but in heritage documents and management discourse it still appears, with sacredness associated with stillness, silence and awed reverence, and hence a 'sacred site' being in need of careful preservation. Within this dualism, sites such as Stonehenge become analogous to Christian cathedrals where peaceful reverence is (now) key and as Hubert (1994) says, even secular visitors speak in hushed tones; long-term endurance of a site is paramount – or else such sites are nothing. Some pagans align with this view also, as they are uncomfortable with 'partying' at Stonehenge managed open access events (see Chapter 3). But there are many other approaches of pagans to place. Animist pagans align with indigenous understandings, approaching 'sites' as living places where spirits should be engaged with in order to maintain respectful relationships with the other-than-human-people who dwell there. These 'alive' sacred sites – whether marked or not by ancient monuments – are seen as embedded within living landscapes, so that it is as much the wider context as the sacred site which is significant, and the sacredness of landscape is not of human determination. Another point – also made by Hubert – is that of the categorising of sites as preservation-worthy or otherwise, based on rarity value. A site may be one chosen as the 'best' exemplar from a particular period. Rather than being sacred in themselves, then, selected sites become examples of sacredness – examples reflecting current theory and dominant paradigms and political narratives (see chapter 4 regarding the 'sacred landscapes' of Stanton Moor and Thornborough, and debates around issues of local and national significance and 'nationalism' in interpretation, e.g. between Ronayne, Cooney and Thomas [all 2001]). Ivakhiv (2001) draws on Foucault in theorising the sacred sites of Glastonbury (Somerset, UK) and Sedona (Arizona, USA), places of spiritual tourism and pilgrimage, as heterotopic: spaces where meaning is created, contested and negotiated by a variety of agencies (only some of whom are held to be human). In this sense, *heterotopias* are cognate with the 'third space' articulated by Bhabha (1994) and Soja (1996), places of manifold potential and transformation, and pagan engagements with sites and landscapes may be seen as heterotopic. In a similar vein, Hetherington (2000) discusses 'new age travellers' (or better, following Martin 2002, simply 'new travellers') occupying 'a place of alternative order, an as-yet-uncertain order' (Hetherington 2000: 175), 'an unrepresentable "place of otherness" ambivalence, paradox and shifting representations' (Hetherington 2000: 28).

If the term *sacred site* is so contested and so obscured, why employ it in this volume, indeed make use of it to index the entire project? In brief, we do so deliberately, as not only a term used, but a term central to the various competing discourses of site use and landscape that we explore here as constituents to practitioner meanings and identity. This volume does not offer a particular definition of sacred site, but avoids a definition that is fixed and indeed any singular definition per se. We argue for fluidity of meaning in order to engage with and explore the diversity of perspectives that construct, and are constructed within, *sacred sites*. We maintain that ongoing theorisation of the term by all concerned is essential in order to maintain a climate of inclusivity and respectful dialogue. At the very least, application of the term 'sacred site' should provoke heated remarks, invite contest and encourage debate, all of which is healthy to what we see as the emerging sub-field of 'sacred sites studies'. Further, all of the discourses on sacred sites are permeated by an issue which we have implied but not yet explored – the preservation ethos; it is to this issue and its implications for understanding pagan (and other alternative) *vis-à-vis* heritage management engagements with sacred sites, that discussion now turns.

The preservation ethos

The dominant, legitimised, contemporary discourse pertaining to the past and its artefacts (including sacred sites) is that largely articulated by the archaeologists who excavate and interpret them, and heritage managers entrusted with their management; and it relies on what might be termed the 'preservation ethos'. This ethos maintains that (pre)historic artefacts and sites are intrinsically valuable – a value understood principally as intellectual but containing an inherent fiscal value as driven by the art dealer-critic system and evinced by the illegal trade in antiquities. As such, it is deemed that these material remains – or examples of such, where they are many – should be preserved 'for the benefit of future generations', 'for posterity'. As with all discursive practices (sensu Foucault) such a notion appears reasonable and common-sense, but privileges and legitimises certain modes of interpreting and engaging with the past to the detriment of others. Theoretically informed archaeologists (principally academics influenced by the interpretative/discursive 'turn') are well aware of this (e.g. Bender 1993, 1998; Holtorf 1998, 2005; Holtorf and Schadla-Hall 1999; Dowson 2001), and recognise that this ethos is of recent or modern origin: until the activities of antiquarians in the seventeenth and eighteenth centuries brought prehistoric sites to more widespread attention, sites tended popularly to be regarded, at best, with indifference (see Chippindale 1994) – although there are archaeologically attested instances of reverence (or 'sacredness', or possibly aesthetic appreciation, or simply laying claims to an ownership of pasts) of some kind, such as the re-use of prehistoric burial mounds by Anglo-Saxons (Semple 1998; Williams 1998).

The preservation ethos rests on modernist assumptions of 'progress' – ultimately, upon an often-disputed Hegelian idealism in which culture and society move ever onwards in a process of continual betterment, leaving behind symptomatic artefacts, as fossils of the zeitgeist, and evidence of the evolutionary trajectory. For a society in which origins and ultimate destinations are of central importance, this discourse displays how the continuing existence of artefacts from the past matters: 'the remains of the past, both moveable and immovable and also including the intangible – the historic environment – should be protected and preserved for their own sake and for the benefit of future generations' (APPAG 2003: 6). The preservation ethos privileges intellectual and visual engagement with the past and its material objects over other (most obviously spiritual and tactile) engagements, and promotes dedicated professionals (principally academic archaeologists and historians) as final arbiters of meaning. This discourse also supposes that a linear, purposeful, or directed 'progress' requires that the past is in some sense unobtainable.

Though 'knowable', or interpretable, to some extent, it is ultimately unreachable because it is closed. Both the delineation of the past as 'closed' and the privileging of visual/intellectual engagement with artefacts have important implications for pagans and other alternative practitioners. Before attending to this issue, we first explore the practical ramifications of the preservation ethos for the heritage and archaeological professions.

The preservation ethos and heritage management

Not surprisingly (given the preservation ethos), the results of the Monuments at Risk Survey (MARS 1998) were met with dismay and '[a]n estimated 22,500 ancient monuments – one per day – have been destroyed since 1945, with cultivation the single greatest cause of loss' (English Heritage 2000a: 16). Nevertheless, the heritage industry is faced with a contradiction. The preservation ethos derives from the notion of progress, and without progress and change there would be no material objects from the past to preserve, even as heritage management recognises this: 'There has always been change; indeed, without change in the past there would be no historic environment and the past would be identical with the present' (English Heritage 1997: 7). However, progress and change necessarily destroy or transform the majority of those material objects. It is incumbent on heritage managers to decide which are the symptomatic and most valuable artefacts meriting preservation, whilst acceding to, not resisting, the forces of change and progress. A similar process is imposed upon 'dirt' archaeologists who increasingly must work under the prohibitive time pressures of rescue archaeology conditions in the face of aggressive road and house building projects, mineral extraction operations, and ongoing urban development.

Recent documents (e.g. English Heritage 2000a, 2002) show that heritage managers are keen to democratise the process of evaluation, not only because '[p]eople care about the historic environment' (English Heritage 2002: 2), but also because public involvement, as exemplified by the success of the recent BBC *Restoration* programmes, can lead to conservation implementation. Furthermore, in a climate of accountability, managers have sought to make the evaluation process more rigorous, and quantifiable, according to set objective criteria: '[p]olicy needs to be based on evidence' (English Heritage 2002: 16). In addition to the use of the new methodology of 'character assessment' (English Heritage 2000a), 'research frameworks' (Olivier n.d.), indicators of 'historic capital' (English Heritage 1997: 7), and 'community vibrancy' (PDNPA 2000: 16), managers are expressly borrowing terminology from the 'hard' environmental sciences. Documents speak of a historic 'environment' (e.g. English

Heritage 1997, 2000a, 2002, 2006), attained or facilitated through the current (in 2006) 'Historic Environment Enabling Programme' (<http://www.english-heritage.org.uk/>) with consideration of 'environmental capacity' ('the capacity of the environment to absorb or accommodate activity or change without reversible or unacceptable damage' [English Heritage 1997: 9]), the 'carrying capacity' of a site such as Stonehenge (English Heritage 2000b: passim), and 'sustainability' (English Heritage 1997: passim).

Whilst such terminology gives the impression of objectivity and the ability to quantitatively measure 'value', 'character' and so on, it defers subjective decisions by one remove. As with the environmental sciences, deciding what constitutes 'acceptable damage' remains subjective and discursive, however good the indicators are (e.g. Irwin 2001 on problems inherent in the term 'sustainability'). The language used privileges archaeologists and heritage managers as final arbiters of historic value, rendering the claims of democratisation somewhat hollow. The statement that '[g]ood new design will create a rich historic environment for the future' (English Heritage 2000a: 18), for example, implies an objective set of criteria by which 'good' design may be determined, but actually privileges the authors' values and tastes. Indeed, whilst heritage managers claim to respond to the needs of minorities – ethnic, disabled, and, occasionally, religious – the 'glossy' (and hence produced for a wide audience) summarised reports *Power of Place* and *State of the Historic Environment 2002* (English Heritage 2000a, 2002) photographically portray these minorities as *consumers* of the historic environment, but white, middle-aged, middle-class men and women as *managers*. The inclusion of a much wider and more democratic range of industrial and modern buildings into the discourse of 'heritage' has not succeeded in separating conservatism from conservation.

The problem remains that the preservation ethos provides no 'objective' criteria by which material objects may be evaluated, although as previously indicated and as will be exemplified in Chapter 4, rarity and apparent state of preservation may be discussed as if they were factual attributes of sites rather than theoretical constructs. That heritage managers are aware of the lack of objective measurement is evidenced by the space devoted to the problem within the documentation, but there is only an implicit acknowledgement of the discursive nature of such decision-making. The indicator of value most often used is a default mechanism of the modernist paradigm – an artefact's economic potential for generating income (e.g. 'The historic environment enriches the quality of our lives. As a result, it is a major economic asset'; and 'An empty building is an underused asset' [both English Heritage 2002: 5]).

Implications of the preservation ethos for the non-specialist

Our interest here is the negotiation and contestation between competing discourses pertaining to sacred sites, and in particular between those espoused by practitioners of alternative spiritualities and heritage managers. The routine discursive application of the preservation ethos has two important implications for the former parties. First, the assumption that the past is *closed* marginalises the activities of contemporary practitioners at sites, as these activities – frequently stated by pagans as reviving, reconstructing or at least reconstituting ancient practices, and therefore approaching the past as alive and accessible in various ways – are seen as lying outside the arbitrary boundary of closure. Archaeologists interested in the 'religious' significance of, say, Stonehenge, tend to limit themselves to activities detectable within the archaeological record, even the historical record, but rarely to those of the present day (but see Chippindale 1994; Bender 1998; Edmonds and Seabourne 2001; Wallis 2003). Contemporary ritual activity is invalid as a form of archaeological knowledge; it cannot be considered 'authentic', because it lies outside this arbitrarily defined boundary of closure. What counts as being of interest are the ritual activities of the 'original' culture(s). This widespread dismissal of contemporary religious activity as academically irrelevant is made more tenuous by the interest of archaeologists in the re-use of sites in the past as well as ongoing representation and consumption: for if ancient re-usage merits interest, then it is unstated why the contemporary does not.

The preservation ethos also reifies the activities of people in the past, and the impact that these activities may have had upon a site, to the detriment of contemporary activities and any resulting amelioration. Since a site must be preserved in its current state and change constitutes 'degradation', contemporary activities must necessarily be regarded as potentially threatening sites' stability and continuity. The ethos creates the situation in which sites are regarded as being continually and permanently under threat. The discursive nature of this position becomes apparent when, for example, the history of Stonehenge is examined: rather than being a singular 'thing', Stonehenge is a palimpsest, resulting from many phases of intervention, as discussed further in chapter 3. Throughout its long history the monument has been altered, changed, developed, abandoned, and reused (Chippindale 1994; Bender 1998; Wessex Archaeology 2003). The name, *Stonehenge*, dates to the Anglo-Saxon period, some 2000 years after its construction. The familiar layout of the monument dates only to excavations at the turn of the twentieth century and since then, particularly during the 1950s. Whilst any contemporary 'damage', such as alleged carvings, is denigrated in the press as 'desecration', Bronze Age carvings count as archaeological evidence –

and Victorian ones are conveniently ignored. The felt need to 'preserve' Stonehenge as it currently exists is a comparatively recent development.

Notably, the preservation ethos privileges a visual, rather than physical, embodied, or emotional engagement with sites: to appreciate sites fully they should be *looked at*, like museum exhibits, and preferably from a distance so that they can be appreciated in the full context of their archaeological landscape (but for archaeologists challenging this see e.g. Bender 1998; Thomas 1993; Wallis 2003). Management plans repeatedly stress the importance of landscape and distance views (e.g. again regarding Stonehenge: 'From the highest points on the downland ... views are extensive and landscape features can be visible from a considerable distance' [English Heritage 2000b: 3.13]). The visual bias inherent within the preservation ethos is consequently influential upon current archaeological interpretations which foreground spatiality, distance and perspective, and vice versa. It has also contoured thinking regarding the planned improvements to visitor facilities at Stonehenge and the proposed 'visitor experience', in which (in various versions of proposals over several years) one road will be removed, another possibly replaced by a tunnel, and visitors bussed to vantage points from which to view and wander through the panorama (for critical discussion of this approach by archaeologists, see Baxter and Chippindale 2002).

1.4 Stonehenge today – 'a dramatic ruin, devoid of people'. Visitors are restricted to the tourist path around the monument.

Finally it determines the repeated representation of Stonehenge and
other sites, through photographic, video, and postcard images, as a
dramatic ruin (Hetherington 2000; Letcher et al. forthcoming) devoid
of people (e.g. English Heritage 2000b passim.).

Pagan discourses

The diverse groups of people seeking access to sites for spiritual ends
might be broadly divided into those who wish to work within the
preservation ethos, and those who rail against it, though the division
is not hard and fast, but one of degree and emphasis rather than
formal group membership. Andy Letcher, as ESRC-funded researcher
for the Sacred Sites project, conducted an extensive discourse study of
pagan periodicals and heritage documents up to 2003, and we have
outlined these findings on usages elsewhere (see Blain, Letcher and
Wallis 2004). The former includes contributions to largely Wiccan-
inspired magazines such as the journal *Pagan Dawn*, and the writings
of those whom Letcher (2001a) terms 'personal-growth druids' artic-
ulating opinions in later editions of *The Druid's Voice*. The latter
includes so-called 'counter-cultural druids' (Letcher 2001a) such as
the Secular Order of Druids and celebrants campaigning for the
return of the Stonehenge free-festival (see Festival Eye magazine
passim, and below).

Preservation ethos and 'personal-growth druids'

For pagans in the former group, a range of prehistoric sites including
stone circles, barrows, standing stones, examples of rock art, fogous,
Iron Age forts and later features such as holy wells, are interpreted as
commensurate artefacts of pre-Christian paganism, and as such, sacred.
Access to sites is therefore of central importance to practitioners, but
not at the expense of preservation for future generations – the preservation ethos is reified and upheld. Thus, many articles in *Pagan Dawn*
and *The Druid's Voice* complain about ritual detritus and damage caused
by unscrupulous pagan ritualists (see also comments by Carpenter
1998; Prout 1998; Fleming 1999, n.d.a, n.d.b). And, many pagans
regard themselves as the 'guardians' of their chosen sacred sites.

Somewhat contrarily, the voices within these pagan journals seek
both an identity of alterity *and* acceptance by mainstream society:
'Druids were once more allowed back into the temple only because
[management appreciates that] Druids exist who want nothing to do
with the free festival, who live with or within mainstream society
instead of spitting at it' (Restall Orr 1998: 23). Thus, various groups
seeking to preserve sacred sites (e.g. *Save Our Sacred Sites* and the
Ancient Sacred Landscapes Network [ASLAN]) are delineating a

distinctly 'pagan' campaigning area, which presents pagans as respectable society members concerned with the conservation of heritage. Archaeology as a discipline is viewed positively amongst these groups and the presence of archaeologists at pagan events and conferences is remarked upon favourably because it is interpreted as conferring legitimacy/authenticity upon pagan practices (appropriated/reconstructed from the past) (e.g. Bannister 2000: 8). This view is not precisely reciprocated, although some archaeologists and heritage managers already regard pagans sensitively (sometimes because they are themselves pagans), while others are beginning to realise the benefits of having a pagan community wedded to the preservation ethos and willing to patrol sacred sites as guardians; indeed, the needs of pagan practitioners are beginning to be accommodated in management plans (e.g. Lambrick 2001).

Counter-cultural Druids and festival celebrants

Not all pagans are sympathetic to the preservation ethos. 'Counter-cultural' Druids (Letcher 2001a) and other festival celebrants (including many pagans and new travellers), adhere to an alternative discourse which calls for mass public celebration, especially at the summer solstice, at the 'people's temple' of Stonehenge. Preservation, where considered, is put second to access. The origins of this discourse may be traced back at least as far as the late 1960s at which time Stonehenge was becoming an icon of the 'hippy' counterculture (and used in adverts for the latest albums by psychedelic and 'prog-rock' bands in publications such as *Gandalf's Garden* (e.g. 1969, 5: 30). The front cover of *International Times* issue 59 (4–17 July 1969) shows a hippy or Druid ritual event at Stonehenge, and in 1970 the launch of Hawkwind's first album was indicated in *International Times* with an image of the band in front of their sound equipment which is stacked to resemble trilithons (Letcher, pc.). This counterculture began to regard its activities in mythological terms as a utopian struggle against a corrupt mainstream society: celebrating the solstice at the Stonehenge free festival (started in 1974 by Phil Russell, a.k.a. Wally Hope), whether in Druidic or less structured rituals, became a means in itself of magically transforming society and restoring 'harmony' to the land. The banning of the festival and clash between the police and new travellers at the 'battle of the beanfield' (1985) reinforced the notion that the festival had threatened to transform 'society' and that festival goers were freedom fighters against state oppression (*Festival Eye* passim). In this counter-cultural discourse it is the denial of access, and not preservation, which provides the central narrative: until the free festival is restored, adherents feel their rights are violated. Stonehenge is not a ruin but a living temple and mass gatherings restore it to its 'original' purpose. It becomes a place

of protest and a place of freedom, not symbolising these but constituting them in association with festival use. MacKay (1996)
comments of the Stonehenge Free Festival that:

> Latching onto the solstice rituals of Druids at Stonehenge
> which themselves go back only to the turn of the century, the
> hippies invent an instant and powerful tradition. Squatter and
> original Hyde Park Digger Sid Rawle . . . explained: "we come
> to Stonehenge because in an unstable world it is proper that
> the people should look for stability to the past in order to learn
> for the future".
>
> (McKay 1996: 18)

Today's attendees at managed open access will likewise index both
stability and transformation, and the need for assembly in order to
celebrate, as outlined in Chapter 3.

So, pagans seeking mainstream respectability and supporting the
preservation ethos attempt to distance themselves from such 'less
spiritual' new travellers who apparently 'knock down the perimeter
fence, stop a Druid ritual and clash with the police . . . No true pagan
would show such disrespect' (Coughlan 1999: 46). It is incumbent
upon researchers of pagan, alternative and heritage discourses to
demonstrate the diversity of perceptions within the interest groups
and make available to the groups themselves the ways in which their
speaking is constituted so as to develop constructive dialogues and
relationships between them. Such is one aim of this book.
Preservation and access, discursively constituted, are dearly held, and
discussions where one or other is undervalued become not merely
frustrating but actively counterproductive. The chapters that follow
return to the theories and issues raised here. This chapter ends,
though, with an overview of why it is that pagans engage with sacred
sites, what they might do there, and how a rapprochement of pagans
and archaeologists may be timely.

Pagans at sacred sites

There is a wide variety of reasons why Pagans engage with sacred
sites. Gordon 'the toad' MacLellan, a 'shaman' and environmental
educator, thinks ancient sites 'offer places of stillness, connection
with ancestors' (pc). 'Barry', also a neo-Shamanic environmental
educator, suggests there are dangers: 'too much activity of the wrong
kind can cause harm to the natural energies of a famous or popular
place...I've found a lot of sites that were closed down or seriously
abused because they were well known' (pc). This abuse may, accord-

ing to some, also take place on a 'spiritual' level. Fleming suggests meddling with a site's energies is 'psychic vandalism' (Fleming 1999) and argues – in a markedly uncompromising tone – that many forms of Pagan ritual constitute site damage:

> I find it unnecessary to perform any ritual at a prehistoric site unless the site is actively involved in the ritual . . . [I]f the ritual could be performed in exactly the same way in any other location then the site is providing no more than an atmospheric backdrop and that is insufficient reason to expose a delicate and unique monument to the risk of damage.
>
> (Fleming n.d.a; see also n.d.b)

The Druid Philip 'Greywolf' Shallcrass, formerly Joint-Chief of the British Druid Order, offers a different, more detailed and community focused perspective on why places like Avebury and Stonehenge are spiritually important to Druids (and by implication other pagans):

> Many Druids like to make ritual at ancient stone circles since there is a strong feeling that they are places where communion with our ancestors may be made more readily than elsewhere. There is also a sense that making ritual at such places energises and benefits both the sites themselves and the land around. . . . I am drawn to Avebury . . . because it is my heartland, i.e. the place where I feel most spiritually 'at home'. The first time I visited, more than twenty years ago, I felt I belonged there. That feeling has never left me. I work with spirits of place. This is a strong part of Druid tradition. I feel the spirit of place most strongly most often in Avebury. Six years ago, I was asked to make a Druid rite for an eclectic gathering at Avebury. I composed a rite that left space for people of all traditions to experience their own faith together in one circle with those of other faiths. It worked so well that similar open, multi-faith ceremonies are still being held there and elsewhere, both in Britain and overseas. Avebury is a very welcoming place in which to make ritual. I am not the only person who has experienced the spirit of the place as a great mother with open arms, welcoming all who come. (pc)

This diversity of approaches notwithstanding, there is a common theme underlying Pagan engagements with sacred sites: such places are perceived as special, spiritually so, or more simply, as 'sacred', whatever this is held to mean; more specifically they are places that are 'alive' today, where connections can be made with 'ancestors', where deities and 'ancestors' can be contacted, and where the spirit/energy of the land, the genius loci and local land wights, can be felt most strongly. Increasing numbers of people make pilgrimages to these places throughout the year, with a surge in numbers around the eight most well known pagan festivals. In terms of preservation, this direct physical contact is being noted, increasingly and necessarily, by archaeologists and site managers. Pagans also propose interpretations of these places which may contrast markedly with those of site curators (e.g. Dames 1976; Devereux 1992; Cope 1998; Gyrus 1998b).

There is no single Pagan relationship with such places. Many pagans claim individual divine inspiration for whatever practices seem appropriate at the time, often involving the deposition of the votive offerings – flowers, food and drink of various kinds, which might in turn comprise 'ritual litter' for other visitors – candlewax, tea-light holders, incense sticks, charcoal and coins, as well as the decoration of specific places with symbols such as spirals or pentacles; and the insertion of crystals, coins and other materials into the cracks of megaliths. The most destructive practices involve lighting 'ritual' fires with detrimental effect on the stones, and there have been instances of deliberate vandalism. Much Pagan use takes place with little knowledge either of archaeological interpretation, or of what practices are detrimental or problematic for other users.[2] In an extreme example, Peak District archaeologist John Barnatt (1997) describes a stone circle being 'altered' by a group who apparently held that the stones were wrongly positioned, according to their information obtained from dowsing. Pagans have also come forward as 'guardians' of sites, as noted in subsequent chapters, and in Cornwall Pagan groups worked with English Heritage to restore Men-an-Tol, a monument which had been vandalised with an ersatz napalm-like substance by a group calling themselves, bizarrely, 'Friends of the Stone'. Indeed, the late 1990s saw the emergence of preservation ethos aligned organisations explicitly focusing on pagan interests in sacred sites and as such either formed by pagans, as in the case of *Cruithni* and *Save Our Sacred Sites* (SOSS), or with substantial pagan involvement, as in the *Ancient Sacred Landscape Network* (ASLaN). The activity of *Cruithni* and SOSS has petered out, while ASLaN has endured in association with The Rollright Trust which curates the sites of the Rollright complex in Oxfordshire. ASLaN produced a 'Sacred Sites Charter' offering a guide to pagans as to how approach sites respectfully when visiting and conducting ceremony. Initially, this was available on-site at the Rollrights and was also publicised online and in publications with a pagan readership including the magazine of the Pagan Federation, *Pagan Dawn*, and the magazine of the Rollright Trust, *The Right Times*. The charter is less in evidence at the current time, but a synopsis is still available online on the Rollright Trust website (<http://www.rollrightstones.co.uk/aslan.html>).

The politics surrounding Pagan uses of sacred sites are extremely complex. The situation at the timber circle dubbed 'Seahenge' at Holme-next-the-Sea in Norfolk in 1999 (Champion 2000; Pryor 2001) exemplified the diversity of Pagan and other opinions. Some Pagans were outraged at the proposal by English Heritage to *not* conserve the timbers:

> [I] asked if I could arrange a meeting with all of them, in a sacred manner. They all agreed so last Tuesday [22.6.99] we had eleven people from wildly different backgrounds holding hands, invoking our Ancestors and Great Spirit (which saves a lot of explanation and debate) and Awening.[3] And within five

The Ancient Sacred Landscape Network

Sacred Sites Charter

Please take care when visiting sacred sites to leave them as the next visitor would like to find them. Respect the land and all its inhabitants - spirits, people, animals, plants and stones.

Digging holes for any purpose will damage plants and probably insects and archaeological remains. Damaging any aspect of nature will not please the Spirit of Place. Damaging archaeology may upset the official guardians or owners of the site and lead to it being closed to all. Lighting fires can cause similar damage to digging. A fire can damage standing stones - if they get too hot, they split. Fires can spread quickly in summer, killing wildlife, and it can be very difficult to make sure a fire is truly out. Heat, candle wax and graffiti damage moss and lichens which can take decades to recover.

The Spirits of Place are more likely to be displeased at fire damage than upset that you haven't lit one.

If an offering seems appropriate please think about all its effects. Don't leave artificial materials. Choose your offerings carefully so that they can't be mistaken for litter. Please don't bury things. Please don't leave biodegradable materials that may be offensive as they decay. If the site is already overloaded with offerings consider the effects of adding more.

Taking things from a site needs similar careful thought. Much of the vegetation around sacred sites is unusual or rare so don't pick flowers. Don't take stones - they may be an important part of the site in ways which aren't obvious.

In times past it was traditional to leave no traces of any ritual because of persecution. This tradition is worth reviving because it shows reverence to nature and the Spirits of Place.

Don't change the site, let the site change you.

ASLaN can be contacted via The Right Times

1.5
The ASLaN Charter, distributed at the Rollright Stones. Scanned and reproduced with permission from Andy Norfolk.

hours we had a remarkable agreement. The timbers would be removed and preserved but returned to the village, possibly within a new Bronze Age village that would be built to house them. In the meantime, the site would be recreated with new timbers, with the proviso that if it caused tourism that impacted the birds it would be removed. And any ceremony for the removal of the timbers would be welcome . . . [A]ll those who were in the meeting were gracious and giving and we got a fabulous result.

(Prout in submission to Nature Religions email discussion list 7 July 1999 [used with permission])

There are other, conflicting narratives of the Seahenge fiasco. Some Druids protested against the excavation of the circle (as shown on the Channel 4 *Time Team Special* on Seahenge). And meanwhile, the local community felt their views were completely ignored, with the result that one of them supported the legal actions of druids against Norfolk Archaeological unit. Local pagan Chris Wood describes the controversy in terms of local wishes (for the circle to remain until it was eventually taken by the sea) being overruled by outsiders, notably archaeologists, who stressed preservation (see Wood 2002). Arguably the situation was more complicated than this, there being some dissent amongst archaeologists. An article in the widely read journal *British Archaeology* by its editor, Simon Denison, expresses disgust with the way Seahenge was 'yanked out of the sands': 'The excavation . . . was destruction, nothing short of vandalism' (Denison 2000: 28). Controversially perhaps, for an archaeologist versed in the preservation – or at least conservation – ethos, Denison argues:

The only way to truly cherish an ancient monument or other historic feature is to leave it alone, avoid it, plan round it. And if it is necessary, *absolutely necessary*, to plough a road through it, or abandon it to the waves, then my judgement is we should photograph it, film it, write about it – and let it go.

(Denison 2000: 28, emphasis in original)

In *Heritage Today* (Issue 47, September 1999), on the other hand, English Heritage is presented as having a common-sense approach (excavating the timbers as quickly as possible for preservation) in contrast to the rather hysterical responses of Druids and others in this presentation (see also Pryor 2001) – as might be expected in the magazine publication of the organisation distributed to members.

One theme which may unite pagan approaches to sacred sites, whether they are preservation-ethos-supporting or counter-cultural pagans, is their implicit contest to the rapid 'consumption' of sites (by tourists, archaeologists or indeed other pagans). This same theme might unite archaeologists (both academic and 'dirt-digging'), even if heritage managers concerned with annual budgets and cost-cutting might find such an idea challenging. Places which have endured for millennia cannot be understood or appreciated in a thirty-minute tour or a hurried excavation. At a conference at the University of Southampton in 1999 (*A Permeability of Boundaries? New Approaches to the Archaeology of Art, Religion and Folklore,* co-organised by Wallis) the question was asked during a chaired debate, 'alternative archaeology, has it happened?' The intention was to address the extent to which archaeologists, heritage managers and other custodians of the past were prepared to engage with rather than dismiss as eccentric such alternative archaeologists as earth mystics and pagans. During this discussion, Richard Bradley, Professor of Archaeology at Reading University, suggested that we must:

> get used to monuments, spend time with them, be patient with them, contemplate them, before insights arise. There is an analogy between our instant consumption of monuments like Stonehenge, and the deficiencies of traditional archaeology; we have no patience. We have no patience as tourists and we have no patience as academics. It's no good having forty-five minutes access to Stonehenge whether you pay or not. What you need is the possibility for spending a long time at it, of being able to look at it in different lighting conditions, for instance. And that goes for all monuments, not just Stonehenge. The health of the discipline as a whole depends on a change in mindset and the way we expect people to experience these sites.
>
> (Bradley cited in Wallis and Lymer 2001: 117)

Pagans find that current heritage management may not, however, have sufficient time to address this issue. We read Bradley as saying that we need, whether pagan, archaeologist, anthropologist, tourist or 'other', to have patience with place and landscape, spend time with them, engage with them, walk slowly over the terrain and return many times. For pagans this may involve peaceful contemplation or celebration and partying, returning in many moods to a changing landscape over seasons. So known, the site becomes a friend or a colleague, yet the time of place and the time of human people are very different: in our short lives, how do we know the changes of landscape and how some places come to be sacred?

The question of time (explored brilliantly by Fabian 1983; also Gell 1992) raises the issue of a different kind of consumption, on which to end this initial exploration of issues, constructions and representations: some of the places discussed here are under threat from a variety of external processes and human needs of late modernity – from rapid transportation to the West Country (regarding Stonehenge), to demands for quarried dimensional stone or gravel (at Stanton Moor and Thornborough). The sacredness of place and the wish for in-depth understanding – in pagan or archaeologist – are in tension with other issues. Our contention is that, despite differences of opinion and approach, moves towards dialogue and mutual understanding are not only possible but highly important for the presentation of – for the want of a better phrase – *the sites' points of view* within political processes. While the example of Seahenge marks dissonance, there are other instances where dialogues are already in effect, and though perhaps strained, are resulting in reciprocal negotiations. In the chapters which follow, we examine some of these situations and their complexities.

CHAPTER 2

Avebury

'Twas here that our game began, and the chase led us (at length) through the village of Aubury, into the closes there: where I was wonderfully surprized at the sight of those vast stones, of which I had never heard before: as also at the mighty Bank and graffe about it: I observed in the inclosure some segments of rude circles, made with these stones, whence I concluded, they had been in the old time complete. (John Aubrey, *Monumenta Britannica – Templa Druidum* 1648:1, transcribed as 'Notes from Aubrey' by Glastonbury 2004)

I feel the spirit of place most strongly most often in Avebury. Avebury is a very welcoming place in which to make ritual. I am not the only person who has experienced the spirit of the place as a great mother with open arms, welcoming all who come. 'Greywolf' (Philip Shallcrass), pc.

The Avebury landscape

The sacred sites at Avebury are, to use a term much in use in the heritage industry, 'unique': its best-known prehistoric stone circle is the largest in Europe, and within the stones is a village with a history from Saxon times until today. The prehistoric Avebury complex (West Kennet Long Barrow, Avebury Henge and its stone circles, the Avenue, Silbury Hill, Windmill Hill, the Sanctuary and various associated barrows and monuments) is managed by the National Trust (which owns approximately one-third of the land, and most properties within the village) in association with English Heritage which is closely involved with project management and development of plans, and which funds a World Heritage Site officer. Avebury and its environs constitute the Avebury World Heritage Site (WHS), listed together with its relatively close neighbour Stonehenge (22 miles away), in accordance with the UNESCO World Heritage Convention. The local and national management has responsibility for maintaining the site in ways which, according to the long-term objectives of the Avebury Management Plan, 'Meet Britain's obligations under the

World Heritage Convention in relation to the effective management of the Avebury WHS' (Pomeroy-Kellinger n.d.). The local council website comments that 'A measure of Avebury's uniqueness is its appeal to a wider variety of people. 350,000 annual visitors are attracted to Avebury, including a large element of international tourists. Pagans also visit the site as a place of contemporary celebration and gathering' (Kennet District Council n.d.).

Many sacred sites are small, remote, or isolated from daily living. Avebury is an exception. National Trust properties at the site and open to the public include a shop, a restaurant, and the Alexander Keiller Museum. Avebury is also home to *The Henge Shop*, which sells an assortment of books, magazines and cards, T-shirts and other textiles, and items such as ornaments and jewellery often with a 'celtic' emphasis. Where the National Trust shop attracts a more conventional range of heritage tourists, much as would be expected in National Trust property shops elsewhere, *The Henge Shop* includes what the popular media might consider a more 'new age' set of wares, thereby attracting a more alternative clientele. Other properties in the village include the various houses, the post office, an antique shop, a church and the *Red Lion* pub, approximately in the centre of the great circle, and a notable part of the local community (including archaeological and pagan) life. But here we are getting ahead of the narrative.

Archaeological interpretation of the prehistoric Avebury landscape has varied over the years, but has come to focus on 'ancestors' and 'landscape' (e.g. Pollard and Reynolds 2002; Whittle 1997). The last twenty years have, however, seen immense growth in 'visiting' by pagans who may regard Avebury as a 'living temple' and its associated sites as places where spirits or ancestors may be met with; and by others who visit Avebury as a place where folklore accrues and unexpected or mysterious events occur and are documented by popular authors (see e.g. Richardson 2001 for some description of Avebury and Silbury as places associated with Earth Mysteries). Associations of Avebury with modern Druidry date from the antiquarian John Aubrey in the seventeenth century, and today Avebury is a principal location for the meeting of 'the tribes', consisting of various groups of Druids, Heathens, Wiccans and others such as new travellers, and including those living locally and others from all areas of Britain and overseas. As such, Avebury is the home of the Druid-orientated Gorsedd of Bards of Caer Abiri, and on various equinoxes or solstices Druid rituals may include induction into this informal Gorsedd, which is less an organisation and more of an idea about how people, mainly pagans, may attain their potential as poets or artists (see <http://abiri-gorsedd.org.uk/>). Several Druid orders celebrate at Avebury on a regular basis (usually arranging a schedule enabling avoidance of one another – Druid politics are complex), and numerous groups from other Pagan traditions will attend, often from other areas of Britain, while local Wiccan and other groups conduct their own rituals according to their own calendars. The village lying within Avebury Henge, and most of its surrounding areas and sites, are open to the public – excepting Silbury Hill, fenced off due to damage and potential danger to both site and public. In this 'contested landscape' (Bender and Winer 2001) issues arise both over the celebration of pagan festivals, site use more generally, and parking restrictions, and over protection issues with pagans and local people attempting to put pressure on heritage organisations – for example, to 'Save Silbury' (Blain and Wallis 2006d; see also Heritage Action website at <http://www.heritageaction.org>).

The sites within the Avebury complex are described in detail by Pollard and Reynolds (2002; and previously by Ucko et al. 1991; Burl 1986 [1979]), and the geology of the landscape is also indicated in their account. Diagrams and maps are available as part of the online Management Plan (Pomeroy-Kellinger 2005). Summarised, according to these analyses (which present their own discursive constructions of what is 'Avebury'), Avebury is in the area of the headwaters of the Kennet which rises at the Swallowhead Springs south of Silbury but is fed by the seasonal Winterbourne, earlier known as the Sambourne, which flows past Windmill Hill and Avebury village to join the Kennet. The landscape is one of chalk downland, just west of the Marlborough Downs, and nearby areas were in the past studded with large sandstone boulders known as sarsens – used for construction purposes since the Neolithic. The landscape has been modified by humans since the Early Neolithic,[1] with the construction of wooden monuments, earthen long barrows, henges, enclosures and other earthworks, field clearance, and dwellings from prehistory, with further modifications through the Anglo-Saxon and Mediaeval periods until the present day. Most obvious and most famous of these monumental changes are the banks and ditches of Avebury Henge with their large standing stones within, and the constructed mound of Silbury Hill south of the henge.

Avebury's monuments have been described from the sixteenth century (when John Leland mentioned them in his *Itinerary*) to the present, most famously by both John Aubrey in the late seventeenth century (including his finding of them during the 'chase' described in the quotation which begins this chapter) and, extensively, William Stukeley in the 17th and early 18th centuries. Images of Stukeley's Avebury sketches are much found in art shops and on the internet, and Aubrey's earlier statement that 'This monument does as much exceed in greatness the so renowned Stoneheng, as a Cathedral doeth a parish Church: so that by its grandure one might presume it to have been an Arch Temple of the Druids' is extensively quoted in pamphlets, articles, websites (and here from the Avebury Tour CD, Glastonbury 2004). The progressive descriptions of stones, place, landscape not only document change – the destruction of sarsens of the Avebury circles and use of their fragments for building – but each piece of writing delineates a different Avebury, a 'sacred landscape' altering over time or seen with different eyes, constituted within ideas about pasts, humanity and sacredness, current at the times. Writings of early chorographers, such as Aubrey and Stukeley, may emphasise the 'temple of the Druids', whereas today's archaeology is more likely to deal in 'community' and 'ritual' associated with 'ancestors' as a focus of the people who built the great circle; the twentieth century attempted to locate Avebury within the series of 'ages' invented a century previously.[2] Excavations have had their own impact on the landscape: most notably Keiller's uncovering and re-erection of some of the stones, in the period from 1934 to 1939. However excavation reports and finds have constructed imaginal Aveburies both past and present: Gray's work in the early twentieth century still influences archaeological accounts and tourist literature in its descriptions of the ditch and bank, and recently Whittle's (1997) work in the area between Silbury and the West Kennet Long Barrow has provided knowledge of structures which leave no obvious (visible) traces, the palisaded enclosures used for some ritual or at least seasonal purpose. Accounts and interpretations from various excavations have added to the folklore of Avebury. Visitor leaflets and booklets repeat some of these: that the stones of the great circle are of two shapes, representing 'female' (lozenges) and 'male' (thinner rectangular stones), for instance, which seems to have originated with Keiller, or that stone 9 (in the south-west quadrant) in Mediaeval times in its falling killed a barber-surgeon who was helping to fell it, his occupation indicated by the toolkit he carried with him. The first of these is disputed by at least some archaeologists and pagans alike, the second has been shown to be unlikely by archaeologist Mike Pitts (in a story given by him in *Hengeworld* [Pitts 2000], the tale of his discovery of the remains now becoming its own part of new Avebury folklore) and others, but they are still repeated in popular interpretations and on websites about Avebury (see e.g. <http://www.prehistoric.org.uk/wiltshire/avebury.html>, although the tale of the re-finding of the 'barber's skeleton' is now starting to appear on other sites such as <http://www.avebury-web.co.uk/>).

The Avebury complex as defined by the Avebury WHS covers an area of 22.5 square kilometres. Within this boundary (arbitrarily delineated by modern features) are 67 areas protected as Scheduled Monuments, the number having increased through, for instance, sites identified by aerial photography since the first demarcation of the WHS. Some sites are of course relatively recent (there are 85 listed

2.1 'Tourist Avebury' immediately before summer solstice, photographed from the south bank.

buildings including those of the remaining buildings within the Avebury village, for instance) but around one-third of the identified 383 sites are, according to the Management Plan, prehistoric burials and monuments (AMP part one). The WHS includes several areas of 'unimproved chalk grassland' or chalk downland, rich in wildlife species, and exemplifying an internationally-threatened habitat. The WHS designation makes specific reference to six monuments which are listed as 'guardianship' monuments: Windmill Hill, West Kennet Long Barrow, Silbury Hill, with the three linked monuments of Avebury Henge, West Kennet Avenue and The Sanctuary. These six are also the best-known components of the Avebury landscape and they are what tourists – including spiritual tourists – come to see.

Avebury has national and international significance, archaeologically, historically and scientifically, and as such it is an attraction for many people who journey there for their own reasons. Avebury is a 'honeypot' site with its own idiosyncratic history: it is 'the village in the stones' (so named in a BBC2 documentary), from which people as residents and farmers have been removed, first by amateur millionaire archaeologist and entrepreneur Alexander Keiller to facilitate excavations in the 1930s, further by the National Trust, which became landowner in 1942. The village today is smaller than in the time of Keiller's excavations, when houses were bought and demolished with their occupants moved to nearly Avebury Trusloe, the National Trust continuing this policy formally until 1976, although, paradoxically, some of the demolished dwellings seem to have been Mediaeval cottages (Chandler, 2001, 2003, n.d.; Edwards 2000). Tensions endure between site management and local people. Pagan pressure (most noticeably in the form of numbers of visitors) on the village and associated monuments is mounting, and disputes ensue, particularly over use of the National Trust car park at festival times, but also over the stream of 'outsiders' who walk and drive through the village, create their own meanings with the stones, sometimes attempt to set up tents, and crowd out the local pub. National Trust site managers have changed several times in the past ten years. The period from 2002 to 2005 saw an immense growth of obvious pagan 'visiting' at Avebury, together with a series of disputes involving management with both pagans and local people. An 'Avebury Forum' established (in 2005) to ease tensions and develop guidelines for 'visiting' through negotiating access includes representatives of some pagan groups, though these seem very restricted; two recently-local pagans are also part of the forum, though pagans with a rather longer period of attachment to the place do not seem to have a voice, and the forum itself has its critics.

Avebury and the Sacred Sites project

Our work as the Sacred Sites project is most obviously about what people, principally pagans, do at places such as Avebury, and why: the meanings involved and how these are developed, and how sites and people are together part of these constructions of meaning. Practices and meanings change as they are developed within contexts which are political and cultural as well as spiritual. The increasing pressure of numbers at Avebury affects not only what can occur but how people experience place and event; and the interpretations of policies and negotiation of space and meaning alter with changes in heritage management personnel. These are clearly significant issues; yet there is no sustained, critical commentary on them outside the *Sacred Sites* project. By way of example, the Negotiating Avebury Project (see Gillings et al. n.d.), initially a collaboration between archaeology departments of the universities of Leicester, Newport and Southampton, despite the apparently reflexive use of 'Negotiating' in its title, does not consider pagans or other alternative engagements in its discussion documents (to date). Given its remit of furthering knowledge of prehistoric Avebury, perhaps one should not expect any attention to paganisms today in such studies. But pasts are always represented and negotiated in the discursive milieu of their present telling, and the present can only be engaged with by virtue of the memory of the past preceding it. Archaeological research does not, to state the obvious, exist within a political vacuum. It is, we argue, incumbent upon archaeologists and other professionals engaging with Avebury and other ancient sites (whether all agree that they are 'sacred' or not) in various ways to address alternative archaeologies. Here, we redress this imbalance and, specifically, explore social, political and economic implications of increasing pagan engagements with sites. Particularly at Avebury, we are interrogating how these practices and engagements constitute fragmented selves and competing/contested identities of person, place and community.

The focus here is on how the Avebury Complex becomes part of the construction of paganisms (Druidry and other forms), through exploring what people do there and the interplay of pagan, heritage management and local understandings and responses. Thus this chapter examines perceptions of sacredness and its inscription and performance in the Avebury landscape, within the specific political and historical constitution of that landscape, and the emergent tensions arising (which may be themselves mythologised as foundation myths of paganisms within post-modernity).

The Avebury landscape is not 'fixed' either within archaeological or pagan interpretation. 'New' or 'discovered' features may become points of interest, and management delineation of features as archaeological may legitimate pagan focuses of practice. Some features remain to be discovered by tourists or discursively constituted as ancient. Local photographer Pete Glastonbury has described his recognition of a mound (which he terms 'Silbaby' as a small version of the nearby giant Silbury Hill) which he has since reported to the Negotiating Avebury project. Within the tourist gaze, this mound is not visible. He comments that:

> I am bemused by the fact that Avebury is now being used extensively for various Pagan rituals all around the landscape and there is this one spot with its own mound, spring and pond that no one uses or even recognizes. Amazing as its only 500m from Silbury, West Kennet Long Barrow and Swallowhead.

> I was at West Kennet Long Barrow recently and pointed it out to a tourist and he couldn't see it! It shows that there are still major discoveries to made at Avebury by Amatuers and Professional archaeologists alike. (Glastonbury, pc)

Pagan 'performances' of spirituality and site include druid rituals which have come to have a standardised form in many instances, described later in this chapter (including processing around part of the banks, with associated erosion issues – at least in dry spells – according to some heritage management), but are not restricted to these. Several druid groups will undertake ritual on different days over festival weekends (to avoid 'druid politics'): they include two loosely-defined groups which we, following Letcher (2001a), have called 'countercultural' druids (those campaigning for improved physical access to sites while seeing themselves as part of an active global peace campaign) and 'personal growth' druids (who focus on self-improvement); though both groups may follow an idea of progression through stages of bard (poet), ovate (seer) and druid (ritual specialist and knowledgeable or wise person with magical abilities). Both groups attempt to negotiate with site management over camping and parking, particularly during festivals. Issues of preservation versus access may come to the fore, and there are differences in how these are balanced and how sacredness and reverence for place are constituted through *being* and *doing* within a site which we return to throughout this volume. It is important to point out not only that some druids (and others) have been frequenting Avebury for several years – twenty or more possibly – but that there are pagans who live locally, whether in the village itself, surrounding villages, or nearby towns such as Devizes or Swindon, and others who once lived locally but do so no longer, though feeling it as 'home' and returning regularly. Those pagans who are 'local' or 'regular' may differentiate themselves from 'festival pagans'. Meanwhile, pagans and others attempt to lobby heritage organisations to preserve archaeology, notably Silbury, creating their own pressure groups or joining with others who may likewise see spiritual meaning in ancient sites (e.g. <http://www.heritageaction.org/>).

Avebury therefore serves as an introduction, in this volume, to our investigations of culture, meaning and accomplishment of pagan spiritualities within site and landscape. In theorising pagan spirituality at Avebury we draw on ideas of the formation and accomplishment of 'pilgrimage' by pagans from Britain and overseas, with associated creative dimensions of *irony* and *play* (cf. Coleman and Elsner 1998); issues of 'authenticity' and 'new-indigeneity' (Blain and Wallis 2002) including constructions of 'Celticity' (Bowman 2000); and performance/construction of self, gender, and indeed countercultural identity (Letcher 2001a,b), all within the political and economic structures that constitute today's Avebury.

Pagans and sites in Avebury

Among a variety of visitors, Avebury attracts tourists and media. These groups arrive for a variety of reasons, including archaeology, scenery, photography or filming, and the (spiritual or non-spiritual) artefacts sold in *The Henge Shop* and the National Trust shop. The *Red Lion* pub, meanwhile, is frequented by locals, tourists, and a biker club. Pagans at Avebury therefore perform on an open stage, so that pagan engagements or their consequences are quite noticeable, observed and to some extent documented. In the circles, Druid rituals attract tourist observers with reactions ranging from interest and approval to laughter and suspicion, and there is evidence that many tourists may expect to see 'Druids' and photograph their rituals. Postcards showing older – that is, early twentieth century – Druid rituals can be found in the Henge Shop, arguably priming some tourists for a specific 'Avebury experience'. More explicitly, the *Red Lion* advertises the schedule of forthcoming Druid ceremonies – Druids being particularly well-known for enjoying the hospitality available at public houses. We have heard some tourists complain if *no* rituals are evident, and we have seen the observers gather not only for larger 'public' celebrations but even when a single practitioner engages in chanting or other less intrusive practices in an out-of-the-way part of the circle.

This public nature of paganism comes with a price. Around midsummer (actually 19 June) in 1996, white and black 'pseudo-magical symbols' (Carpenter 1998: 24) were painted on some of the megaliths of the West Kennet Avenue, Avebury. While these images may simply be graffiti, connections to paganisms were made in the media, with the archaeological journal *Antiquity* suggesting they may have been executed by 'New Age crazies' (*Antiquity* 1996: 501). In various newspapers, 'Kevin', a self-proclaimed 'King of the Witches', claimed responsibility. Two more stones of the avenue were vandalised in the June of 1999, one covered in red and green paint, the other painted with the word 'cuckoo', apparently in a statement against genetically modified foods (Chris Gingell, National Trust site manager, pc). Then, enigmatic markings were scratched into stones of the central chamber in West Kennet Long Barrow at the Summer Solstice in 2001. These are serious instances of vandalism, but they cannot all be linked reliably to pagans and in our collating of them here we do not suggest a cohesive link; at the very least, the decentralised and heterogeneous nature of paganisms signals these are isolated and rare events. Yet, the public nature of Avebury and of paganisms there means that pagan-seeming events or symbolism may be adopted for reasons of protest or publicity, or simply to cause trouble.

2.2   Inside West Kennet Long Barrow, after winter solstice 2004, with offerings of mistletoe and rosemary, coins, joss-sticks and a charred smudge-stick.

Other forms of damage may arise from thoughtlessness or careless-ness. This concerns what pagans do at sites, and indeed what some feel is expected of them, particularly those new pagans who have read popular, often American, books and attempt to adopt or adapt the rituals they find in these, which usually include candles and other commercial items. West Kennet Long Barrow and various parts of Avebury Henge have been subject to fire damage and scorch marks, with one sarsen fragment from the barrow, fractured due to a fire positioned immediately next to it, having to be restored with a gluing agent. More obvious and regular impacts on sacred sites which can be reliably linked to either pagan or 'new age' site-users, are in the form of votive offerings – of flowers, tea-light holders, incense, coins, and so on. For some pagans, these offerings are perceived to forge and strengthen links with sites, and/or honour wights, goddesses or some other local 'spirits'. Indeed, some will travel long distances to leave their offerings at a well-known site, with West Kennet Long Barrow

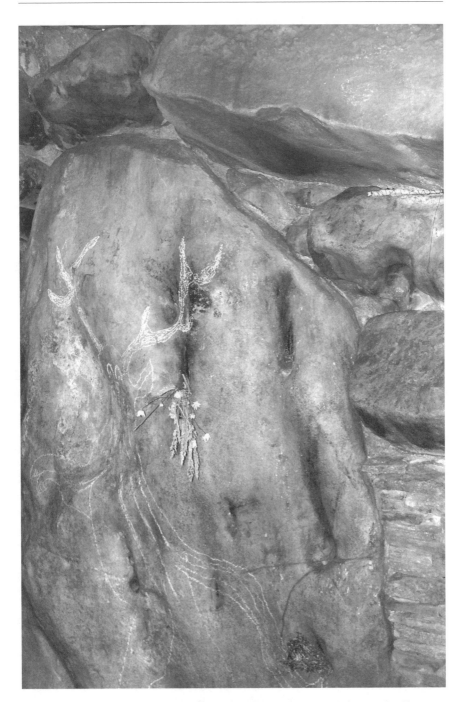

2.3   West Kennet Long Barrow, chalk-art showing an antlered figure, with offerings. This orthostat displays soot marks and cracking associated with tea lights.

2.4
A poster and litter-bag:
pagans associated with
Avebury request that
visitors 'respect this
sacred site' at summer
solstice 2003.

attracting offerings from all over the world. For others, particularly
those who visit the same site regularly and who also uphold the
preservation ethic, this is 'ritual litter' to be cleared up and discour-
aged, as outlined in a variety of pagan documents, but particularly
the ASLaN 'Sacred Sites Charter'. Local pagans often attempt to keep
a careful watch on the activities of 'outsiders' – as demonstrated by
reactions to a notification in spring 2002 that a 'Prophets'
Conference' was to be held in Oxford with trips to Avebury,
Stonehenge and the Rollright Stones, with the goal of 'awakening the
stones' through ritual. (Numerous representations from pagans associated with these places and from the Rollright Stones site management appear to have been linked with the postponement and
eventual cancellation of the conference.)

Such signs of pagan involvement are obvious, but it would be
'monolithic' to suggest that all pagan engagements with sacred sites
are destructive or non-cognisant of issues of conservation. From our
observations and discussions, many or even most pagans do not leave
destructive traces. Some pagans, as indicated above, attempt to clear

up and to educate others about the destructive nature of candles and wax, and participate in the founding of conservation-minded groups such as the Ancient Sacred Landscapes Network (ASLaN). At Avebury, also, a more formal National Trust Guardianship scheme was instituted in the 1990s, under which local pagans and others joined forces with the National Trust to clear up ritual litter, monitor impact on sites, and provide on-site guardianship during annual pagan festivals. According to Chris Gingell (then site manager at Avebury) as reported in the pagan magazine *Pagan Dawn* (Oakley 1997), this Guardianship Scheme was very effective, and after reading the piece so many pagans 'from all over Britain' offered voluntary help that Gingell had to write a reply to the journal (Gingell 1998) pointing out that the National Trust was too 'decentralised' to deal with all the inquiries. This formal relationship fell into abeyance, but individual pagans have continued to do 'site clearing' – with some referring to spiritual energies as well as ritual and other litter. The 'Avebury Sacred Sites Forum' (ASSF) of 2005 offers its own guidelines for visiting which are clearly aimed at pagans (available online: <http://www.national-trust.org.uk/main/w-vh/w-visits/w-findaplace/w-avebury/w-avebury-guardians/w-avebury-guardians-guidelines.htm>), Under the ASSF, an 'Avebury Guardian' scheme was again instituted, though information on the National Trust website may tend to suggest that one must be formally involved and that the concepts involved are new.

By now it will be plain not only that 'pagans' do not form a unified whole, but also that relations between the National Trust, pagans, local people and other interested parties are neither simple nor straightforward. Although 'the village in the stones' seems to accommodate all comers, Avebury exists today as a partially reconstructed monument within very specific contexts of recent history and policy. Today some pagans are local (or some locals are pagan) and pagans, particularly at festivals when they outnumber the bikers (and, for that matter, any other visitors), swell the tourist trade of the *Red Lion* pub. In 2002, several thousand people converged on Avebury at the summer solstice, particularly after Stonehenge 'closed' on solstice morning, until the National Trust 'closed' the car park to solstice celebrants on the Saturday. Media perceptions of pagans and new travellers there drew on rather mild sensationalism; for instance Rod Liddle's account in *The Guardian* of circumstances surrounding a pagan handfasting (a form of usually informal pagan wedding):

> Nobody, however, wished to leave. One of the main objections to moving on was that they were so utterly and totally drunk that they would constitute an enormous traffic hazard on the A303 – an excellent and, I would have thought, incontestable, defence . . . Badger – a cheerful, lank-haired hippy – intended

The
Avebury
Guardians

The Avebury Guardians is a volunteer group dedicated to caring for the stone circle, the Sanctuary and Kennet Long Barrow at Avebury.

The group has developed out of the ASSF. It aims to support the Trust's own small wardening team.

Volunteers will be active in patrolling the site, litter picking and monitoring erosion issues, as well as talking to visitors about the different aspects of Avebury – spiritual and historical.

The group is not exclusive to pagans and anyone is welcome to get involved.

The Avebury Guardians aim to help bridge a gap between the archaeological/historical interpretation of Avebury and the spiritual one.

The founding of the group has led to a much better mutual understanding of the different interpretations of Avebury, as well as increasing our capacity to care for Avebury.

2.5   Text of 'Avebury Guardians announcement, online at the National Trust website, <http://www.nationaltrust.org.uk/main/w-vh/w-visits/w-findaplace/w-avebury/w-avebury-guardians.htm>.

to marry his beloved in a ceremony conducted by some similar creature known as Arthur Pendragon. But nobody was quite sure when it would all happen. A policeman who was asked surveyed the scene with good-natured concern: 'Dunno,' he replied, 'all depends what time they find Arthur Pendragon. He's probably drunk and asleep in a hedge somewhere . . .' But the authorities were immovable. Get out of town or you will be locked up, was their response to the exquisite romance of the moment.

(Liddle, 30 June 2002)

While this points, albeit humorously, to tensions between the 'authorities' and pagans, it conveys nothing about sacredness or meaning, and pokes fun at (homogenously) drunken pagans to make a (political) point. This stereotyping does nothing to promote dialogue and co-operation between the authorities and pagans. And other tensions have manifested: the National Trust had, in recent years, operated an unofficial camping policy in the Avebury environs, so long as it was small-scale and brief (Chris Gingell, pc.). More recently there have been rulings designed to prevent camping on the site other than controlled camping in the small overflow carpark – instituted as part of the court ruling supporting the National Trust's eviction of a small new traveller community known as the 'hedglings' of Green Street, in March of 2002. Tentative attempts to create a parking/camping field for summer solstice 2003 misfired and no satis-factory solution has been reached in subsequent years. So Avebury, too, is constituted within tensions and competing discourses, which heighten as the pressure of numbers increases.

Since the 2002 solstice events, pagans and other 'spiritual' atten-dees have been writing to the National Trust, challenging interpreta-tions of 'visiting' and site management; our interviews indicate that friction between the National Trust and many local people is if anything increasing, and the historic tension between 'management' (or ownership) and 'locals' has grown. A change of management in 2004 has brought some relief: yet before that, at the 2003 summer solstice, in association with exceptional numbers at Stonehenge, roads were packed (with the police towing away cars parked 'illegally', some of which turned out to belong to local people) and parking in Avebury car parks full. In 2004 parking at Avebury was further restricted, with fresh painting of double yellow 'no parking' lines along the roads into the village, to the extent where local businesses suffered from reductions in trade, and 'closing time' came at midday on the 21st of June. Indeed a Pagan group, though having previously arranged use of the car park to facilitate a hand-fasting on Monday afternoon, elected to go elsewhere rather than add to confusion in the car park. Here there are many versions of 'ownership'. Avebury is constituted today within ambiguous political and spiritual contexts, and the people who come and go – and wish to park their cars – include locals, pagans, new travellers and 'stones' enthusiasts, together with tourists (many of whom subscribe to aspects of so-called 'new age' thinking), bikers and other 'publics'. The categories are neither monolithic nor exclusive, but pagan/spiritual use is growing, and pagans are now appearing as concerned and often irate citizens who claim a say in planning and are active and vocal critics of events and management.

The institution of the Avebury Sacred Sites Forum has raised hopes for dialogue and negotiation of the issues, notably the situation with regard to parking. Avebury is open to all comers, but public transport can make it difficult to access without a car: buses from Swindon or

2.6   Pagans and others begin to assemble at the Red Lion in the centre of Avebury on solstice eve. This would normally be the busiest time of the year, but in 2004 parking restrictions hampered the pub's trade.

Devizes run during the day, so visitors who need to arrive or leave in the evening are dependent on their own cars. The problem is increased by situations pertaining at Stonehenge where 'the stones' are available for 'managed open access' for an hour around dawn at winter solstice and spring and autumn equinoxes, and approximately eleven hours, plus several extra for the car park, at the summer solstice. When Stonehenge 'closes' at summer solstice, crowds descend on Avebury. The car parking restrictions give a measure of control, which is hotly contested by some pagans. Negotiations through the Avebury Sacred Sites Forum, however, in 2006, led to one leading Druid, Arthur Pendragon (of whom more anon: see Pendragon and Stone 2003), leaving the forum, questioning whether it was designed for 'consultation' or simply for 'telling' pagans what had been decided elsewhere. In the meantime, residents have been required to cope both with periodic pagan crowds, and with a biker club that meets weekly in the centre of the village.

'Paganism' is not entirely leader-free – or at least does not appear so to some heritage managers, police officers and other official personnel – and those who become 'leaders' may be challenged by other pagans. Druid orders seem particularly prone to splitting, as new groups diverge from older ones. No leader can claim to represent all pagans or all groups. Pagans cannot speak 'with one voice' because paganisms are varied, based in different worldviews and histories, with different relationships to place, land, and spirit. While most pagan 'leaders' recognise this, it sometimes appears that heritage personnel do not, that for them the lack of unity of doctrine and worldview is problematic and that they seek to negotiate with a small range of leaders or officers rather than with the 'new tribes' who seek a voice at the negotiation table. It is a scenario familiar in other contexts and other cultures, with the need for a bureaucratic or colonial officialdom to find 'headmen' with whom to negotiate, and possibly to invent such.

At the time of writing, tensions over use of the National Trust car park and juxtaposed overflow car park have been brought to a head: after complaints from locals relating to crowds, noise, drugs and other issues, Kennet District Council has issued a legal order to the National Trust requiring them to deal with festival visitors and to forbid overnight camping. The National Trust has expressed some dismay over this enforcement notice, its Regional Director commenting to the press on 11 October 2006 that 'By forcing the Trust at this stage into a position where it has to find instant solutions, the council risks alienating many of the partners who are working hard to find a mutually acceptable solution' (quoted in Cork 2006). Comments from readers on the online version of the *Western Daily Press* (Cork 2006) include sympathy for both local people and pagans, with calls for a carefully managed campsite to cope with the demand. If, as the article suggests, '49 pagan events are planned in Avebury over the next 12 months', such a site might need to be a permanent fixture, and it will have to include campsite facilities such as toilets. The National Trust Property Manager at Avebury, Scott Green, has since emphasised in a letter to the *Western Daily Press* that plans for a long-term solution are in formation and that a proposal will be presented to Kennet District Council at the end of November 2006, saying that 'The National Trust is committed to protecting the World Heritage Site, both respecting the rights of pagan worshippers and minimising the impact of camping at pagan celebrations on local residents' (Green, 2006).

Avebury continues, therefore, to be a contested site, constituted politically and geographically in shifting alliances of pagans, management and locals as they attempt to negotiate these issues of conservation, celebration and daily life. In the meantime, the *Western Daily Press* holds out images of a return to the days of new travellers and pagans being moved on, while an increasing number of pagans, through mediums of internet fora and email lists, and letters to the press, express sympathy with the villagers and distaste for the large crowds at festival time.

Performing Avebury

Avebury is a stage, or linked set of stages, on and in which people constitute paganisms. Druid rituals are the most obvious, performed usually in 'the eye of the sun', that is in the middle of the day. Large-scale druid rituals have come to take a standardised form, which may be followed by several different groups over the course of a weekend near a festival date. In general there is an understanding that people associated with LAW (the Loyal Arthurian Warband, <http://www.warband.org>) and/or the Secular Order of Druids (SOD) or the Glastonbury Order of Druids (GOD <http://www.archdruid.co.uk/>) will meet on Saturday, while the Druid Network (<http://www.druidnetwork.org/>) or the British Druid Order (BDO <http://www.druidorder.demon.co.uk/>) make ritual of a similar form on the Sunday. Yet though the form is similar, the feel and performance of the rituals can vary greatly.

After meeting, the gathering of druids, other pagans and friends divides into two groups: the party of the Goddess and the party of the God. The Goddess group proceeds directly from the meeting place to the stones which form the south entrance to the great circle, within Avebury Henge. There they will sing, drum and dance while one woman undertakes to faithfully represent the Goddess of the place, and sits in the 'devil's chair', the huge stone to the west of the entrance which has a place which looks designed for one to sit (and has a folklore attached to it). She may enter an altered consciousness, in some forms of the ritual. Meanwhile the God party has processed from the northwest of the henge monument, on its bank, to the eroded chalk path that leads to the south entrance. Arriving there, they are challenged as to their intent, and make offerings (often seasonal flowers or fruits, mead and bread) to the Goddess through her representative. All proceed through the entrance and to the south circle which is known as the circle of the sun, within which they form a circle and proceed with a ritual form which includes calling for peace in all directions, casting a circle and honouring directions and often ancestors, and invoking goddess and god to be present. What takes place varies with the participants, but may involve healing, hand-fasting (usually at the Ring Stone) and child-blessings, sharing mead and bread, and sometimes inductions into the Gorsedd of Bards of Caer Abiri. It will usually involve some form of the Druid Prayer and Druid Vow (see e.g. Harvey 1997), chanting, and often an eisteddfod,

2.7   Druids make an arch of staffs at Avebury as part of a summer solstice ritual.

with poems, songs or stories performed by individual people within the circle, as the spirit moves them. In the shortest Avebury druid ritual we have observed, on a cold winter solstice day, only the Druid Vow was spoken. On other occasions, and particularly if it is warm and if the ritual leaders are given to more poetic expressions, the ritual may take over two hours. Sometimes announcements are made, calls for assistance to defend sacred spaces, calls for healing for people not present. Bereavements may be notified, and the people mourn. An induction in the Gorsedd involves those who would welcome greater creativity in their lives forming a small circle facing outward, while those who are already members form another circle around them: all chant the 'Awen', the Druid's call to inspiration and creativity.

This is the Druid ritual that participants and tourists alike are coming to expect. Other pagan rituals at Avebury, including druidic ones, may be much less elaborate. The most common is simply for an individual or small group to walk around, touching the stones and 'listening' to them. Heathens might simply offer mead and sing a rune row[3] or offer a praise poem, to honour ancestors at the site. Sunrise, at solstices or equinoxes, is a time of waiting and stillness, a time for standing by a stone or on the banks of the henge, watching

2.8   Tourists and media crowd around the Druid solstice ritual.

for the sun. Some rituals celebrate the full or new moon. Some combine lunar and solar events: Terry Dobney, self-styled 'Keeper of the Stones', a druid now living locally, says that he began coming to Avebury in 1969. He celebrates both solar and lunar festivals (13 lunar and eight solar in the year, he says) and speaks of having 'brought the moon to the sun circle' regularly (pc). He also performs as many as 200 hand-fastings, each year. Rather elaborate hand-fastings may be conducted, particularly by Wiccan groups. Other areas of the Avebury complex see less-public ritual, some formal and some spontaneous; individual or group meditation or chanting among the stones of the henge, full-blown Wiccan or Druid rituals at West Kennet Long Barrow, shamanic singing and altered consciousness work in the Avenue and again, particularly, at West Kennet. Ritual may also be as simple, and as private, as quietly sitting on Windmill Hill, watching kestrels hovering, or singing softly on the hillside where few human people go.

Performance is also movement in space, and here we investigate how people relate to place and constitute 'sacredness', in part through ritual. Here are some examples, as narratives from ethnographic fieldnotes:

> Picture the summer solstice of 2003 at Avebury: it is early afternoon and people are sitting on the grass, in groups by the stones of the south circle, in view of the *Red Lion* pub. Later there will be a ritual. I (Jenny) am with a small crowd – they include a leading Druid, Tim Sebastion (Secular Order of Druids), several academic writers on paganisms, various other Druids and pagans. Dressed in jeans and T-shirts, we don't attract attention from the red-shirted BBC radio crew who are occupying the next stone over.

> Enter from the *Red Lion*, an obvious 'Druid'. Last year he had been talking to me about doing his first ever handfasting at Avebury. He'd been nervous, as a relatively new practitioner; apparently it went well. He's often about the place, becoming an expected figure in the landscape. Now he's walking across the road, in white gown and feathered hat – wearing, that is, the public symbols of Druidry. He sees us and starts to come over to pay his respects to Tim and others. The radio crew, however, see, at last, 'a Druid' and reach him just as he reaches us. We watch: they fix an interview with him later, and depart back to their stone where they are readying equipment. The Druid stops by our small group to pay his respects and moves on. In a little while, when the ritual is about to start, we gather our belongings and Tim dons his (rather splendid) robes, startling the radio crew who suddenly recategorise him as a 'druid leader'. (I think they did manage to speak with him later.)

The public performances of paganism are most evident at places such as Avebury, but they can be understood in many ways. Part of the remit of our project is the study of the constitution of identity and meaning through 'performance' at sites. When the 'performance' of ritual or interpretation is itself in contention, both as the right to access place and space, and the ability to define what is done there, the term 'performance' becomes problematic, even while it indexes anthropological theory, when applied to issues of dealing with other-than-human people, as discussed elsewhere (Blain and Wallis, 2006a).

. . . We sat out in West Kennet Long Barrow at Yule for a specific purpose, to engage with ancestor spirits. Wearing shamanic regalia, surrounded by (human) companions, I (Robert) was initially a 'master of ceremonies'. Vigorously shaking my shrill sounding belled rattle I opened the sacred space, and while others sat expectantly, I welcomed the spirits . . .

> Gungnir, Draupnir, Woden's Eye;
> Sleipnir, Hangatir, Gondlir's Cry;
> Galdr-father, Vardlokur sing . . .

Starting up a galdr – chant or sung spell – for the god Woden I was soon accompanied by a monotonous drum, my friends beating out the rhythm with their hands, and other voices joined the chant, drowning mine. Was this a performance? Who was the performer? Who was the audience? Where did the 'performance' begin and reality end? – Where are the boundaries? . . .

. . . Knowing there was work I had to do, though I had put this to the back of my mind, I (Jenny) sat on a cold, cold night in a sacred space, hearing the 'performance' of chant and drum-ming. With a slight effort of will, I was elsewhere, then dealing, negotiating, with the chant (of which I was barely aware) fuelling, driving the interaction: 'vardlokur' for the spirits, Dísir, (female ancestors) that I had not planned to meet there. The chant, drawing on symbolism, names, imagery, mythology – however it worked for its practitioners – became a 'performance' on a different level for my Dísir, and a vehicle that I could use to meet them. The 'performance' persisted after its time, so that it was 'overheard' (half an hour after it ceased) by a friend on a mobile phone, and it still resonated in the space the following day, when I returned to tidy up some spiritual 'loose ends' and state aloud to my Dísir my under-standing of what had occurred . . .

These occurrences absorb the 'performer', who works with intent to achieve something through acts of *doing* or creation whether these be physical procession, dance or song, or stillness and mental imagery. All are ways in which meanings are inscribed in and by person and place. Rather than 'performance' we prefer to talk about agency or active accomplishment of meaning. It is important to stress, though, that accomplishment of pagan or of ethnographic meanings blend practical and alternative or magical activity, and that contexts of accomplishment include onlookers and everyday events.

In July 2005, I (Jenny) am driving through Avebury, on a detour to wave at the stones in passing. In the avenue, though, are people clearly intent on what they are about: a neo-shamanic group from the Toronto area, I find, the 'wolf clan'. They have brought water from their own land to offer to the stones.

I park, take photographs, and discover on returning to my car that the silencer is falling off it: well, Avebury is a better place for this to happen, by far, than the M4 or M1 motorways! In search of a shady spot where I can get mobile reception, I am in the south circle when the neo-shamanic group – who have processed around the landscape – descend from the banks, so I watch as they attract the few tourists, with cameras, on this non-festival day, and watch the onlookers who carefully do not watch them, as they engage with space and place.

Later, I speak to their apparent 'leader', who says she does not want to 'intellectualise' her group's engagement but that their practice is both *Celtic* and *Seneca* (an Iroquoian nation from what is now the Canada/US border area). While I am rather puzzled by the association of either with Avebury, and by her asking if I know the 'great white mother', I respect her tiredness and the work that she and her people have done at the site – a pilgrimage in process, in the heat of the day, walking to and touching each stone. I respect, also, their abstinence from leaving traces that will affect the engagement of others. She says she has noted, and respected, my acknowledgement and partial avoidance of their engagement with the site. I talk of pilgrimage, and, to make a link to show that I am not straightforwardly an observer, of my own 'shamanic' practices. In short, both her people, and I, have 'performed' Avebury – each the Avebury that we know – and both been noted by the other, as have those watching (us both) with cameras in hand.

In this analysis, meanings are constituted through doing and through discourse – in post-modernist accounts of 'self' there is no separation of interpretation, perception and experience; we perceive discursively and bodily, though interpretations and meanings change as experience is re-told, re-storied. Pagan accomplishments, at Avebury or elsewhere, are not simply 'experience' but are constituted from understandings of the world(s) – that is, they are theoretical and political, historical and discursive products, with deliberate and non-deliberate elements, events and outcomes. And they are accomplished within sets of relationships, through different modes of consciousness, by attending to and interpreting different inner and outer events within space and time.

Silbury Hill and Silbury Hole

The artificial hill known as Silbury has, since 2000, become a place of concern to pagan activists and 'stones enthusiasts', who have followed the stories of the appearance of 'Silbury Hole', its spread, and attempts by heritage management to deal with this problem. The hole – resulting from the apparent collapse of the cap on a shaft from an excavation – was first identified in May 2000, when a person who had gone up Silbury Hill for personal or spiritual reasons found it and reported it. Silbury was then a site that many pagans attempted to visit and climb. Such a pilgrimage was first encouraged by Michael Dames (1976, 1977) who suggested that ancient pagans had gathered on the summit in order to celebrate the harvest at Lammas (1st August). This was extended to incorporate midsummer, perhaps inspired by Paul Devereux's (1992) account of the 'Double Sunrise' and 'Silbury Glory' viewable between Beltane and Lammas (1st May to 1st August).[4] Silbury was and is embedded in folklore accounts, chief among them the tale of 'King Zil' supposedly buried on a golden horse at the foot of the mound; numerous excavations have been attempted, chief among them those of Atkinson in 1968–1970, funded by the BBC. Atkinson had tunnelled from the side, following the course of an older excavation tunnel from the nineteenth century. The shaft from the top of the mound had been made in 1776, by the excavations of Colonel Drax and the Duke of Northumberland. Chadburn et al., writing for 'a more general audi-ence' (than receive English Heritage technical reports) say that, 'Accounts tell us only that they found a small sliver of oak and "a man", presumably a skeleton, at the base of the shaft, though a newly discovered report says the hill consisted "of chalk and gravel thrown together by the hands of men" and that "there were many cavities in it"' (Chadburn et al. 2005).

Attempts to deal with the problem of 'the hole' involved photog-raphy and analysis of cores obtained from seven boreholes. This initial investigation persisted into 2003, and gave considerable infor-mation about the structure of the mound, as well as confirming that excavations had either not been backfilled, or inadequately back-filled. Subsequently, temporary measures for stabilisation, involving polystyrene blocks, were undertaken. English Heritage reports that plans for permanent stabilisation are now decided upon, involving the removal of inadequate backfill from tunnels and its replacement with a more permanent backfill, and hopes to commission these repairs from spring 2007 (see <http://www.english-heritage.org.uk/server/show/nav.8613>).

The current Avebury World Heritage Site Management Plan phrases it thus (Pomeroy-Kellinger Part 3: 118):

D.4 As a matter of priority, a long-term solution to repair the structural problems identified at Silbury Hill should be implemented by English Heritage. English Heritage has agreed to develop a proposal, with partners, to remove the existing backfill and consolidate the lateral tunnels. This will involve refilling the collapsed shaft at the top of the hill and infilling depressions on the slopes as a means of ensuring the long-term integrity of the monument and the archaeological remains within. The aim is to complete this work after 2008, subject to funding.

Initially, the hole was covered with corrugated iron sheeting, which remained in place until further work could be undertaken. The mound was declared unsafe for people to ascend – and it was already a Site of Special Scientific Interest (SSSI) which people were requested to not ascend (to protect rare flora), although many pagans, as aforesaid, did so. Issues arise here concerning the extent of cooperation between organisations and individuals, in what was perceived by many as a very serious threat to a unique part of heritage: and a perceived lack of information, and hence accountability.

The following year, in 2001 at midsummer, ASLaN (Ancient sacred Landscapes Network) collaborated with local National Trust and

2.9   Pagans and others at the 'Save Silbury' demonstration, May 2004.

English Heritage representatives in seeking volunteers to protect the hill (from pagan pilgrims) and prevent accidents, many of these from within the pagan community. One of those who responded, Matt, described some events of the night (pc). Numerous people attempted to climb the hill, and when he explained its precarious situation (and risks to themselves at the summit) almost all went to celebrate elsewhere. Very few insisted on 'rights' to ascend to the top: a little polite education provided by a volunteer – albeit one who was 6'7" high, leaning on a large oak staff – went a long way. Matt also talked extensively to the English Heritage personnel there about Heathenry, his religious path, and why prehistoric sites were important to him. These events point towards a spirit of co-operation between heritage managers and pagans, but the situation is complex and not straightforward nevertheless.

Prior to this pagan festival, there had been little word from English Heritage on the progress of assessing and repairing 'Silbury Hole'. So, a protest was called by Clare Slaney (of *Save Our Sacred Sites*) and others including locals and pagans, who organised a demonstration, on the road because of on-going foot and mouth restrictions, to draw attention to the problems of the hill (which had slipped from public awareness). Two press releases were forthcoming from English Heritage, within a few days, to the effect that the hill's situation was under study. Pagan activists in this case considered that their actions pushed English Heritage into at least indicating what it was doing, and certainly displayed that there were interested people out there. English Heritage would, perhaps, argue this timing was coincidental. The showing of the 'Silbury Hole' TV documentary (BBC2, 14 March and 8 August 2002) met with considerable criticism from pagan activists: first, when it was shown only in the West of England, and second, after national screening as it implied that the situation was now under control.[5] Pagan activists pointed out that the situation was neither straightforward nor rectified. An activist constituency became evident, growing and calling for public discussion of the problem and of the scale of funding required for a solution. In the meantime, the hole had been growing, under its corrugated sheeting, due to the effects of subsidence in wet weather.

The attraction of monuments and landscapes, and an interaction between unthinking damage and self-publicising, can be seen in these developments. Silbury lies at the centre of 'crop circle' country, and in 2000 and 2001 several people billing themselves as crop circle enthusiasts 'under cover of darkness' abseiled into the 'hole' – taking photographs and making video recordings which they then attempted to sell, via the internet, to the crop circle community. An online account – interspersing the abseilers' text with critical editorial comments, and linking to outraged comments from pagans, local people, crop circle followers and archaeologists alike – is given at Silbury Hill Damage 2001 (<http://members.fortunecity.com/crop-signs/>. According to this account, those involved lifted a corner of the protective sheeting, and a combination of weather and the activity of the abseillers enlarged the hole.

In 2004, when repeated requests to English Heritage for information had again proved unfruitful, a demonstration was called by the recently-formed Heritage Action organisation (<http://www.heritageaction.org/>), on 29 May, the fourth anniversary of the discovery of the 'hole'. The action featured a walk from Avebury Henge via a path through fields to the south and past Silbury, and along part of the A4 to the Silbury car park and the south-west of the mound. The demonstration featured King Arthur in leading the walk, and various people from Heritage Action spoke after assembly at the destination. While this organisation does not describe itself as 'pagan', it seems associated with pagan sensibilities and its initial formation arose from the *Modern Antiquarian* group based in the writing and campaigns of the musician Julian Cope (e.g. 1998), who has himself been associated with Avebury issues. In this demonstration, Arthur and others were calling not only for action on the preservation of Silbury, but for the sharing of evidence and information, and for the publicising of such action. Here and elsewhere, issues have focused on a perceived lack of information stemming from English Heritage and other organisations. In short, many pagans see themselves as protecting the monument and calling for action, and see official heritage management as requiring to be prodded into action – or, and perhaps more problematically, as deliberately concealing from public interests the extent of damage. Here, and elsewhere, a problem preventing more targeted or coherent cooperation appears to be that of an unwillingness to publicise material, especially the details of excavations and the deliberations of committees. While to many heritage personnel this may be seen to result from under-funding and staff shortages, or simply from the time involved in the process of publication, to many pagans it appears as evidence of a culture of secrecy, or of a reluctance to share information; or, importantly, a perception of pagans (or other involved people) as less able to deal with technical materials. Pagans do not like to be 'talked down to'.

Archaeologists and pagans: performing ownership

Despite the above, some archaeologists attempt to engage with prehistoric 'religion' and pagan identities in ways including experiential research and ethnographic comparison. Others may feel that these approaches have no place in 'serious' interpretation, but may at least serve to attract tourist 'visitors'. Still others appear vaguely embarrassed by the expressions of interest and spirituality that come from 'visitors' to place and landscape at Avebury. Some of the more extreme tensions have resulted from pagan encounters with excavations: on which pagans attempt to place their own interpretations, by, for instance, walking from Avebury to 'bless' the archaeological dig at the Longstones in the summer of 2000; or by protesting against excavations. We have had expressed to us views, from some (few) archaeologists, that pagans are axiomatically wishing to delay or prevent excavation;[6] likewise, we have had expressions, from some pagans, that archaeologists are latter-day grave-robbers, disturbing the sleep of the ancestors and their association with land and artefacts (a topic continued in Chapter 7). Such expressions constitute knowledge claims over the interpretation of Avebury's 'pasts' just as in the case of present-day excavations and other archaeological fieldwork. We see individual people caught within these situations (on any side), having to deal with the extreme claims, and forging their own understandings within contexts which include their own locations in theory as well as within site and landscape

Yet, taking the differences in perspective and even the complexity of understanding among archaeologists into account, there remains an understanding among archaeologists and heritage managers that 'they' as experts have knowledge and 'the public' (whoever that may be) do not. At a conference in 2005, a presenter asked, 'Whose cultural heritage are we talking about, and for the benefit of whom?' This was relating to indigenous knowledge, elsewhere, but seems to us pertinent here. For heritage management, it appears that the performance of site – such as Avebury – is one of:

- excavating
- publishing (or not)
- relaying archaeological knowledge as top-down distribution.

Ideas that, for instance, people chanting within the West Kennet Long Barrow may be able to contribute *perceptions* as *knowledge*, seem fairly foreign to most archaeologists. Those who do take such ideas on board often ally with other sources. Archaeologist Mike

Parker-Pearson's association with indigenous Malagasy collaborator Ramilisonina (e.g. 1998) in order to re-appraise the meaning of Stonehenge, for instance, comes to mind, akin to Wilson's (1994) account in the seminal volume on *Being Changed by Cross Cultural Encounters: The Anthropology of Extraordinary Experience*, when he found, in teaching a class, that his students would listen carefully to a tribal Medicine Man, but that he, Wilson, was expected by the class to not engage with theories which did not meet conventional standards of rationalism. 'Indigenous Peoples' are able, in the western mind-set, to have or adopt seemingly 'irrational' views which might contribute to our interpretation of 'irrational' (religious, spiritual) views of past peoples. Members of our own 'western' societies are not afforded the same qualities, and so the exotic other is maintained. But chanting in West Kennet Long Barrow – described as 'inexplicable' or 'bizarre', or sometimes (possibly patronisingly) 'experimental' – has many stories attached to it, of meeting ancestors or Woden, or simply seeking the experience and letting the swirling sound alter consciousness in ways that are akin to, but cannot be measured by, the instruments which deal only with frequencies and standing waves. In our locations as insider-researchers, spanning boundaries of several disciplines, we see different epistemologies and different types of understanding converging on some of the practices and interpretations that we uncover. A scientist may be fascinated by the experiments of Aaron Watson and others into the acoustic properties of Avebury Henge, and their explanations; an ethnographer looking at people's engagements with place, may be both fascinated by, and repelled by, the patterns and decorations that some (not all or most) pagans or neo-shamanists leave in chalk or as offerings. Likewise, an ethnographer may be equally intrigued by why the offerings, or indeed the rituals of the pagans and neo-shamans we describe here, *are so puzzling* to heritage management and archaeologists or to some other visitors and tourists. How can we – bringing together the situated knowledges of academia and practitioners – combine or broker these perspectives?

'What *are* they doing?' a couple asked at Avebury in July of 2005, when they found in conversation that they were talking to an anthropologist. 'Why *do* they leave these things?' heritage people have likewise asked. The simple answers, because they want to, or because they see it as fitting, or indeed because it has been asked of them, by their gods, ancestors or wights of the landscape, do not enter academic discourse and seem counter to the ideas of 'rationality' that need to be indexed within heritage management discourse. Yet they may be ones that make sense, not only to the practitioners but to others who share in the landscape and are attempting to form their own associations with place. In whatever way they can, a huge assortment of people, in coming to Avebury, are acknowledging the land, its and their pasts, the history, the generations of people. In so doing they are constituting themselves, not as abstract identities, but in relation to time and place. And in so doing they are – we are all – performing Avebury.

Stonehenge

Thro' the middle of the principal entrance, runs the principal line of the whole work; the diameter from north-east to south-west. This line cuts the middle of the altar, length of the cell, the entrance, the entrance into the court, and so runs down the middle of the avenue, to the bottom of the valley for the almost 2000 feet together. This is very apparent to any one at first sight, and determines this for the only principal entrance of the temple.
(Chapter III, p. 18, Stukeley 1740)

The Avenue of Stonehenge was never observ'd by any who have wrote of it, tho' a very elegant part of it, and very apparent. In answers, as we have said before now, to the principal line of the whole work, the north-east, where abouts the sun rises, when the days are longest. Plutarch in the life of Numa says, the ancients observ'd the rule of setting their temples, with the front to meet the rising sun. (Chapter VIII, p 37, Stukeley 1740)

Stonehenge, once famously described as 'a national disgrace' is at last to be rescued from its current shameful state and given the dignified setting it deserves as an iconic World Heritage Site. The £57 million scheme announced today will help to transform the ancient landscape, uniting it with the Stones and dramatically improving access for millions of visitors from across the world.
(English Heritage News Release, Wednesday 31 July 2002
<http://www.thestonehengeproject.org/news/pressreleases.shtml>)

'Stonehenges' in discourse

'Every age has the Stonehenge it deserves – or desires': Hawkes' axiom (1967: 174), however oft-quoted, is a reminder that Stonehenge is always subject to the vagaries of interpretation. Despite the apparent singularity of the statement, even at the time Hawkes was writing there was not a single Stonehenge desired; there were then competing perspectives, as indeed there probably always have been. It might be easier to say this now, in a postmodern 'age' of interpretative archaeology. So, now, perhaps more than ever before, the various publics 'desire' a variety of Stonehenges. Indeed, Stonehenge, 'the world's most famous prehistoric monument' (Richards 2004: frontispiece), is infamous as a contested site. Even the quotations from Stukeley's 1740 volume, above, were composed to argue configuration and interpretation with others of the period, notably Webb.

The contested Stonehenge of heritage management, curated 'for the nation' by English Heritage, is one of the best known Stonehenges. This Stonehenge is not only an 'icon of Britishness'[1] (Bender 1998), but as a World Heritage Site (designated in 1986) it has 'outstanding universal value' (English Heritage 2000b: 1.2) for all of humanity. As it is unique, unchanging, ancient and fragile, it is fenced-off, denied tactile human attention and available for visual consumption alone (during daytime opening hours), narrated in a series of official guidebooks (e.g. Newall 1981 [1959]). In the interests of preservation (or at least conservation) it should not be touched; it is a frozen moment of prehistoric grandeur. Of course there have been plans to change this widely criticised re-presentation of the past, the

3.1   The impression of 'splendid isolation' is maintained by a rope which separates tourists from monument.

Stonehenge World Heritage Site Management Plan (English Heritage 2000b, now become the Stonehenge Project) being the most recent of these. But until change is instigated, the Stonehenge we have today is an encaged monument, surrounded by fences and major roads. 'The stones' of this spectacle are made familiar by the cameras of tourists: the average visitor stay is around twenty minutes (Stone 1999) but many visitors do not pay the entrance fee, choosing to spend only a few moments standing beside the A344 to take their photographs. This Stonehenge of the tourist's gaze is, inevitably, subject to consumer tourism, with miniature replicas, tea-towels and collector's plates available in the English Heritage shop. And, this image is reproduced over and again elsewhere in the visual culture of advertising and popular press.

Stonehenge also exists, of course, as a subject of archaeological research – of 'later prehistory', 'phenomenology', 'interpretative discourse' and 'landscape context'. Archaeologists recognise that Stonehenge should be approached from the Avenue, not via a modern tunnel from the car park. Some of them ask us to imagine the stone circle and its landscape populated with humans, humans who were much like us (at least in modern human anatomy). Those interested in phenomenological approaches ask us to move around the landscape thinking about the relationship between 'the stones' and the Cursus, the Cursus and the Avenue, the mounds of Old King Barrow Ridge and other round barrows, as well as the way ancient users moved around this landscape of monuments included within today's World Heritage Site, including Coneybury Henge, Woodhenge and Durrington Walls. With more emphasis on the people who produced and used the Stonehenge landscape, rather than the stones as, simplistically, a grand 'observatory' or 'temple', current research has investigated Stonehenge as, for instance, a site of wide-scale ritual feasting, as well as a monument to the dead avoided by the living (with neither possibility being exclusive in the long prehistory of the site). This is the Stonehenge of the past in the scholarship of the present. From our heathen, animistic perspective, we wonder, furthermore, whether the stones were perceived not as inanimate objects but as living 'persons' in themselves, perhaps as 'ancestors'.[2]

No list of imagined, desired or imaged Stonehenges can be exhaustive. Other Stonehenges pertain to alternative engagements. There is the Stonehenge of alternative archaeology, of earth mystics, dowsers, ley-line hunters, crop-circle enthusiasts and alien conspiracies. By and large, these Stonehenges are dismissed as 'fringe' by scholarship, although there is a growing interest in alternative representations of the past and the implications of this for archaeology and archaeologists (see in particular Bender 1998). And, there is the Stonehenge of

3.2   Images of Stonehenge are reproduced on tea towels and many other items, for sale in the Visitor Centre shop.

alternative lifestyles, with free-festivalers and party people seeking a Stonehenge festival site. New travellers themselves view Stonehenge as a special meeting place, a place where 'the tribes' can come together, form communities and celebrate, before returning to the road. Meanwhile, many pagans approach Stonehenge as a ritual site, a special site of ancestral spirits, and book special access or campaign for open access in order to perform ceremonies celebrating their gods, goddesses, spirits and ancestors in a living landscape.

All of these Stonehenges coalesce and collide in many instances, for archaeologists who are English Heritage personnel, for English Heritage personnel who are pagans, for pagans who are new travellers, and for travellers who ley-hunt. There is no single 'visitor' type to Stonehenge, just as there is no single Stonehenge. The Stonehenge landscape, the Stonehenge experience, are constituted within a discursive web, a weaving together of different threads of discourse, even if each discourse might be viewed by its own adherents as authoritative or authoring 'truth'. In writing this chapter we are interested in the discursive weaving of today's mythic fabric of Stonehenge, as much as in the ancient monument on Salisbury Plain itself. The focus is, as a matter of course, on pagan discourses, worldviews and practices. But these do not exist in a vacuum – they challenge Heritage discourse but also take on aspects of it (in the planning of druid rituals at the summer solstice managed open access event, or in negotiating special access on other days around the solstice), as well as new traveller discourse (for example, some travellers feel marginalised by English Heritage-legitimated druid rituals). And so the wheel turns on. The argument in this chapter so far is explicitly intended to complicate Stonehenge, to disrupt the search for a singular truth, for a single Stonehenge, and to demonstrate how any singular discourse becomes confused by those competing with it.

Stonehenge is often described as a palimpsest, or composite, resulting from many phases of intervention. Yet, even this phrasing denies agency to the monument: a palimpsest is written on, not itself inscribing meaning in its users. Throughout its long history the monument has been altered, changed, developed, abandoned, and reused (Chippindale 1994; Bender 1998; Wessex Archaeology 2003). The name, Stonehenge, dates only to the Anglo-Saxon period, some 1500 years or so after it was 'abandoned'. The layout of the monument with which today's visitors and archaeologists are familiar dates back to the opening of the twentieth century when certain fallen stones were re-erected and stabilised, followed by excavations and further conservation in the 1950s, with the remaining fallen stones left as examples of 'decay' from ancient times. The choice was made not to resurrect Stonehenge entirely. There is good reason for this: which Stonehenge would then be presented? – Stonehenge has never been a singular thing, and the re-positioning of stones would not represent 'Stonehenge as it should be' or 'Stonehenge complete'. While calls are still periodically made to 're-erect the stones', the Stonehenge we have today is as much a part of the recent past as of distant times. Physical inscriptions of meaning in the monument include those construed as damage (recent graffiti), those seen as archaeological evidence (Bronze Age dagger and axe-heads – constituted as ancient 'art' or 'graffiti' depending on which discourse one subscribes to), and those which occupy a grey area between damage and evidence – such as Victorian carvings of names. The felt need to preserve the monument as it currently exists is a comparatively recent development.

Our fieldwork at Stonehenge over more than six years has involved attendance at public solstice and other pagan festival events, observation at private pagan ceremonies and participation in the 'tourist experience', leading academic fieldtrips, occasional participation in 'round table' meetings, monitoring of online discussion and debate, interviews with site managers, tourists, new travellers, pagans, and so on. Ethnographic work of this nature is by definition multi-sited: Marcus (1998) encouraged ethnographers to 'Follow the people . . .

the thing . . . the metaphor . . . the plot, story or allegory . . . the life or biography . . . the conflict . . .' (pp. 90–4). In a sense, the Sacred Sites project has had to do that in attempting an understanding of each 'site' and in moving from an initial focus on Avebury and Stonehenge to broader engagements with the politics, metaphors and policies of relationships of heritage and paganisms.

The following sections offer a detailed discussion of Summer Solstice, Winter Solstice and other alternative events at 'the stones' based on ethnographic and historical interpretation. Here we analyse a number of issues raised by this data, including the concept of 'sacredness' and its constitution in heritage and pagan discourses; how constructions of sacredness create debates over an atmosphere of 'partying' at the monument at solstice events; and issues over artificial lighting, the length and timing of open access, and privileging of certain pagan perceptions (particularly Druid) over others. We conclude by addressing the contests to site and landscape relating to planned future(s) of Stonehenge (primarily in terms of the proposals of the Stonehenge Project), how alternative and pagan voices are engaged within these, and raise some issues of landscape and new-indigenous perspectives.

'Managed open access'

Summer Solstice 2006, with sunrise on Wednesday 21 June, was the most recent managed open access event at Stonehenge at the time of writing (FIGURE 3.3), and English Heritage facilitated free entry to the stones for eleven hours, and to a car park in a nearby field for 17 hours (8 p.m. on Tuesday to 1 p.m. on Wednesday). This event encompasses a range of issues, debates, concerns and celebrations which have permeated the history of alternative engagement with Stonehenge over the course of the second half of the twentieth century and first few years of the twenty-first.

The event in 2006 was the seventh 'managed open access' at the summer solstice. Although there have been ongoing low-key access events at spring and autumn equinoxes and the winter solstice, these do not (as yet at least) attract the crowds which flock to the summer event. The numbers at winter solstice, however, have grown: to 700 in December 2005. At 'managed' events, this setting becomes a stage on which the 'sacred' in 'sacred site' is constructed and played out amongst a diversity of interest groups and amongst, and in part for, the cameras of press and tourists. Meanings in the stones are complex, and the various discourses on Stonehenge – the diversity of Stonehenges – become intensified and stark in the instance of alternative access events. Stonehenge as a component of English national identity (see the 'scenic nationalism' discussed by Thomas [2001]) clashes with Stonehenge as a British tourist symbol, Stonehenge as a new traveller meeting-place, and Stonehenge as a pagan temple or sacred site.

This history of contest can be traced further back through the twentieth century to tensions between landowners, local people, druids, archaeologists, and the army. For instance, the collapse of a sarsen and lintel (which broke in half) during a gale in 1900 raised concerns over the safety and stability of the monument and the owner, Sir Edmund Antrobus, elected to fence off Stonehenge (from May 1901) – and for the first time at the site, charge for admission. The move was not popular, with the residents of Amesbury performing, without success, a mass protest at the site in the same year. Druid ceremonies at Stonehenge in the twentieth century began with a visit of nearly one thousand members of the Grand Lodge of the Ancient Order of Druids in 1905, reported negatively in the *Star* newspaper as a 'train load of sham druids' indulging in the 'childish tomfoolery' of 'cotton-wool beards, calico nightshirts and tin insignia', culminating with a 'protest against the simple majesty of Stonehenge being invaded by these shoddy mysteries and sham antiques' (Richards 2004: 32). Official resistance to Druid interests became evident in the 1920s when the Church of the Universal Bond was denied the right to bury the ashes of their dead within the stones (Richards 2004: 35). Around this time, the impact of the Royal Flying Corps with its aerodrome situated close to the monument, as well as the Royal Artillery based at Larkhill Camp and military traffic on trackways including those crossing associated earthworks, raised additional concerns for the future of Stonehenge.

The recent history of contest with which we are concerned begins with the emergence, growth, and eventual suppression of the Stonehenge free festival (with its origins in the 'Peoples Free Festival' in Windsor 1972–1974). Running for ten years from 1974 to 1984, the festival, with its celebration of alterity and overt contravention of societal conventions and drug laws, and with its black market economy (Hetherington 1992), unsettled the authorities; its proximity to the archaeology of Stonehenge, in turn, unsettled the site custodians and some archaeologists. Its demise was inevitable. What the authorities underestimated was how important the festival, and Stonehenge, had become to those attending. Not only did people construct their identity and lifestyle around it, but also, through its utopian vision and entheogen[3] consumption, it met a fundamental need for re-enchantment. The festival, and its ending, are documented visually by photographer Alan Lodge or 'Tash' at <http://tash.gn.apc.org/> and historically by Andy Worthington (2004, 2005).

People were attached to the festival in a very deep sense, and would act to further its continuity. The free festival together with stories of its founder, Wally Hope, and his death, the later suppressions and the 'battle of the beanfield', have become part of the narrativised context and folklore of Stonehenge today, and hence components to the discursive positioning of those who seek to celebrate there today.

The forced closure of the festival resulted in a clash between the police and a 'peace convoy' known as the 'battle of the beanfield' in 1985, aspects of which are recorded in the television documentary *Operation Solstice* (see also the BBC website <http://news.bbc.co.uk/onthisday/hi/dates/stories/june/1/newsid_2493000/2493267.stm>). This film, said *The Guardian* commentator C.J. Stone, 'should be seen by everyone . . . so that they know that evil [in the form of the police under Thatcher's government] exists' (1996: 153). Alternative presentations have made much use of the testimony and eye-witness narrative of Lord Cardigan, whose status as a member of the establishment prevented the 'official' account being read as the only truth on this event.[4] Yet, thereafter, new travellers and festival goers were demonised. The following years saw Stonehenge surrounded by an 'exclusion zone' around the time of the summer solstice, to prevent a recurrence of the festival. Essentially, members of the public were not allowed within four miles of the monument. Various attempts were made to break the exclusion zone, with further confrontations and arrests. This served to give Stonehenge a powerful new meaning. It became an icon of freedom and alterity for anyone dissatisfied with Thatcher's Britain (McKay 1996). Going to Stonehenge, or at least making the attempt, became an act of resistance. There was a long-running, well-documented (e.g. Chippindale 1986; Bender 1998, Worthington 2004) history of protest after the demise of the free festival, and free-festivalers, new travellers, pagans, druids, and other 'alternative' interest groups campaigned consistently for improved access to 'the stones', particularly for summer solstice celebrations. Various access schemes were negotiated for groups or individuals in the years since 1985, but the summer solstice retained its 'exclusion zone' until 1999. In 1998 a partial-access ticket scheme was problematic for those not 'invited' and those who considered that the tickets scheme was discriminatory. In 1999 the four mile exclusion zone was removed after it was ruled illegal by the House of Lords under the Criminal Justice act, after an appeal by two individuals arrested for 'trespassory assembly', and an attempt by English Heritage to allow access to the area (but not the stones) resulted in a breaching of fences so that some were able to reach the monument (observed and described by Wallis, 1999b). In 2000, after a further year of negotiation, the first free, 'managed open access' event was achieved, policed

English Heritage is pleased to be providing Managed Open Access to Stonehenge for the Summer Solstice. Please help us to create a peaceful occasion by taking personal responsibility and following the Conditions of Entry set out below. We have a duty of care to ensure public safety and are responsible for the protection of Stonehenge and its surrounding Monuments. Please read and observe the entry conditions. If we are to ensure that future access is sustainable, it is essential that everyone abides by these Conditions of Entry.

English Heritage continues to work closely with the many agencies and people from all sectors of the community and would like to thank them for their help and support.

Parking and entry will be free, subject to the Conditions of Entry. Please do not arrive at the Solstice Car Park or Stonehenge in advance of the opening time.

SOLSTICE CAR PARK OPENS: 2000 hours (8pm)
Tuesday 20th June

ACCESS TO STONEHENGE: 2200 hours (10pm)
Tuesday 20th June

STONEHENGE CLOSES: 0900 hours (9am)
Wednesday 21st June

LAST ADMISSION TO SOLSTICE CAR PARK: 0600 hours (6am)
Wednesday 21st June

SOLSTICE CAR PARK TO BE VACATED: 1300 hours (1pm)
Wednesday 21st June

Sunrise will occur at 04.58 on Wednesday 21st June 2006

We would like to wish you a happy solstice.

(<http://www.english-heritage.org.uk/server/show/ConWebDoc.5067>)

3.3   Prior to the summer solstice 2006 managed open access event, English Heritage released this statement as well as a comprehensive list stipulating 'Conditions of Entry'. Similar conditions were made available in previous years, accessible online on the English Heritage and other websites including those of pagans and festivallers, also distributed as hard copy at the event. Issues are raised over how 'open access' is restricted, and how these conditions might be made more flexible.

3.4   A Stonehenge of alternative lifestyles. Memories of the Battle of the Beanfield and the years of the exclusion zone, now part of the folklore of Stonehenge and resistance, remain behind today's celebration of managed open access. This image is from 2001.

internally by the (pagan and alternative) communities, resulting in an event with no arrests – possibly facilitated by heavy rain which kept numbers attending down to approximately 5,000, and including many local Wiltshire residents as well as pagans, new travellers, and druids (observed and described by Blain 2000 audio-diary). A further year of negotiation, discussions and roundtables preceded solstice 2001, with an estimated 14,500 attendees. The summer 'managed' event has grown massively since then, with 23,500 celebrants in 2002, 31,000 in 2003 when the day of 'managed access' fell at a weekend, and with numbers stabilising at around 20,000 for weekday solstices in subsequent years, reduced in 2006 due to bad weather. Resistance, campaigns, negotiations and managed events have created their own folklore and their own notable people: King Arthur (see Pendragon and Stone 2003) as a focus of resistance with many arrests, now negotiating access; George Firsoff who initiated the Stonehenge Peace Process and StonehengePeace email list and whose

3.5   Nora Morris, celebrated and loved by all who knew her: a veteran of Greenham Common and a stalwart campaigner for Stonehenge to be open to those who would celebrate there, latterly representing the Pagan Federation on the Stonehenge Round Table. She died in January 2006.

death has been mourned by many including even those who saw him as too close to the heritage line; Nora Morris, a veteran of Greenham Common protests and representative of the Pagan Federation on the Round Table, whose death in early 2006 resulted in many tributes from 'the community'.

We have described the Stonehenge Summer Solstice event elsewhere (e.g. Blain and Wallis 2004a): the accounts here are summarised from fieldnotes. In 2002 we watched seemingly vast numbers of people – around 21,000 – pouring into the small, confined space of 'the stones', and our ethnographic perceptions were of problems resulting from both 'management' and 'user' groups, but much more from the situation in which both were embedded. Essentially this was a situation of mutual distrust – reproduced in all the years we have attended Stonehenge events. People came to Stonehenge, in their marked diversity, constructing and signifying identity through their dress and accoutrements, green branches or face paint, police uniforms or steward 'yellow-jackets', mayoral robes or England flags (2002 and 2006 summer solstices aligned with the football World Cup), peace-steward badges, microphones, cameras and videocams, and druid, wiccan or other priestly/ pagan robes. Their constructed meanings and emotions included rejoicing, ritual, dancing, sadness, annoyance, bravado, watchfulness, worry, fear, boredom or dismay, loss or finding or seeking something unknown, listening to the stones, talking, performing, trancing and weeping.

People came to Stonehenge, with their families or friendship groups, alone, or to meet others, to make new acquaintances and renew old ones. On the way in, they had to pass through gate checks. Questions were raised about musical instruments and blankets. Dogs were impounded. Tents and associated camping equipment were confiscated. All glass containers (such as bottles containing alcohol) were confiscated, although plastic containers were provided in their place in some instances. A small drinking horn brought to toast the sunrise was taken for examination and consultation by an official who, though friendly and polite, did not seem to know what it was. Bags and backpacks were thoroughly searched, and people were asked to leave behind sleeping bags or anything that pertained to an overnight 'camp' – even when they had young children who were obviously going to need to sleep, or when the blankets or sleeping bags were brought to wear as garments for warmth. People also brought with them those things they thought were needed for a celebration or a party: drums, candles, cannabis, magic mushrooms, alcohol, occasionally pipes or a flute or fiddle, ritual equipment, and more drums. Some of these worked, and were non-invasive of others' space – some less so. The morning's litter included large amounts of beer cans and shredded plastic.

People came to Stonehenge for the experience and to share that experience with others. Many people broke the strict rules issued as a condition of entry. As such, the conditions are seen by many people as too restrictive and even dogmatic, and some flexibility might be in order (for example, allowing people to carry blankets in order to keep warm, while still denying tents). Yet an assumption of flexibility in turn requires responsibility within the 'community' of celebrants, and herein lies a problem, identified by numerous people connected with the negotiations. Where, here, do the bounds of 'community' lie, and where does the interaction of 'authority' and 'community' remove decision-making from those who choose to come to 'events' while seeing these as only entertainment, or merely a venue provided for some 'happening' which might, marginally, be called 'spiritual'. Here lies a profound dis-ease that we have with some managed open access events. What is 'spiritual', and what is a non-spiritual 'partying', is an issue which has been raised on many occasions. We see no clear dichotomy. Partying can be spiritual – as documented not only anthropologically, but specifically at Stonehenge 2001 where, as addressed in more detail below, a leading druid commented: 'And it is about – a lot of people partying. There's nothing wrong with that, that's a spiritual thing too, or can be'.

Yet there remains a sense of how spirituality can be conducted or communicated among very large crowds. There may be different and diverse manifestations of both 'spirituality' and 'partying', some allied, some in opposition. In the context of the recent history of the Stonehenge Festival, its suppression, and attempted negotiations in recent years regarding a 'park-up' for those needing a place to be between solstice and the start of the Glastonbury festival (a reminder that paganisms and 'solstice' exist within a wider context of today's Britain including 'alternative' and 'partying' culture), there was, and remains, a tension between authority and resistance which requires considerable exploration and theorising. Put simply, the strict appli-cation of rules on bag-searching and sleeping bags, etc, did not help to make the occasion more 'spiritual'. And while partying for some was indeed spiritual, for others, a peaceful space in which to ritualise or meditate was hard, if not impossible, to find.

At the 2002 'event', some had come specifically and deliberately (and sometimes with some fears) to experience an alternative and perhaps more specifically 'pagan' happening; others had come as pagans to an occasion meaningful to them. Still others had appar-ently come to be seen – by pagans or others – and have their presence noted in the context of the World Cup (England played Brazil on the morning of 21st June, 2002). There remains potentially a large number who attended simply to be there, perhaps to party, perhaps to get drunk, perhaps to sell things (from handicrafts to drugs) – and a further point of contention is the restrictions on trading in the car park area. There were some who had come specifically to show resist-ance to authority. The memory of the Stonehenge Festival is strong, so that the summer solstice at 'the stones' is the archetypal 'party' site 'for the tribes'. It is easy for a 'spiritual' event to become simply a 'party' and vice versa, depending on how it is constituted for specific groups, and the circumstances and discourses surrounding it. Further, while many pagans profess a desire (at conferences, in email discus-sions and other forums) to not be 'political', the summer solstice cele-bration is inherently political, and many of the crowd choose to express their political-spirituality at Stonehenge, rather than at some quieter venue, in order to add to the numbers seen to be 'resisting' what may be perceived to be non-spiritual appropriation by English Heritage and other bodies. Many people came for multiple reasons – as indeed did we – and moved in the course of the night between positions of spiritual meditation or celebration, partying, playing with meaning, performance and, on some level, resistance. More important, perhaps, is the specific interaction of all these people with the site and the specific, overlapping, multiple landscapes they were constructing or experiencing.

By most accounts, these events have been successful and joyful, yet they consistently display the same tensions: English Heritage and the police express concerns over drunken behaviour and articulate a discourse of 'health and safety'; attendees express concern and annoyance about lighting which obscures the sunrise (though there has been some improvement over the years with the strong and blinding floodlights dowsed in rotation around the site) and about the impact of police presence on a 'sacred' event. There are a handful of arrests, usually for drunkenness, and a few people attempting to scale the stones are escorted off the premises. English Heritage complain that some people have been standing on fallen stones and the small bluestones, and raise potential issues of 'damage' to the monument; their discourse is, once again, one of conservation and preservation, although they also voice a 'health and safety' mantra. But there is substantial self-policing at these events: members of the community volunteer as 'green' or 'fluffy' security known as Peace Stewards, identified by badges but otherwise dressed down – visibly a presence but not 'establishment' – asking people to avoid standing on stones or even placing candles on these, and explaining why. Fluffy security consistently had their voices and actions supported by other members of the community, demanding that those climbing trilithons descend – often with success, particularly when a dignitary such as King Arthur pitched in.

Many attendees – not only those involved with heritage management – worry about the impact of huge numbers of people on a tightly focused site, the vast amount of litter as a result, and how the ongoing debate – and monitoring – of this 'event' has been seen to result in a swing towards a 'party' rather than a 'sacred', 'spiritual' event. Celebrants also protest over the time constraints: typically open access is only from around 10 p.m. to 9 a.m., and there are calls for a much longer event, taking account at least of the day-to-day closing time of 5 p.m. to 9 a.m. English Heritage is reluctant to extend the opening hours since there are the aforementioned 'health and safety issues', camping is not allowed, and this might open the flood-gates to a perceived 'festival' of the old days (at its height the free festival attracted 70,000 people [see <http://news.bbc.co.uk/1/hi/entertainment/music/3662921.stm>] and lasted, in 1984, for six weeks). And finally there is disagreement among celebrants, with some rejoicing in the cacophonic percussion of 'The King's Drummers' (of the 'Samba' sort), while others would prefer something more restrained (read less intrusive); and while the Druid procession to Stonehenge from the car park and ceremony in the stones is now a long-established 'tradition' (the ceremony extending at least to 1905 [see Richards 2004: 32]), this exclusivity is viewed as marginalisation among some other druids, pagans and new travellers. Equally, Druids or other pagans who see Stonehenge as a ritual site may find themselves excluded from the centre of the monument by drummers and party-people, whose drumming and monopoly of the centre persists all night. Some would prefer to celebrate at midday 'in the Eye of the Sun' and some at the moment of astronomical solstice, but the limited hours of 'managed access' focuses only on sunrise. Year after year, the same events are played out, the same issues voiced: but at least it is not the battle of the beanfield, or the annual arrests for trespass of the 1990s. If the sun shines on solstice morning, it all seems worthwhile – as those not attending glean from the press, or from the countless websites displaying photographs of the occasion.

Media attention

Access to 'the stones' has always, from Druid events in the early twentieth century, attracted media attention. Media reports may not be an accurate reflection of the thinking of a diverse 'public', but it is interesting to note the shift in tone in coverage of summer solstice access. After the 'battle of the beanfield', the tabloid headlines read 'Sponging scum', 'Invasion of the giro gypsies', and 'Stonehenge scarred in raid by travellers' (cited in Bender 1998: 162). Similarly, when some pagans, new travellers and others gained unauthorised entry to Stonehenge at the summer solstice in 1999, the press described them as 'Smellies' (in *The Sun*), 'Hippies' (*The Daily Mail*), and the somewhat less derogatory but no less sensationalist 'New Age travellers' (De Bruxelles in *The Times*:; Fleet in *The Daily Telegraph*; and articles by Davison et al. and Orr in *The Independent*). Interestingly, though, there were also 'ravers' (3rd *Stone* magazine 1999), with this shift in terminology indicating something of a diversification of interest in Stonehenge – from 'free festival' site to 'party' place. The actions of all of these persons in 1999, none the less, were, the press agreed, an 'Invasion'.

The press has generally been more forgiving since 1999, probably because legitimate 'managed open access' began in 2000, with a 'New dawn at Stonehenge' (*Salisbury Journal*). For other journalists, 'Peace reigns as 7,000 attend first open solstice in 16 years' (*Western Daily Press*), 'It's a Stonehenge love-in: disturbances of the past forgotten as 6,000 celebrate' (*The Times*), 'Modern pagans reclaim Stonehenge'

(Simon de Bruxelles in *The Guardian*), and 'As the midsummer sun rises, crowds gather to see what Stonehenge has been missing for 16 years' (*Daily Express*). Clearly, authorised, managed access went down well with the media. This was repeated the following year, in 2001: 'Thousands see the dawn of a peaceful party at Stonehenge' (Sarah Getty in *The Guardian*), 'Magic of Stonehenge summons up the sun' (de Bruxelles in *The Times*) and 'Stonehenge solstice revellers see the light: crowds police themselves in peaceful sunrise ceremony' (Jeevan Vasagar and Sasha Blackmore in the *Financial Times*).

In 2002, emphasis was on the peaceful celebration, with a note on the rise in numbers of attendees and pagan interests: '14,000 in good-natured gathering at Stonehenge' (*The Guardian*), 'Travellers and druids party as summer solstice sun rises at Stonehenge' (Maev Kennedy in *The Independent*), 'Whistling witches and druids with drums greet solstice at Stonehenge' (Paul Peachey in the *Daily express*) – although the *Daily Mirror* focused on arrests for possession of drugs: 'Stoned henge: drug arrests at party for longest day'. In 2003, the number of celebrants reported increased dramatically: '22,000 at stones for summer' (Richard Smith in the *Salisbury Journal*), and the atmosphere was celebrated: 'Stones solstice celebration "best in memory"' (*Reuters*). And from 2004 to 2006, the positive coverage continued: 'Sun arise . . . happy crowds at Stonehenge for summer solstice' (*The Independent*, 2004), 'Peaceful solstice is celebrated at Stonehenge' (John Bingham, *BBC News Online*, 2004), 'Peaceful start to summer solstice' (*BBC News Online*, 2006).

From 1985 to the present day, therefore, there has been a softening of attitudes in the press. The fact that access is now managed and authorised must play no small part in this. But it is clear from our research that year by year the attendees have diversified, with its own impact on the press and wider public perceptions about what Stonehenge, solstice events, and indeed pagans, are 'about'. Of course, there are 'robed-up' druids, Wiccans, heathens and other pagans. There are also party people, new travellers and others with alternative lifestyles. But there are in addition local villagers, personnel from the armed forces, mothers pushing twins in pushchairs, local teenagers, and tourists. Where once the event was assumed to be significantly 'pagan' or at least druidic, with the celebration including ritual, and while both the ritualising and the event at the stones itself was certainly 'alternative', these two have become increasingly mainstream or non-specific, as much a 'party' as ceremonial. Ethnographic research at the managed open access events, and at the summer solstice in particular, evinces a diversity of voices among attendees, with various implications for how these events are managed.

Alternative voices

Stonehenge, at the summer solstice particularly, during managed open access, is a place of 'celebration and subversion' (Worthington 2004), against the backdrop of heritage management concerns. In contemporary Paganism for at least some southern Druids, Stonehenge is the 'temple of the nation' (Sebastion 2001), and Tim Sebastion's Secular Order of Druids (SOD) claims to have the aims of new travellers and other revellers at heart. Many travellers have strong links with Stonehenge (e.g. Craig 1986; Bender 1998; <http://tash.gn.apc.org>); the free festival marked a time when this nomadic group was able to gather together and celebrate their lifeway at a meeting place which is thousands of years old, a monument which may have been used for similar seasonal rituals in prehistory. This is not to say that new traveller or pagan interests in Stonehenge should take precedence over others; it is to recognise a unique valid-ity of their discourse as played out amongst other, competing and supportive discourses. Stonehenge is therefore a contemporary meeting place for 'the tribes', as a noted pagan and peace activist, the late George Firsoff, pointed out to us at the end of the 2001 summer solstice celebration. His discourse explicitly links meeting place, 'tribal celebrations' and the music improvised during the night and the dawn. And his views exemplify the way in which the different 'camps' of pagans, new travellers, free-festivallers and so on have boundaries which are blurred.

> People were I think trying to recreate primitive music in this environment here. I spoke to a druid gentleman who said, oh the music in the ancient times must have been very similar, you know very, very heavy on the percusssion, a few horns, and maybe bagpipes, and so very similar to what's actually been happening here. And I thought that was interesting 'cos they were producing some of the, some very weird sounds, you know it was like, very totally spontaneous, you know, and again that's very like tribal music that we know about, isn't it? Because there's a strong sense of there being a tribe at Stonehenge, and one of the problems is, people couldn't meet each other any more, when their gatherings here were banned, and the bless-ings of children and the marriages in some sections of the community . . . it was very important to come here.

In the new folklore of new travellers, such events are continuing a long tradition, an idea connecting/legitimated by ideas about circles as prehistoric meeting places, feasting places, market places, and so on. As one 'visitor' to the 2001 solstice event stated: 'standing here, looking in, with all these people among the stones, it looks like any period in time – like it may have looked in prehistory', and others we talked to at this event repeatedly drew on these concepts. Early in the night, an anonymous celebrant told us that:

> I've never been to the stones before, but of all the circles I've been to in the British Isles, and old sites, it actually feels like the most normal . . . It seems like it's really OK for loads of people to be here. And this is probably something that's not new – people being allowed into the stones; it's something that's very old, so seems quite a normal thing to do.

His friend added:

> It's like as ancestral memory that's stored up . . . You're drawn here, quite simply the bottom line is you're sort of drawn here, there's all sorts of, well a myriad reasons for that you see. To me it's like charging my batteries, it's kind of like these sort of gatherings are like getting a new life really. And you don't have to *be* anything here. There's no real kind of code here at all, and that's what I love about, there's such a diversity of people and it is real mixing . . . because everyone's allowed to be what they want.

Others commented that 'it's the place you really should be on solstice', and that it was a place where the stones held 'ancient knowledge', hence giving a connection with ancestors, a sense of continuity. This sense of identity through continuity ran through many accounts.

And at dawn, one Druid at the same event explained his own attachment to the place, and his joy in the celebration:

> My first summer solstice here was 25 years ago. And this time, this summer solstice, it's like a holiday . . . there's all sorts of people here. There's crusty traveller hippy types, there's little old ladies, there's – everybody's here . . . The Hari Krishnas, over there. And yeah, they're here for one reason, because it's a place to be on the summer solstice . . . this is a holiday, it's a Holy Day, it's special, and people I think feel it's special. And I think the site likes us to be here, as well. Stonehenge wasn't built as a museum. It was built as a place for people to come, for worship, to use it . . . Come here at other times, and it's quite quiet, and still and peaceful . . . but I always think *this* is like New Year's Eve or Christmas or your birthday, all rolled into one. And it is about – a lot of people partying. There's nothing wrong with that, that's a spiritual thing too, or can be.

3.6 In the growing light, people wait for sunrise at Stonehenge on summer solstice.

Eventing at the 'right time'

The timing of 'solstice', both winter and summer, is significant; not only for being perceived by pagans and others as auspicious and therefore the 'right' time to be at the stones, but also because of disputes over appropriate opening times for pagan festivals. Winter solstice 2005 marks a case in point. Sunrise at Stonehenge, around 8.10 a.m., was the focus or highlight of the event. The moment of Winter Solstice planetary alignment (21 December 2005 6.35 p.m. GMT), however, was not a time of open access; the period of dawn on the 21st was, and the stones were opened from 7.45 a.m. to 9 a.m.

At the winter solstice in 2001, a number of druids, heathens and others planned to make their pilgrimage to Stonehenge on the 21st – 'as we always have done', as Tim Sebastion of the Secular Order of Druids put it. English Heritage deemed the 'right' day for solstice to be the 22nd, according to their own astronomical information. People turned up on the 21st anyway, and English Heritage refused to allow people access to the stones. After some time the police, however, concerned over public safety, with people gathered next to and buffering into the A344 in the gloom of the early morning, instructed English Heritage to open the gate. With little further encouragement, the celebrants entered and a pleasant if bitingly cold sunrise was experienced by all. This situation is particularly interesting: English Heritage are not only controlling the terms on which Stonehenge is accessed, but also stipulating which is the correct day of the festival – in effect telling pagans and other celebrants when their festival days should be. Graham Harvey, writing an emailed account soon after the event (used with permission), stated: 'Without permission from Clews Everard . . . [English] Heritage were doing nothing, insisting we were there on "the wrong day". So much for freedom of religion!'.

Since then, there has been a growing call for open access for the Winter Solstice sunset. Pagans have encountered archaeological or astro-archaeological sources or their popularising – literature, websites and television programmes such as *Ancient Voices: Stonehenge* (BBC May 1998) and its accompanying booklet by Millson (1998) (also North 1996; Ruggles 1999; Prendergast 2002: see also <http://www.tivas.org.uk/old-site/stonehenge/stone_ast.html>; Cornwell 1999) suggesting that the winter solstice sunset, not summer solstice sunrise, was the most significant time to the builders of the site: or they have simply made this observation for themselves, from the road outside the fence, at sunset. Clearly, even if they are not bound to authenticity, many pagans and other celebrants of ancestral wisdom are interested in historical accuracy where possible. They find that it is one thing to wear a white robe based on Stukeley's notion of ancient druids which has now, through use over a century or more, become 'authentic tradition'; and quite another thing to want to honour the ancestors in the most appropriate way possible by following the (current) archaeological orthodoxy by celebrating winter solstice sunset rather than sunrise. The understanding of times and their relation to place is a matter of worldview and approach. We watch with interest this changing discourse among pagans and pagan dialogue with English Heritage *vis-à-vis* open access to Stonehenge – and Stonehenge itself as the location for these situated performances. We anticipate that there will be growing calls for managed open access to be extended – not simply to lengthen the 'party' or 'celebration' (depending on your point of view), but in order to facilitate sunset events alongside those of the now-traditional sunrise. The enduring issues we see emerging, whenever the event is planned for, are both how interpretive rights, not only access rights, are challenged by celebrants, and how what happens at the stones reinforces, contravenes or re-constitutes, the preservation ethos.

Sacred partying

The preservation ethos of the heritage industry comprises an essential part of the 'informed' 'visitor experience'. If, as heritage managers suggest, these sites should be preserved for posterity, then this gives good reason for fencing off Stonehenge in order to minimise visitor impact and avoid unnecessary damage. When 'sacredness' is used in this context, it is on a par with the sacredness conventionally associated with the passive, humble and serene Protestant sobriety many observe (congregation and tourists) at nearby Salisbury Cathedral, for instance. Clews Everard, recent manager at Stonehenge, suggested (pc), that in contrast to the ways in which pagans and others have behaved at the large solstice events in recent years, the site is not an appropriate place for 'a party' and 'drunken behaviour'. English Heritage evidently feel 'partying' and associated raucous behaviour compromises the preservation ethic, compromises their definition of 'sacredness', and also compromises their view of Stonehenge in the past, when, presumably, 'parties' did not occur. Quietude, essentially, is assumed to be appropriate, including for druid and other pagan rituals. The preservation ethic-informed notion of sacredness promulgated by the heritage industry is accepted or accommodated in the discourse of some pagans, most obviously in the organisations Save Our Sacred Sites (SOSS), ASLaN (Ancient Sacred Landscape Network) and Cruithni, but not others. 'Partying' at Stonehenge is 'spiritual' for some pagans, however; what is deemed to be secular and non-spiritual by the authorities can constitute 'sacred' practice by others (see

3.7   The fenced monument as seen from the A344 today (2006).

especially comments by Pendragon 2000/01). After the Winter
Solstice events at Stonehenge in 2001 at which these issues of contest
to the 'sacred' were made apparent (e.g. Harvey 2001), one member
of the Stonehenge Campaign commented '[W]hat they [English
Heritage] want is tame druids' (on the Stonehengepeace email discussion list), meaning those Druids who are prepared to accept English
Heritage's agenda for solstice events and their concept of sacred-
ness/heritage-cum-preservation ethic. The approaches of 'partying'
Druids and others align more closely with the 'folk carnival' (e.g.
Bakhtin 1968) in pre-Reformation churches, permeating the boundaries between Durkheimian definitions of 'sacred' and 'profane'.

In previous published work, we have discussed how 'sacred sites' in
other times may have owed as much custom to social events or
'partying' as to an appreciation of sombre 'sacredness' (e.g. Wallis
1999b, 2003; Wallis and Blain 2003), citing the use of Salisbury
Cathedral as a market place, horse fair and location of the 'feast of
fools' as an example of the permeability of boundaries between

'sacred' and 'profane' in the Middle Ages: 'The villager drew no clear distinction, whatever the learned might think, between the spiritual and the otherworldly on the one hand, and the material life of the present on the other' (Pounds 2000: 340). (See also discussion of dualisms including 'sacred/profane' in Chapter 1's section on 'the sacred'.) Current understandings of exclusively passive engagements with this and other church buildings are a post-Reformation – and particularly a Victorian – innovation. Archaeological interpretation suggests that it is possible Stonehenge was a meeting place for large-scale feasting and while such events may have required ritual obser-vances, ritual need not be sombre and is by all accounts not passive. Yet where partying is part of resistance with the 'sacred' element omitted, this leads to other implications for the site, the human traffic it can bear, and most importantly the ways that people inter-act with the landscape and with each other. There is also 'sacred resistance' which motivates many attendees and has informed considerable amounts of the negotiation and the peace process, and which links the spiritualities here with various indigenes elsewhere. It is possible that there may be other cultural ways of seeing the distinc-tion. Is behaviour respectful to the landscape and the 'spirits' of the land which many pagans perceive as an intrinsic part of that land-scape? When is dancing on stones respectful? When is it something else? How does it form part of acts of resistance, and what situations have created these?

The memory or myth of the Stonehenge Festival is strong for many attendees (Worthington 2004) so that the summer solstice at 'the stones' is the archetypical 'party' site: partying is memory (even though, as Hill [2006] points out, most of the attendees are 'too young to remember the troubles of 1985'). Email discussion lists and online fora are filled with calls, every year, for a return of the festival. It is then easy for a 'spiritual' event to become simply a 'party' (and actually vice versa) depending on how it is constituted for specific groups, and the surrounding circumstances and constitutive discourses. Further, while many pagans profess a desire (at confer-ences, in email discussions and other forums) to not be 'political', the summer solstice celebration is inherently political, situated within policy and practices over more than a century, and many of the crowd will express their political-spirituality at Stonehenge, rather than at some quieter venue, in order to add to the numbers seen to be 'resisting' what may be perceived to be *non-spiritual appropriation* by English Heritage and other bodies. We make these points not necessarily to support 'partying' at Stonehenge (though as Heathens and academic researchers of paganisms and sacred sites we do attend solstice events at this or other locations) but to demonstrate that not only are concepts of 'sacred sites' exceedingly diverse in both pagan and heritage management communities, but that these conceptions are not always commensurable. 'Sacredness' does, though, appear to be forming a focus point where some of the interest groups can debate and negotiate the issues, as in the Stonehenge 'round table' and peace process set up respectively by heritage management and by wider interest groups.

Stone-standing and solutions

English Heritage's public comments on the 2002 managed access (echoed since) have praised the 'spiritual' dimensions, emphasised the diversity of attendees (a large number of children were there, for instance) and, beside their problem over partying, pointed to another cause for concern: people standing on various smaller and fallen stones. They would prefer to have no 'stone-standing' for conservation reasons, but the crowd draws a different line. Some wonder how such a permanent monument can possibly be damaged by a few people standing on stones. This view may not be cognisant of the fragile state of the monument at the turn of the twentieth century when, on 31 December 1899, a sarsen upright and its lintel on the western side of the circle blew down in a gale (the lintel broke in half); yet it must be stated that extensive excavation and restoration projects over the following sixty years significantly stabilised the stones and removed much of their immediate context. It has been commented by leading archaeologists (e.g. at the Theoretical Archaeology Group meeting in December 2005, where we presented material from the Sacred Sites Project), that archaeological excavation has done more damage to Stonehenge than could be done by pagan celebrants; and many celebrants are also aware of this. Other conservations may not be too visible, such as English Heritage's argument that rare lichens are damaged by stone-standing – unlike, say, rhinos or whales, lichens might not appear near the top of a celebrant's conservation agenda.[5]

More obviously, it is also the case that in the circumstances of darkness, (over-)crowding, and simply wanting space and wanting to see, several people – inevitably – stand or sit on fallen stones. That is, they break the rules of access. There are ambiguities inherent in definitions and narratives of site and 'rules': power inherent in setting rules, and negotiations around acceptance are implicit in the situation. In 2002, we saw two very young children who stood on a fallen sarsen look upwards at the great stones around, with delight and wonder in their eyes, and joy on the face of their watching adult attendant. Even stewards did not seek to remove those children from the stones, although they were in contravention of the 'terms and conditions of entry'. The attending, pagan or other, crowd therefore draws a distinction between upright stones (which should not be climbed) and fallen stones (which are deemed more appropriate for standing on by some), and a further distinction between small upright (bluestones) and sarsens: and the element of resistance at the event seizes on stone-standing as an activity which expresses meanings of many kinds. Each year there have been attempts to reach the lintels. Some revellers, however, perch on bluestones, and some dance on them – the latter constituting a safety hazard to others as well as to the dancer on (e.g. in 2002) a stone slippery with rain. One person attempting to scale a sarsen in 2002 did fall. This was caught on camera by an independent media team, who had been attracted to the location by another camera team's lighting. Robin Pender of *Back Hill TV* gave us an account of the circumstances, which illustrates some of the complexities and problems of the situation.

> My cameraman and I were wandering around the site filming revellers, when we noticed a commotion; lights and shouting, coming from the edge of the trilithon ring. We made our way around, where a young man in climbing shoes had shimmied up between two high stones, and was trying to inch round to the top of the trilithon. There was another cameraman there, with a camera-mounted light illuminating the scene.
>
> Eventually the climber, unsuccessful in his efforts, slipped, and fell into the crowd, where he was promptly apprehended by two security personnel and escorted away from the stones. The other cameraman followed them away. We stayed in this position for a while, as it gave us a great position for filming the party that was going on inside the central ring. About 30 minutes later, we were approached by two women from English Heritage who were concerned about film crews encouraging climbers, particularly by lighting them; we discussed it with them and they left, apparently satisfied that we were being sensitive. (pc)

Attendees and campaigners were aware of tensions and problems, and have suggested several possible solutions, notably that a way to avoid some of the tensions and to turn the occasion to something both more spiritual and more enhancing of community is to move the hours of managed access into daylight of the longest day. The current event, indulging a 'night-club' approach, has elements that are exclusionary. We, like many others, did not spend much time in the centre of the stones which was crowded and where the 'partying' (spiritual or not) was focused, where the monotonous drumming was amplified by the acoustic properties of the site – less inspiring, at least to us, than an earlier year's bagpipe-playing. Long-standing campaigner and negotiator Brian Viziondanz voiced two suggestions in 2002:

> So next year, a daytime gathering, so that the 'nightclub/intox-icated' environment can be replaced with a more wholesome family gathering that will include 'Middle England' because they will feel more secure in that environment. (Also) a longer gathering close to the stones area to allow our community to develop, renew relationships and grow stronger – for some this 'alternative' community is their only family.

It did not happen. The 2003 event ran from midnight to midday – enabling some daytime access to the stones but bringing its own problems of long traffic queues in the middle of the night, and exclusion before the precise time of solstice. The situation in 2004 and 2005 again restricted daytime access, with car park access officially (in 2004) from 8 p.m. and entry to the stones from 10 p.m. until 9 a.m., drawing 21,000 people – the reduction in numbers for this Monday morning indicating that contrary to some of the more sensational press notices previously referred to, many celebrants work 'conventional' hours. The opening times of the 2006 event were similarly restricted to 10pm – 9am. While the non-local police in attendance seemed friendly in 2005, their numbers were described by celebrants as 'over the top' for the size of the gathering; stewards examining bags seemed again uninformed and celebrants complained of inconsistencies in applying rules – some being asked to leave behind blankets or having them confiscated, while others were allowed to bring in blankets for children to sit on. 'Blankets', worn as a cloak, are an article of dress in new traveller and other alternative communities and very practical while on an all-night vigil, so that some experienced a removal of clothing not bedding. For future years, a longer period of daylight access seems unlikely to be approved, as there are implications for the cost of policing and other services. As we write, negotiations are underway for summer solstice 2007, and various options have been proposed including a possible shifting of the 'window' during which the stones (the 'monument field') are open.

Brian's latter suggestion is in line with an idea voiced by many (e.g. Sebastion 2001) to facilitate a music event, at some distance from the stones, to draw 'partying' towards it and so offer reduced impact on the stone circle and perhaps allow a more peaceful 'spiritual' event there; this is a difficult area, a fine line between 'access' and 'festival'. The suggestion has meanwhile been repeated, or re-invented, in numerous discussion groups, email lists and other forums, gaining some popularity, though numerous problems surround the organisation of such an event by any other than official bodies. In 2003 a group of volunteers attempted to form a limited company and actively work for such a gathering, preparing a press release about a potential 'licensed, non-profit making, week-long celebration of life, love and unity' (see <http://www.infinitepossibility.org/stone-henge11/intent.html>). The event did not materialise. Further attempts for 2004 ran into problems of meeting insurance and other costs. On the StonehengePeace email group, the question of a return to a 'festival' – over several days, with camping – circulates every year: the same arguments, the same competing agendas, 'freedom' versus 'health and safety'. Such polarising, on both sides, marginalises people who find themselves outside of either position – the pagan representatives or invitees to the Stonehenge Round Table, who find *their analyses* disregarded by authority and themselves regarded as traitors by some members of the community which they may or may not be seen to be serving or representing. Anthropologists have seen it all before.

The summer solstice open access event at Stonehenge is not self-contained and has an impact on other sites. Access to 'sacred sites' is a wider issue, but managed open access at Stonehenge has a direct, physical impact on sites located nearby. In 2002 several thousands of those leaving Stonehenge on solstice morning headed for Avebury, around one hour's drive northwards, where a more spiritual ambience persisted until, once again, 'closing time': since then, parking and hence attendance has been restricted at Avebury (see Chapter Two). Issues of the Glastonbury music festival – will it happen, which week,[6] and what do people do in between solstice and the festival? – affect Southern English sites and colour perceptions of police and heritage personnel. The issue of people seeking spiritual space – with camping and somewhere to sleep – at the summer solstice is not going to go away. It is now part of the British cultural scene and other areas are becoming increasingly affected – which on the whole is a positive development, problems notwithstanding.

Strategies to address 'appropriateness' of behaviour at sites are necessarily site specific: where the limited space available at Stonehenge makes the presence of a 'party' problematic, the open areas at monuments of the Avebury environs result in reduced – though by no means insignificant – impact; and where the perception of Stonehenge as an 'icon of the nation' means it is currently fenced off, other spaces – most evidently Avebury, but also those up and down the UK, at Castlerigg in Cumbria, Arbor Low in the Peak District, Kilmartin in Argyll, now Thornborough in North Yorkshire and many smaller places – are being 'reclaimed'. Specific to Stonehenge is how visiting (pagan and other) can be managed, particularly within a confined space formed by massive stones, with further issues of longer term plans for the improving of site access and site management.

> **Why can't we go into the centre circle?**
>
> The stone circle has had a lot of footfall over the past few centuries and for conservation purposes it has to be roped off. We do, however, have out of hours Stone Circle Access which allows us to monitor numbers.

3.8   A vague and simplistic reason embedded in heritage 'preservation ethos' discourse for why the stones are inaccessible during usual daylight opening hours, from the 'Frequently Asked Questions' of the English Heritage website devoted to Stonehenge. See <http://www.english-heritage.org.uk/server/show/conWebDoc.4189>.

Widening participation and engaging diversity?

The current presentation and access arrangements at Stonehenge do not permit visitors to walk amongst the stones or touch them during usual opening hours (FIGURE 3.8) – a setting which is problematic for all interest groups, from tourists to new travellers. An unobtrusive rope cordons off the stones and English Heritage personnel who patrol the immediate environs of the site swiftly stop anyone who attempts to circumvent this barrier. The managed open access events stand as anomalies within this conventional setting. Clearly, as an important site of World Heritage status, it is important to avoid unnecessary damage to the stones, and when the current mode of presentation was implemented, it must have been deemed necessary to delimit direct contact with the stones. By and large, visitors accept this approach, with hundreds of thousands (from 300–400,000 in the early 1960s [see <http://www.britarch.ac.uk/stonehenge/>] to 834,318 in 2005 (discussed in the house of commons: see <http://www.publications.parliament.uk/pa/cm200506/cmhansrd/cm060626/text/60626w1200.htm>) flocking to the site, paying the entrance fee (£5.90 per adult in 2006), and walking the circular path around the stones – without ever getting closer than thirty metres or so to the megaliths (except the heel stone, situated close to the A344). It is possible to request 'Stone circle access visits' but there are financial restrictions and time limits: £12 per adult in 2006, for one hour, out of usual opening times, and bookings must be made well in advance; effectively there is a queue. The stone circle itself is only part of the landscape; a wealth of archaeological features comprise the World Heritage Site, from the Avenue and Cursus to the New King Barrows, and most of these are accessible on foot. Yet, the stones are magnificent, they do inevitably provide a focus, and there is widespread agreement that their representation is far from ideal.

It is difficult to argue that visitor impact will really have such a negative effect on the stones when much of the site has already been excavated (that is, deconstructed and reassembled) and stabilised with concrete, and the landscape environs have also been damaged by the triangle of surrounding roads. The argument that rare lichens will be damaged by visitor impact is an environmental issue rather than an archaeological one, albeit one of concern. The preservation ethos is enduring and persuasive, yet the felt need to preserve Stonehenge as it currently exists is a recent discourse. Of course the site custodians are cognisant of the fact that preserving Stonehenge in a vacuum would be a misguided if not impossible task, with their concern being to conserve the site in the long term for future generations. Yet, it is difficult to separate conservation from preservation, and the ideology of conservation is not value-free, being deeply embedded in social and political issues.

Critics have long commented that while English Heritage markets itself as an organisation independent from government duress, it is a government quango none the less (established 1984), being therefore reliant on government funding. And both English Heritage and the National Trust have been criticised for elitist tendencies, marketing to the middle classes who can afford membership (£38 and £40.50, respectively, for one adult in 2006) or pay the not-insignificant entrance or special access fees (see above). This elitism filters into the alternative arena with which we are concerned: while establishment-aligned 'personal growth' pagans may themselves be English Heritage or National Trust members, and in general supportive of the preservation ethos, counter-cultural pagans, new travellers and related interest groups feel marginalized by the authorities, excluded from a monument they consider a pagan sacred site – not only due to class status and financial restrictions, but ideologically, with the preservation ethos taking precedence over tactile, intimate engagement. It might be argued that with Summer Solstice managed open access arrangements and other events English Heritage are indeed facilitating access to pagans and others, signifying their willingness to engage with pagan needs and those of the alternative community. But taking into account the limits of access as stipulated in the 'Conditions of Entry', it might also be the case that this concession is simply paying lip-service to interest groups the establishment, given the choice, would rather avoid (as they did for some decades). What sort of visitor is deemed to be 'ideal' or 'average',[7] and what are they expected to 'get' out of a Stonehenge visit? Arguably, there is an underlying specular discourse not only aimed at current visitors but with an impact on the planned development of the site.

It is startling to discover that an estimated 200,000 (based on 2001 figures: Chippindale and Davison 2001) visit Stonehenge without entering the English Heritage managed part of the site (that is, the immediate environs of Stonehenge), apparently content to look through the wire mesh fence beside the A344, for a few moments, and conclude their visit with a photograph (and often a visit to the toilet facilities in the car park). Stonehenge, contained within fences, privileges a visual, rather than physical or tactile mode of engagement with the site. Stonehenge is not alone in this regard, although its situation is unique. In order to appreciate sites fully, it seems that they should be *looked* at, like museum exhibits, but preferably from a distance so that they can be appreciated in the full context of their archaeological landscape. Once again, the preservation ethos is at the root of this discourse. Management plans for Stonehenge repeatedly stress the importance of landscape, and distance views. Stonehenge is 'not so much a site as a "cultural landscape"; a relict landscape preserving evidence of a long history of man's interaction with the environment' (English Heritage 2000b: 2.4). 'Typically much of the WHS [World Heritage Site] is an open landscape in which the sky dominates' (English Heritage 2000b: 2.15). 'From the highest points on the downland (often the location of the most significant archaeological remains), views are extensive and landscape features can be visible from a considerable distance' (English Heritage 2000b: 3.13). This approach, widening perception out from the stones and into the surrounding landscape of monuments, owes much to the 'landscape archaeology' of the 1990s.

The visual bias inherent within the preservation ethos is consequently influential upon current archaeological interpretations which foreground spatiality, distance and perspective, although the dynamic here probably works both ways and is not straightforward. Furthermore it has contoured thinking regarding the planned improvements to visitor facilities at Stonehenge, and the proposed 'visitor experience'. While there is no decision on the sort of changes that will be implemented (discussed in more detail below), a new visitor centre is planned some three miles from the Stones, although its future is, as everything else connected with this landscape, uncertain. (In 2006 Salisbury District Council gave approval, although a very similar scheme was rejected in 2005. There is an appeal, the application has now been 'called in' and a local public inquiry scheduled, but it is possible that Salisbury District Council may not defend the appeal: see Fielden [2006] for a brief account of current situations.) If the centre is relocated, visitors will be conveyed by 'land train' to vantage points from which to view the panorama of the landscape (now apparently untrammelled by recent human architecture), and thereby to appreciate the perspective of archaeologists. What people will see is Stonehenge manufactured for the twenty-first century, but whether this is actually what visitors want remains a moot point (Baxter and Chippindale 2002).

This specular approach is displayed throughout the Management Plan and Stonehenge Project documentation, and the description of the future of Stonehenge on the English heritage website:

> Land trains, running on low-emission LPG (Liquified Petroleum Gas) will transport visitors from the new visitor centre to drop-off points within the World Heritage Site.
>
> From these points, visitors will be able to walk the final short distance to the Stones and explore the surrounding landscape. By approaching on foot, visitors will be able to fully appreciate Stonehenge's dramatic landscape setting and its relationship to the other monuments. For those visitors who are less able to walk, there will be special arrangements to ensure that they too are able to reach the stones.
>
> (<http://www.english-heritage.org.uk/server/show/nav.876>, 'The future of Stonehenge')

The 'visual drama' of Stonehenge is further evinced in the images produced or reproduced by heritage managers and archaeologists. These representations typically show Stonehenge from a variety of dramatic, unusual, and long-distance perspectives (i.e. from the air, silhouetted against the sun rise etc.), reinforcing the notion that the grandeur and 'mystery' of the place can only be experienced from a distance. Moreover, and in contrast to most people's experience of the site, they show a Stonehenge devoid of humanity. Hence the Stones are rendered not as architecture but as 'natural', framed as part of a dramatic landscape in which humans no longer play a part. The Stones appear frozen in time, hence they are 'timeless', 'unchanging', and ultimately 'mysterious' – qualities set in stone which heritage managers have committed themselves to preserving.

The role of archaeologists in this discourse of visuality and preservation is problematic. Those who regularly feature in documentaries tend to reinforce the preservation ethos through clichéd images and sounds. Archaeologists, as 'experts', are seen striding purposely through deserted sites, or through virtual tours of 'stone age' Britain, as it is currently imagined. A surfeit of digital editing shows stones 'looming' from unusual camera angles (compare with similar representations of cathedrals), shrouded in dry-ice, and accompanied by a soundtrack of stereotyped vox-effect drones. Archaeologists are of course eager to promote their discipline and use such documentaries to espouse and visually present their latest interpretations. However, in doing so, and in conceding to the demands of 'good' television, that is, with high ratings, they end up portraying stone circles more often as mysterious, enchanted places, not as interesting pieces of archaeological evidence. The archaeological message is thereby obscured by visual trickery, a romanticisation which makes both the programmes and the sites themselves extremely appealing to the wider public. It is a well-known irony that the images and representations of these sites, as with many others, are instrumental in generating the very tourism which they believe threatens sites' stability and continuity.

'Stonehenge is perceived internationally as a "must see attraction"' (English Heritage 2000b: 2.11), but for heritage managers wedded to the preservation ethos, the current numbers of visitors to Stonehenge are problematic. On the one hand, visitors contribute to the site's tangible value, in that tourism generates considerable revenue, but on the other, visitors present one of the identified threats to the stable continuity of the stones through the steady erosion of so many feet. At Avebury, for example, tourists have been reluctantly accepted, with the earlier management plan stating that the 'purposes of the National Trust embrace the principle of providing public access, where it is consistent with its primary duties of preservation and good neighbourliness. The Operational Guidelines for nomination to the World Cultural Heritage list do not, in fact, require sites to be accessible to the public' (National Trust 1997: 25). The plan is arguably committed to *reducing* visitor numbers; its idealised image of the site, it might be argued, is an engraving from 1724, in which the site is deserted, unnoticed except by antiquarians. The plan, in other words, side-steps the issue of why stone circles have become so popular, or why they have become so meaningful within contemporary culture. The great longevity of Stonehenge means that it, quite literally, represents continuity with the ancient past. Furthermore its inherently unknowable qualities makes this distant past particularly amenable to polysemic interpretation: Stonehenge can support a host of alternative meanings in a way that, for example, a cathedral, with a (largely) known history, can not. For contemporary culture, destabilised by the uncertainties of post-modernity, the appeal of Stonehenge is considerable.

Additionally, Stonehenge has been given an even greater international significance through its inclusion as a 'World Heritage Site': the Taj Mahal is iconic of, and epitomises, 'Indianess', the Great Wall of China 'Chineseness', and Stonehenge and Avebury 'Englishness'. Foreign visitors to the UK go to places like Stonehenge (alongside the

Tower of London and Madam Tussauds) not simply to view a 'past' or hear it through the audio tour (FIGURE 3.9), but also to partake of this quintessential branded English experience. Visitors to Stonehenge therefore find meanings in the site that may or may not accord with the preservation ethos. Whilst some may appreciate the site intellectually for its archaeological interest, the majority seek some kind of *emotional* encounter with it, with its past or with its significance as a national icon (see Baxter and Chippindale 2002). As Baxter and Chippindale have argued, the majority of visitors do not want to appreciate the stones from a distance as part of a landscape, but close at hand. They want to experience exactly those qualities of drama and mystery that they have been primed to expect through the plethora of stereotyped images to which they have been exposed. They want to photograph themselves against the background of the stones so that on their return home they can say 'I have been there'. For Baxter and Chippindale, therefore, the new plans for visiting Stonehenge represent the imposition of an archaeological discourse of how the site should be interpreted and encountered. It is a discourse shaped by the concerns of supply, not demand, and we are not alone in questioning the desirability of a Disneyfied Stonehenge 'world' in order to meet the needs of tourists seeking 'the mystery' of Stonehenge. The extent to which the proposed Management Plan reconciles the preservation ethos with a diversity of 'visitors', including pagans and other alternative engagements, is an issue to which we now turn.

3.9 Tourists, confined to the path, may 'experience' Stonehenge through an audio-tour. Many do not find this sufficient.

The future

Stonehenge, to reiterate once again, is not a singular thing. It is poly-semic, signifying a range of meanings discursively contested through image and text. Indeed, the image of 'the Stones' has been so over-represented that visitors, expecting hyper-reality, often find reality a disappointing second. The henge monument is sandwiched between the A344 and A303, the former severing the henge from the Avenue marking the original entrance-way, the latter being the main, extremely noisy route to the south west of England. The visitor centre, originating in the 1960s, consists of a small conglomerate of shop, turnstiles and café, part submerged, with a concrete tunnel under the A344 taking visitors from the car park to the stone circle. The car park (not submerged) is visible from almost every part of the Stonehenge landscape, glistening starkly in sunlight to the point of dwarfing and often obscuring sight of the stones. Fences criss-cross the fields surrounding the site, disrupting open access. No wonder, then that today's setting for Stonehenge has famously been described by the UK Parliament's House of Commons Public Accounts Committee as a 'national disgrace'. Fenced off, ringed by throngs of visitors and watchful attendants, set off against two heavily used roads, Stonehenge-as-actually-experienced is very different from the popular and insistent images of dramatic and mysterious solitude. The proposed visitor plans have been shaped in large part by the need to fill this 'reality gap', with a protracted and complex history of plan-ning and consultation to the present day.[8] The literal 'maps' drawn to present contexts and roads, which draw attention to specific features, act discursively to open or close off lines of questioning, even as the discourses of 'health and safety' versus 'sacred celebration' and 'free festival' close off each other's lines of approach. The recent story of Stonehenge includes production of its management plan and master plan, now 'The Stonehenge Project' (<http://thestonehengeproject.org/>), in which we are told:

> The Stonehenge Project is designed to improve the setting and interpretation of Stonehenge. It will remove the sights and sounds of the roads and traffic from the area near the Stones, recreate chalk downland from arable farmland and transform the visitor experience with better access to the landscape and a new world class visitor centre.

The negotiations have revolved around the importance of devel-oping an appropriate setting for the stones and the WHS landscape as a whole, which all parties agree is of the utmost importance, and weighing this up – and especially the cost of a new Stonehenge visitor experience – against the needs of an effective road transport system through the site. From the mid-1980s to today, a major problem has been in establishing 'joined up thinking', as ICOMOS put it in 2001, between the various government departments, heritage bodies and other relevant parties. In the past six years, plans have shifted from putting the intrusive A303 into a 'cut and cover' tunnel; changing this, after considerable protest, to a bored tunnel, said to occasion less disruption to archaeology and other features; rejecting the bored tunnel scheme on grounds of expense; and suggesting five possible schemes (both tunnels, north and south bypasses, and a 'partial' solution) – all of which attract their own protest. A number of heritage and conservation agencies, including the National Trust, CPRE and ICOMOS-UK and the Pagan-led ASLaN have pronounced themselves against all five. A large-scale public inquiry was held 2004, and 'consultation' in spring of 2006. A further inquiry, regarding the visitor centre (now estimated to cost £67 million), is scheduled for December 2006. In this issue the boundaries are differently drawn, less polarized and with a resistance positioned well within the mainstream: the boundaries of 'the tribes' are permeable and they shift.

Despite the best of intentions towards site improvement, the discussions have principally focused on the rerouting of the A303, either with an alternative route (all proposals for which have been dismissed as inappropriate), a cut and cover tunnel (considered as a poor fix by those with conservation interests) or bored tunnel (considered as too expensive by the government but an option with less impact on conservation), as well as the siting of a new visitor centre (previously at Lark Hill, currently at the Countess East farm site purchased for the purpose by the National Trust in 1999). So the redevelopment of Stonehenge has often been secondary to road improvements and, of course, fiscal concerns. The removal of the A303, A344 and the relocation of the visitor centre can also be read as cosmetic landscaping exercises to contour the land to hyper-real expectations. If the plans do eventually go ahead (there is still no decision – see Figure 3.10), visitors might now expect to see the long-distance views and dramatic panoramas for themselves. Initially proposals led visitors to expect that they could wander amongst the Stones and encounter their mysterious qualities first hand, though this now appears uncertain. But, in case reality is still not enough, the new visitor centre is to contain the latest virtual reality technology, so that hyper-real expectations can be met. We concur with Baxter and Chippindale's (2002: 5) concern as to whether heritage management is 'imposing *our* beliefs and *our* desires through our control of planning for the future management of Stonehenge on visitors and on the physical archaeological remains themselves in an experimental fashion'.

STONEHENGE IMPROVEMENT OPTIONS UNVEILED

Possible options for the A303 around Stonehenge were outlined today by Stephen Ladyman, Minister of State for Transport, and David Lammy, Minister for Culture.

The options for improvements to the road follow the decision in July 2005 to look again at the planned bored tunnel, which has seen the cost escalate to £510m.

In addition to the bored tunnel, the following alternatives are also being looked at:

- Bypasses of the Stonehenge site, either to the north or south
- A 'cut and cover' tunnel past Stonehenge;
- Changes to the Countess Roundabout, closure of the A344/A303 junction and construction of the Winterbourne Stoke Bypass.

Stephen Ladyman said:

"The Government is committed to improving the A303 past the World Heritage Site at Stonehenge. I hope that everyone with an interest in this important issue will take this opportunity to contribute to the review process. I am keen to take account of as many views of possible before deciding on an option that will be in keeping with the special requirements of the location as well as being affordable, realistic and deliverable."

(Stonehenge Project press release, 23 Jan 2006)

3.10   Stonehenge 'improvement options' current in 2006.

Currently the visitor centre plans and all road proposals are disputed. Further, the long-standing issue concerning both visitor centre and road plans impacts on the status of Stonehenge as a World Heritage Site: The National Trust warned in July 2006 that this designation of World Heritage Status could be lost, and Salisbury District Council (now in late 2006 dealing with the expense of an inquiry demanded by National Government) point out that a decision must by made over the road situation before a new visitor centre can go ahead. Meanwhile, Baxter and Chippendale's call for low-impact and smaller-scale responses (for both roads and visitor centre) has been echoed by the campaigning group Heritage Action (<http://www.heritageaction.org/>), and most recently by Professor Peter Fowler, addressing the Council for British Archaeology (6 October 2006), who 'advocated low tech interpretation at several perimeter points, encouraging walkers, cyclists and horse riders to explore the whole site and its myriad monuments, not just the stone circle itself' (Kennedy, 7 October 2006).

Alternative meanings

If, as Baxter and Chippindale contend, visitor expectations and meanings are largely ignored, then those of pagans, alternative archaeologists, earth mystics, new travellers and free-festivallers are actively marginalized and have even been criminalized. At an abstract level, alternative discourses are incompatible with, and directly challenge, the preservation ethos. For alternative practitioners the past is not closed, nor is it unreachable; its relics are 'living' things, with Stonehenge as a living temple, as sacred now as it was to 'the ancestors'. Through a variety of practices, which include dowsing, meditation, visualisation, ritual, entheogen consumption, and the cartographic search for 'alignments', it is believed that the knowledge of these ancestors can be rediscovered, and the lack in our culture met. It is understandable why traditional academic archaeology, resting upon rational enquiry and the procedures of graduate training, peer review and so on, is suspicious of these alternatives, for – post-modern interpretative archaeology aside – there is a fundamental methodological and philosophical incompatibility.

However, it follows from alternative discourses that intellectual engagement with sites from a distance is not sufficient, and the need to interact physically, emotionally and spiritually with sites is what renders these discourses so problematic for the preservation ethos. That managers perceive alternative visitors as a threat is evidenced by the following statement, unsubstantiated (in the document at least) with evidence: 'Visitor pressure is compounded by the highly seasonal nature of tourism at Stonehenge together with peaks created by the influx of visitors at certain times of the year, mainly at the summer and winter solstices and equinoxes' (English Heritage 2000b: 3.22). The Stonehenge management plan itself perhaps attempts to accommodate these alternative views: 'It is essential that plans for visitor management do not affect the essential mystical quality of Stonehenge, a quality which for many people lies at the root its attraction' (English Heritage 2000b: 3.23) – yet it is just as likely that 'the mystical quality' alluded to here is that of mainstream media representations rather than pagan perspectives. Druidic and other rituals, organised via 'Stone circle access visits', are tolerated and perhaps even welcomed given the revenue they can attract, but these rituals and alternative views are only accommodated to the extent that the preservation of the site is not compromised – the preservation ethos remains non-negotiable.

Those approaching Stonehenge as a sacred site arrive with a variety of interpretations already in place: these include glimpses of history and prehistory, whether gleaned from guidebooks, websites or archaeology books. Of those we interviewed at the 2001 summer solstice, most interpretations focused only on the immediate, the stones as 'home'. Yet landscape was inherent in approaches. The previous year, in 2000, the event was preceded for some by a processionary walk from Woodhenge, led by the late George Firsoff, and accompanied by some ritual at its start. People walked through lanes and field, past barrows, finally joining the last part of the avenue and experiencing the monument rising up before them as they walked the last uphill metres, only to have to turn aside at the last moment because of the separation of avenue and monument by the A344 and two fences. At the 2001 event, foot and mouth restrictions prevented such processions, although they have been conducted subsequently.

The proposed 'Stonehenge tunnel' – to take traffic away from the visible Stonehenge environs – is seen by many of those celebrants as not a removal of intrusion, but *as* intrusion, a gash within sacred landscape, a massive trench scooped out of land (and archaeology) which, according to some, would break lines of energy, to others would destroy links with the past they would rather were left *un*excavated, and to still others would further destroy the relationships constructed over millennia between land, ancestors, stones and people. Consideration of the Stonehenge landscape, therefore, for many of today's pagans, includes both a sympathy to seeing 'the monument within its landscape', and a concern over the process by which this can be achieved (and not merely the achieving of a cosmetic end-product). Some point out that the proposed changes cannot (in any case) return Stonehenge to how 'it was' and that the devastation already accomplished by not only the current A303, but by excavation and concrete, would not be somehow 'cancelled' by the current plans. Further, indications that 'visitors' will not (as initially promised) be 'allowed' to walk amongst the stones, for free, is a blow to many different people, pagans – and archaeologists – included.[9]

Baxter and Chippindale (2002) suggest that most 'tourists' visit Stonehenge to obtain 'primarily an emotional experience' – not to attend extravagant presentations on the monument in its landscape, but to see it for themselves, photograph family members in front of this 'icon', seek some kind of connection to the stones, etc. Few visitors, they suggest, have much interest in the landscape. Baxter and Chippindale do not in this paper mention pagans, who, often, do have some knowledge of the landscape and indeed who may perform rituals on or near the barrows, nor do they mention those people who seek a return to the 'free festival', who already know about the cursus. Nor do they mention the pressure of solstice and equinox celebrations, which have increased since the time of writing of their discussion paper. However, they do suggest that 'the display will give about equal space to historical Stonehenge as to the prehistoric Stones, and will display the multiple and emotional responses to the place' (p. 5). Current experience suggests that tourists do have interest in the responses of others: rituals performed during 'special access' attract their own lookers-on, and those preparing for such an event are questioned by visitors, indeed asked by site-guides to explain their ritual 'performances' to tourists.

Plans for Stonehenge need to acknowledge pagan, new traveller, and other interests – the 'tribes' are not going to go away. There are several separate, though linked, issues here, and a growing public awareness of each of these. They include: issues of access at festivals; issues of access at other times (walking freely amongst the stones); connections with the landscape; the devastation potentially occasioned by a tunnel; and the devastation already occasioned by a serious of factors including excavation, neglect, and Victorian and other graffiti. Pagans and other members of the alternative communities have endeavoured to attend public meetings concerning the plans: these are often held either in London or locally, and often (though not always) midweek, facilitating attendance by those for whom the issue forms part of their job, but not interested parties who work in other fields. Meetings do result in the provision of some information (although 'of what' and 'to whom' may be contested points), and in the raising of some questions. ASLaN member Andy Norfolk was able to attend one which fell on a Wednesday in 2002 in London. He illustrates his perceptions of some of the debate, including difficulties in determining which document, at any one point in time, was most current, along with issues of potential destruction of features through road construction.

> I was also at the meeting representing ASLaN and I recall
> Andrew Lawson of Wessex Archaeology saying [that]the
> geophysical survey of the 135m wide road corridor has shown
> very little in the WHS part of the route as compared to the rest
> of the route near Winterbourne Stoke. He suggested that this
> supported the idea that this area was a special set-apart place.
> George Lambrick pointed out that geophys is bad at finding
> some sorts of archaeological features, such as Bronze Age struc-
> tures remaining only as post-holes . . . I'm still not convinced
> that the road is being properly considered in the context of the
> WHS as a whole . . . It would be a shame, for example, to end
> up with a tunnel portal destroying a barrow group when the
> University of Birmingham study shows how carefully such
> monuments were sited in relation to Stonehenge. If it's right to
> try to explain to visitors that Stonehenge isn't just an odd
> place in splendid isolation but is part of an intricate and inter-
> linked landscape then any impacts of the road including the

construction phase should surely not reduce opportunities for such interpretation. There still seems to be reason for puzzlement, at least, over statements that the Management Plan is the 'overarching' document taking precedence over the Master Plan and what is actually happening.

(Norfolk, on Britarch email list 28 February 2002,
used with permission)

A critique of Wainright's (2000) report on the Stonehenge Management Plan, by Baxter et al. (2000), once again omits the concept of 'sacred site' or 'spiritual experience' while focussing on the 'Stonehenge experience' received by an (apparently) passive, 'ideal visitor' to the site. The multiplicity of meanings relating to this rich complex are in danger of disappearing, yet again. Studies emerging from the archaeological and heritage management communities, understandably, focus on the sites: we see a need to also focus on people, and identify a clear need for foregrounding meaning and its construction among 'visitors' to sites; notably pagans whose meanings and approaches are most at odds with the concept of 'visiting' promoted by management plans. As several informants have commented, 'visiting is what you do in someone else's house'. Members of the pagan and new traveller communities may speak, not of visiting, but of 'coming home'. Further, this discourse of 'coming home' may relate to the construction of community based at, and in, the site itself, with shared modes of expression and shared values emerging, at times, specifically to oppose those of the site managers.

The Stones and their (whether assumed or researched) history and prehistory form an important part of many people's concept of self, place and belonging – but do so differently for each person. For instance: some participants in the 1970s festivals spoke of how the stones had come, for them, to symbolise 'freedom'. The concept of a free festival and open access, therefore, was centrally important for them as a goal in itself. For many pagans the stones had inherent power, or the ground on which they had been placed had this power, so that free access was for them a means to an end, and the rising of the sun to shine onto the stones was a sacred or holy moment. For some in both of these groups, the stones were a place where people in the past (the un-named builders) had held social events, and at the solstice several handfastings (pagan weddings) and child-namings were performed.

In this understanding the monument is a site of construction of meaning, and people engage with it, and each other, actively, in forming their communities. They claim it as 'home', as the place where they meet, exchange news. One young man attended because 'I was conceived here 23 years ago today'. A friend had come because he wanted to touch the stones, and had resented the barriers present at other times. A third friend said it was 'part of her faith': she followed a solitary Wiccan path, and for her the stones were both spiritual, and about 'freedom and resistance'. For all three, they were a focus of identity, and attending was 'coming home'.

Turning to plans for the Stonehenge-area redevelopments indicates that boundaries are differently drawn here, with considerable alliances formed around questions of a tunnel to take the A303, and the siting of the proposed new visitor centre (see e.g. articles linked from the Stonehenge Alliance website). The Stonehenge Inquiry of 2004 (see Planning Inspectorate 2004, <http://www.planning-inspectorate.gov.uk/stonehenge/>) included pagan and druid voices along with those of the CPRE and the National Trust (opposing the current road plans) and English Heritage and the Highways Agency (presenting the plans). Once again, pagan views are not simple. The Pagan Federation and the Ancient Sacred Landscapes Network were associated with the Stonehenge Alliance, campaigning against the planned tunnel. Presentations of The Druid Network raised some questions about the ramifications of the road plans, while indicating a basic support for the proposal to build a two-mile tunnel to take the A303. Not all members of The Druid Network supported the 'official' stance. We were asked to indicate something about the 'reburial issue' and produced evidence which we intended to indicate that such issues go beyond Stonehenge. Our earlier work on pagans and sites has become part of the process – referenced by the Highways Dept environmental statement (now no longer available online), differently referenced by the National Trust in their written submission to the inquiry, and we were asked to contribute to the Druid presentation on reburial of human remains.

Baxter and Chippindale (2002) point out that grass within the monument can stand only around sixty thousand 'visitors' per annum and a 'good Stonehenge experience' (presumably meaning 'majestic silence' unspoiled by too many tourists) would be accessible only if numbers remained below one hundred thousand. We would add to this that with 20,000 or so attending an all-night solstice celebration where the 'visit' includes not only walking but dancing, processing, moving all over the area of the stones, this problem is indeed pertinent, but its solution may lie in attempts to draw people into other parts of the area – the earlier experiences of a music festival on the cursus may be one to re-consider, or reconstructing Avebury's sanctuary to act as a 'new' sacred site and remove the focus from Stonehenge. Yet, negotiations for open access each year have (until a possible 'extra' hour or so in 2007) been more short-term, frequently dividing into discussions of the English heritage plans for a shorter access time – apparently due to lost tourist revenue during the morning access period from a budget-challenged English Heritage, and policing costs. Rather vague schemes for an 'after-party' previously mooted would attract only part of those drawn to celebrate.[10]

However, for archaeologists, pagans, and others to work together here, there is a need to avoid devaluing the discourses of others. While there is evident common cause, this is not perceived when some pagans view archaeologists as saying only that 'we cannot know the purpose' of whatever monument is addressed, and so removing or sterilising any spiritual element; or new travellers view heritage management as interested only in the financial value of tourism; or archaeologists view pagans as irrational, or as inappropriately 'appropriating' the landscapes of the past to avoid a less romantic present. None of these groups are monolithic; and there is need to move between, to translate archaeological discourse into something which becomes accessible but not patronising.

In 2003 a documentary series on the National Trust and Heritage was shown on BBC4, repeated on BBC2 in 2004. The last in the series was on the disputed issue of Stonehenge access, and showed meetings of the 'Round Table' peace process. The director commented, on the BBC website afterwards, that

> You would not believe the passions that this event raises. You are dealing with a group outside society's boundaries. It tells you so much about what works and what doesn't. Tolerance works, beating them up does not.
> (<http://www.bbc.co.uk/bbcfour/documentaries/features/nationaltrust5.shtml>, 'Director's Diary')

The documentary focused on tensions between the heritage organisations involved – English Heritage and the National Trust – local police representatives, and members of the community that wished to celebrate at Stonehenge. However issues raised about the programme have suggested that some participants or campaigners saw direction focused on following 'Gandalf look-alikes' – men with beards – as the only spokespersons or representatives of the diverse pagan communities involved. Women were shown as celebrants, and two women were shown attending meetings but not speaking. Celebrants were mostly referred to as 'druids' or 'hippies', so that the diversity of attendees was masked. One spokesperson – Brian Viziondanz – was however treated seriously and emerged as a thoughtful representative of what might be called the new traveller/pagan community. Some dimensions of the importance of Stonehenge as a spiritual focus, for Brian, have thereby had an airing. This has contributed, in turn, to the further development of paganisms around places such as Stonehenge – even though much of the political content was ignored or bypassed in the making of the documentary.

What the documentary did show clearly, however, were tensions between the icon in splendid isolation, and the site as 'temple of paganism'. We have referred in other work to the iconography of sacred place – the images appearing on websites, English Heritage versus the Stonehenge Campaign. The dominant discourses of *conservation* and (e.g. articulated by Clews Everard, previous site manager for English Heritage) *health and safety* set the terms for negotiation, and during round table meetings Brian and others attempted to use these to address issues of spirituality and of the length of time in which people could remain at the monument and in the car park.

Ramifications from this discourse include the 'pissed off factor' expressed most clearly by a new traveller member of the Stonehengepeace e-group, which Brian attempted to counter, on this mailing list, through presentation of his philosophy of 'light is returning'.

> What you perhaps mean is that without the 'peas process', there would not be the travesty of an event that we have now been saddled with. It is EH's policy to dilute the radicalism of the Stonehenge Free Festival movement by its so called 'free access policy'. This consists of herding thousands of people in and out Stonehenge as fast as possible making any sort of 'event' impossible. The 'peas process' appears to be colluding in this.
>
> (Mark, March 2004)

Brian's response arose from his theology:

> Light is returning and there is nothing anyone can do to stop it.

> Its written in the script, the light ALWAYS wins – this is the velvet revolution and its coming, its sweeping the planet – the water rises in all wells equally, and the wells are each one of us – all of us human beings, on all sides of the equation.

> When we at the round table hold hands in a circle, no matter what has taken place during the meetings, no matter what position we hold in the story, we are in that moment in unity with each other and our commitment to find a peaceful path to resolution of the issues.

The forces that hold all of this stonehenge situation where it is are made up of millions of human beings with millions of stories, fears and agendas.

Each one of us is a well and as the sun rises everywhere in our global culture, it rises within us also and the paradigm dissolves and reforms to reflect our more enlightened global consciousness.

There are no bad guys – landowners are operating within the current paradigm according to the structure/rules/agreements of the current paradigm.

Innocence is universal, humans being human, surviving, desperately clinging on to this spinning rock for dear life.

This is what we all have in common and understanding, this is a fundamental piece of the awakening.

(Viziondanz, March 2004)

Yet, two years later, Brian was expressing frustration with inabilities to negotiate the Stonehenge issues in other than management discourse, emphasising the necessity to take into account how people interacted with landscape and site in the present day in a letter to English Heritage. He has since pointed out his feelings that the round table retains potential for discussion and negotiation, even creativity, saying to members of the Stonehengepeace group that:

The round table has become a hostage situation where the hostages bond with the hostage takers and no one wants to upset anyone, because in reality we quite like and love each other. There is a fear of the return of the festival the way that it became in the latter years. I maintain that if we all collaborate fully on a midsummer community celebration – the authorities included – we can create a wonderful event for the entire community.

He comments that the Stonehenge event is 'an experiment in what is possible when we human beings aspire to be the best that we can be', and adds:

We are regenerating and creating a new future for our global culture. From its mono, youth subculture in the 60's, wild and free, the festival movement has matured and now encompasses all generations and walks of life. We are a living breathing example of a world working for all of us.

The round table is an opportunity for us to work together and move forward – I am not suggesting that we throw out the baby with the bath water – what I am saying is that we need to expand the vision and the remit of the round table.

(Viziondanz, email to Stonehengepeace email discussion list 17 May 2006)

While the BBC documentary illustrates some key points in the issues involved, including the conflicting discourses and also the potential to which Brian points, the description of those assembled by Patrick Forbes in the online 'Directors Diary' notes as 'a group outside society's boundaries' and as '30 thousand whacked-out hippies' has done nothing to increase confidence in media presentations of pagans or other alternative groups at Stonehenge or elsewhere today.

Animism and the landscape

Chapter One in this book, and that on Avebury following it, indicated that pagan representations can contribute positively to more general understandings of the past. Concepts of a feasting-place, a greeting-place, a meeting-place in the present day, and also a place of power, a place of conflict, bear on this. While the notion of Stonehenge as a landing pad for aliens (met only fleetingly in our discussions) might not be the best example of this, we, following Hutton (1996), argue that the more voices that are involved in interpreting the past, the richer our understanding of that past may become. In a tapestry of voices, the richness of depiction and interpretation of this and other landscapes, no single interpretation or discourse is pre-eminent, but plurality of voices reflects the substantial diversity of interests, meanings and interpretations. Description of Stonehenge as a 'druid temple' may seem to hark back to Stukeley (and so may provoke reactionary remarks from at least some archaeologists) yet on closer inspection the current use of Stonehenge by Druids and other pagans and new travellers as a *living temple* where communities can gather to celebrate or 'party', perform hand-fastings, child blessings, honour a life recently ended, and offer respect to previous ancestors, is not so very far removed from academic archaeological interpretations of the site in prehistory as a place for ritual feasting, rites of passage and the maintenance of ancestral connections. Further, a pagan contribution to archaeology may be seen in the revival of animism[11] and the agency of 'objects' with Stonehenge as a focus. For pagans as *new-indigenes*, the Stonehenge landscape is filled with unconventional, if not strictly 'otherworldly', agencies including ancestral spirits, gods and goddesses, wights, and shamanic spirit helpers. It has agency and is a living landscape. The stones of Stonehenge are themselves animate, with 'forces' of their own which affect the people who 'visit'. Theoretically speaking, these pagans are, to use Harvey's (2005) term, 'new animists', turning their attention away from the prevailing idea of the Stonehenge landscape as a blank canvas which has been encultured by humans of the past, towards an approach to this site and its landscape setting which affords agency outside human actions. For these new-indigenous site users, Stonehenge inscribes meaning in its visitors. In a way, this approach aligns with post-structuralist commentary on the agency of all objects which are *a priori* socially constructed. New animism pushes this notion further, disrupting the status of 'humans' as the ascendant species and that of cognicentric emphasis on human (front brain) 'consciousness' over other forms of perception, and moreover extending sociality – the world is filled with persons only some of whom are human, and some of these other-than-human-people are 'objects' such as the stones of Stonehenge. Such a pagan approach to Stonehenge may offer something to a more general understanding of the site in prehistory, resonating with Ingold's (e.g. 2000, 2006) re-animating of western thought and with current anthropological and archaeological interpretation. In this sense, academic discourse and emerging pagan discourses may have much to contribute to each other, as pagans seek out new ontologies including seeing Stonehenge as animate.

Stonehenge as 'site' indicates shifting meanings and alliances which for us exemplify the fluidity and permeability of boundaries of the 'New Tribes' of today's Britain. Identities are formed in the public spaces of prehistory and sacredness is constituted in discourses drawing deliberately on mythology, archaeology and indigeneity. Strands of both preservation and use run through such discourses and identities. Of all the sites that we discuss in this book, we have not devoted so much attention to Stonehenge simply because it is the most well-known prehistoric monument in Britain and one of the most celebrated monuments worldwide (though it is precisely this status, of course, which attracts massive interest, including from pagans). More importantly, the history of contest at Stonehenge is remarkably sustained, deeply complex, and always impassioned. As such it forms the ideal case study with which to build on the previous, related example of Avebury, and to thereby complicate the discourse and explore the way in which a pre-eminent *sacred site* is embedded in contested rites and equally contested rights. The discussion so far has drawn attention to the diversity of pagan contests, how these are embedded in current political and social movements and the way in which they resist generalisation and monolithic attempts at resolution. Central to the understanding of Stonehenge and its landscape today is the importance of engaging with and understanding pagan discourse, on a number of levels, from academic study to face-to-face dialogue between pagans, archaeologists and heritage managers. This attention to dialogue should not be seen simply as a 'politically correct' attempt to entertain a 'fringe minority'. Rather, dialogue and its analysis, informed by Foucault and all theorists since, attends to the inter-relations of discourse and power, and so reveals as much about the politics and complexities of site management and interpretation in Britain as about the variety of paganisms today, with implications for how sites and dialogues are represented and managed.

In the following chapter, we take this analysis beyond the honeypot sites of Avebury and Stonehenge, and a focus on the south of England, to the less well-known sites of Stanton Moor in the Peak District of Derbyshire in central England, and Thornborough Henges in the Vale of Mowbray in North Yorkshire. In both of these situations, a central issue is pagan and alternative protest and activism to save a site from the encroaching threat of quarrying, where many pagans, local people and heritage managers have found common cause.

CHAPTER 4

Derbyshire and Yorkshire: Stanton Moor and Thornborough Henges

*That monuments can change in their significance is demonstrated
all too clearly at Nine Ladies. There were ten stones here, possibly
more. The name has a different derivation, a link to folk traditions
that saw an importance in the number and circles as women
frozen in the act of dancing. . . . Visited by locals out with their
dogs, by hikers pushing through and those clutching archaeological gazetteers, the circle also sees regular gatherings around
seasonal thresholds. In certain years, the signature of these can be
traced in a broader circle of charred and shallow fire pits, each
associated with the debris of celebration. Some come alone to hold
their own communion, others to party; attitudes running from
political or religious conviction through to romantic whimsy.
For many, the circle is a broad church, with the capacity to be
interpreted in a variety of ways, not least because we know so
little. In their shared fascination for these places, others express
their dissatisfaction with the crass materialism of the present. For
some though, meanings are more fixed and more dogmatically
asserted. Claims are made that there is a 'truth' to the place, a
truth held exclusively that establishes priority over others... we
may be catching a faint echo of statement heard in the second
millennium.*
(Edmonds and Seaborne 2001: 168)

At Avebury and Stonehenge, site management may see much pagan
engagement as threatening the monument – yet, as previous chapters
demonstrate, there are instances of reciprocal collaboration which
look towards the conservation of these sites. But while the implementation of management plans, archaeological excavations and
ongoing tourism all have their own detrimental effects, neither of
these sites is currently under direct threat of destruction of its landscape; even the plans for a tunnel for the A303 are attempting to
minimise perceived landscape threats. Elsewhere different boundaries

apply, and management and pagans make common cause, particularly where sites are threatened by such actions as road building and quarrying. In Ireland, motorway plans encroach on the hill of Tara; in England, the Anglo-Saxon cemetery of Prittlewell, Southend-on-Sea (Essex) is directly threatened by road expansion. Thornborough Henges in North Yorkshire and Derbyshire's Stanton Moor, discussed in this chapter, are both under threat of quarrying based on old permissions. Of these two sites Stanton Moor has been until recently better known, and its proximity to Sheffield locates it within a short drive from where one of us lives. This therefore is where we begin our discussion of paganisms as protest and alliances formed thereby.

Stanton Moor, its context and recent history

The Nine Ladies Stone circle is well known to many British pagans, especially those in the English Midlands. Yet while some will think specifically of this circle as a 'sacred site', others extend their interest to the entire landscape of Stanton Moor, considering the cairns, circles and Bronze Age burials as part of a sacred landscape in which spirits of nature, deities and/or ancestors can be honoured. Two other stone circles can still be found on the protected area of upland heath known as Stanton Moor, though a fourth is now fragmentary. Yet the north-east area of the heathland is subject to an application to reopen quarries last worked over 40 years ago.

This application has a peculiar history, involving protestors, local people, high court hearings and organisations including the Council for the Protection of Rural England, in addition to the quarry company and the Peak District National Park Authority (PDNPA). The application submitted in 1999 was to extract 2.18 million tonnes of block sandstone, in high demand as dimensional stone for building, over a period of 42 years. Issues raised by local people, heritage management, and various 'users' of the moor, pagans included, concern destruction of parts of this landscape, and the disruption to the remainder occasioned by the sounds of quarrying, the removal of material and destruction of wildlife habitat.

Since autumn 1999 a protest camp of pagans and 'Eco-Warriors' has occupied land in the proposed quarrying area near the Nine Ladies circle. Many pagans express support for the protesters and for local action group opposition to the quarry, and look to the protest camp leaflets and website (<http://pages.zoom.co.uk/~nineladies/index-01.htm>[1]) and associated sites such as <http://www.stonehenge.ukf.net/nineladies.htm> and the PaganWarriors email list for information. The situation has been 'on hold' while the PDNPA awaited a detailed environmental statement from the quarry company, bought out in 2001 by a bigger quarry company: the environmental statement appeared in December 2003 in the form of a revised application from Marshalls PLC, to remove a greater amount of stone. The company's insistence that the quarry should be construed as 'active' not 'dormant' went before the High Court, with implications for the PDNPA's liability for compensation if quarrying did not go ahead, with determination due in June 2004.

Here some further context is required. Stanton Moor is in the southern part of the Peak District, an upland area roughly divided into the northern and eastern Dark Peak of upland gritstone heathland, and the south-western limestone plateau of the White Peak. Stanton Moor (more properly, ecologically speaking, a heath) is an upland island of pinkish-tinged gritstone in a limestone sea. The Peak District as a whole is rich in prehistoric archaeology, described by, amongst others, Edmonds and Seaborne (2001), more popularly for those who wish to visit by P. and V. Morgan (2001); its heathlands and cliffs or 'edges' are home to many species of wildlife. Like all of England and most of Britain, it is a human-made landscape – as attested by evidences of occupation and use from Bronze-Age clearance cairns to mediaeval and later farms, trackways, roads, reservoirs, industrial works relying on the water-power of the area's swift-flowing rivers, mines and quarries, or indeed the grouse moors which have changed the habitat. In parts of the area it is common to find piled or scattered millstones made from local gritstone quarried through centuries, and a millstone mounted on a plinth will greet travellers on all major roads that enter the boundaries of the park.

The Peak District National Park was established in 1951, and its governing body is the Peak District National Park Authority (PDNPA – whose extensive website at <http://www.peakdistrict.gov.uk/> gives far more detail on history, geology, archaeology and wildlife of the area than we can include here). The park covers much of the area known as the Peak District (including 1438 square kilometres), and includes villages and small towns – approximately 38,000 people live within the park's boundaries. The park is therefore home to industries of various kinds: including over 70 active and inactive sites of mineral extraction. The PDNPA is therefore constantly dealing with applications to reopen or to extend existing quarries and is in the difficult position of balancing the needs of a working landscape with the aims for conservation and recreation of a National Park. The Stanton Moor situation is not alone. In another well-publicised case, quarrying on Longstone Edge has hit headlines, with the PDNPA attempting to prevent extraction of limestone in excess of the permission to a quarry company – in this case MMC Mineral Processing Ltd – to extract other minerals (with limestone only as a secondary product).

But to return, drawing on statements by the Council for the Protection of Rural England (CPRE) and Stanton Lees Action Group (2003) and materials from the PDNPA, to sketch a history: permissions to work quarries at Lees Cross and Endcliffe – the area adjoining Stanton Moor – were granted in 1952. These quarries, then relatively small, had been worked during the 19th and the early part of the 20th centuries. The application (submitted by Messrs. Stanton Quarries Ltd. in 1947 to Bakewell Rural District Council) was for a continuance of this working. After the granting of this permission, according to the CPRE and Stanton Lees Action Group report prepared in 2003, 'It is believed that Lees Cross quarry has not worked since the permission was granted and that work at Endcliffe ceased in 1959'. Confusingly, the permission was not sought or given individually for these quarries, but for six quarries in the area of Birchover and Stanton Moor, of which four received approval (Endcliffe and Lees Cross constituting one unit of the four).

Since the 1950s, considerations of heritage and the environment have gained considerably greater prominence, and subsequent to the Environment Act of 1995 planning authorities identified areas subject to permissions as 'active' or 'dormant': the PDNPA declared the Lees Cross and Endcliffe quarries 'dormant', which Stancliffe Stone (who had bought the permissions) appeared to accept in applying in 1999 to re-commence working. Issues of compensation claims at this time prevented the PDNPA from denying permission outright, but their recommended working conditions (in default of an environmental assessment statement) would have restricted working to one tonne of sandstone per year.

This is not the place to delineate minutiae of the application or the detailed recommendations of the PDNPA, CPRE and others: points have been extensively argued, and sometimes revised, over the seven years since the initial application to reopen the quarries. The history of the application since 1999 has involved a number of dates being set for determination of the application, each time the date being postponed (at approximately six month intervals) until December 2003, when Stancliffe Stone – having been bought by Marshall's PLC two years previously – produced a fresh application related to a new concept, namely that the quarries should not be construed as 'dormant' because there were still active workings relating to the group of four to which 1952 permission had been granted. This revised application was for the removal of 3.28 million tonnes of gritstone (Stancliffe Stone and Glentoal Associates 2003). The High Court ruled in 2004 that the quarries were indeed dormant and this ruling was upheld in 2005 through an appeals procedure. The situation is now one of dates being set for a determination, and again postponed; meanwhile there are suggestions for 'trade-offs' between the Lees

Cross and Endcliffe permissions and other areas which might be less environmentally sensitive.

A news statement from the PDNPA dated 21 October 2005 related to a further extension of deadlines, this time until April 2006:

> The deadline for imposing modern working conditions on two dormant quarries on Stanton Moor has been extended six months.
>
> Quarry operator Stancliffe Stone asked for the extension from October 31 to April 30 next year in order to gather more environmental information for its Lees Cross and Endcliffe quarries.
>
> The Peak District National Park Authority agreed on the basis that it needs the fullest environmental information on the long-unused sites, which are now an overgrown wildlife habitat, in order to make a sound decision on what modern working conditions would need to be imposed if the quarries were to be re-activated.
>
> At the same time, Stancliffe Stone is preparing a possible planning application to extend its active Dale View quarry, nearby.
>
> That application could include the offer to surrender its rights to re-activate Lees Cross and Endcliffe
> (Accessible on CPRE website, <http://www.cprepeakandsyorks. org.uk/pdf_files/PDNPA%20Oct%2005.pdf>) and PDNAP website (<http://www.peakdistrict/gov.uk>)

Indeed, in July 2006 the PDNPA invited people's views on a planning application to extend Dale View quarry on Stanton Moor through a press release, and it was made explicit that the company, Stancliffe Stone, was attempting to trade off an extension of the existing working quarry there for the permissions at Lees Cross and Endcliffe. In November 2006, as we write, a decision is again awaited. Yet the significance of the decision that dormant quarries are, indeed, dormant, should not be underrated. Roy Hattersley, former minister and former leader of the Labour Party, commented in *The Observer* in March 2005, while a ruling on the appeal was pending, that:

> [U]nless the original ruling is upheld other companies with dormant quarries may test their status in the hope of avoiding the obligations to modernise. If that were to happen, the Peak Authority – run on an annual government grant of £7.5 million – would be faced with legal costs it cannot afford. Were it to lose the cases it currently needs to pursue, lawyers fees

would total at least £500,000. Like all poor litigants, it may find the price of fighting the cases too high to pay.

(Sunday 27 March 2005, accessible
<http://www.guardian.co.uk/conservation/story/
0,13369,1446493,00.html>)

The cases of quarrying at Stanton Moor and Longstone Edge, therefore, raise issues that go far beyond their immediate location. These tensions between economic and spiritual interests – here with the widest meaning, quarrying and tourism, older and newer traditions, deal in questions of what today's Britain is about. These contested landscapes may stand for many places where the issues have not been so publicised: but the convolutions of the Stanton Moor stand-off show how the interconnections of today's Britain, the historic and socio-political constructions of each issue, prevent simple solutions. Briefly put, Stanton Moor demonstrates how policy and human rights issues, resulting from past decisions and shifts, return to haunt the policy-makers. Not only the 1952 post-war planning permissions, but the constitution of the PDNPA and the shaping of the 1995 environmental act have contributed to the current situation, as has the changing climate of opinion respecting environment and prehistory or 'heritage'.

Stanton Moor: engagements and reactions, protestors and others

The place

The moor is accessed from the north, south or west. Its stone circles, and others, are described by Barnatt (1990). Stanton Moor is crossed by many paths, including one obviously 'main' path which leads north–south from the small hill road linking Stanton in Peak and Stanton Lees to the south of the moor near Birchover. The simplest access is from a road between Stanton-in-the-Peak and Birchover. One may park near the entrance to a working quarry just north of Birchover, and take the signed path that leads over an entrance stile up to the Cork Stone (a natural boulder of a distinctive shape, high on the moor, which now has climbing handles and footholds) to a crossroads with the main north–south path, beside a large bronze-age cairn. An alternative route, heading north from the Cork Stone by a minor path, winds around older quarries and eventually leads the walker to near the Nine Ladies circle (Stanton Moor II).

From the crossroads by the cairn, a left turn onto the main path heads northwards past the Stanton Moor IV and III embanked circles, buried in heather and unrecognised by most tourists or celebrants or even by those walkers who frequent the area, although at least one of the Bronze-Age cairns is more prominent. Much of the archaeology here is hidden, but the area seems to have been important in prehistory, one of the 'sacred landscapes' of the British Isles. The Nine Ladies circle (Stanton Moor II) is considerably more obvious, as heather has been cleared and the encircling birch trees have been prevented from encroaching on the circle. Also, the embankment of this circle is so small as to be not seen as such, so that the stones, though small, are prominent. This circle, therefore, attracts the attention of pagans and others, as indicated by Edmonds and Seaborne in the chapter epigraph, and has suffered considerable erosion since illustrations from the 19th century which show a mound in its centre. Indeed, some restoration work was conducted at this circle during 2003 after a small excavation in 2000–1 designed to ascertain recent damage to the monument from compaction and erosion.

Many visitors enter from the north of the moor, by the small road that leads from Stanton-in-the-Peak to Stanton Lees, parking in a 'scoop' by the roadside and crossing a stile to walk through a field of cattle before the area of the scheduled ancient monument and the main path are reached. This is the most direct route to the Nine Ladies circle, and often those using it do not realise how much more there is to the moor. If the parking area is occupied, driving further east enables tourists to pass the Dale View Quarry entrance and continue to just after where the road from Rowsley joins from the left. Here they can park along with the vans associated with the protest camp, and a winding rocky path leads through the previously-quarried area which now provides part of the 'home' of the camp and up to the moor. This is a longer route, often very muddy. Where the path forks, protestors have provided notices to the Nine Ladies.

The peace of the Nine Ladies circle is in general only marginally disturbed by audible beeps and sound from the Dale View Quarry. However, the proximity of the Lees Cross and Endcliffe planned quarries would mean that this peace would be considerably further disrupted for visitors, should the quarry plans go ahead, and would occasion more frequent quarry lorries on the narrow hill roads. Further extension to Dale View, in addition, would also affect the ambience of the heathland.

As mentioned above, parts of the Nine Ladies circle and its environs were excavated during 2000–1, in attempts to ascertain the extent of recent erosion, this being followed in 2003 by some restoration work. Notably, local archaeologists took pains to explain purposes of the excavation to protestors and visitors – some of whom decorated the site with a pentacle,[2] whether to protect the land or bless the endeavours of the excavation being unclear. In 19th century illustrations the circle is shown enclosing a small mound, possibly a cairn. This area was by 2000 flat (the restoration has attempted to restore a slight hump). People – walkers, pagans and others – interact directly, and may leave their mark, sometimes quite deliberately. The 'King Stone', an outlier, displays 19th century graffiti of 'Bill Stumps'. An outcrop close to the circle carries more recent engravings, some of which may be associated with a former member of the protest camp, while the related fire-pit and others in the vicinity are used by many visitors. In September 2001, protest rituals by a busload of pagans from Birmingham, accompanied by King Arthur and a Dorset druid group, included an attempt to 'raise energy' to 'protect the stones', as well as a concerted attempt to pick up the scraps of litter and cigarette ends littering the site. The diversity of engagement with the Nine Ladies circle thus illustrates various challenges specific to its location, along with those issues raised at other sites mentioned – issues of multiple meanings, identities and interpretations constructed at, diverse engagements with, and a variety of pressures imposed on sites.

4.1 By the Nine Ladies circle, an outcrop shows new 'rock art', carved about four years before this shot was taken. The green notice on a birch tree requests that people do not cut living wood for fires.

The circles of Stanton Moor seem fairly typical of the gritstone circles of the peak district: fairly small, with low stones (barely a metre above ground, with many smaller). Embanked circles are found throughout the sandstone, while on the limestone plateau there are two much larger henge monuments, at Arbor Low and Dove Holes. The Dove Holes monument has no stones, though there is some indication that there may have been such in the past: now it is within a village and encroached on by houses, a recreation field, and an area for rubbish, and not, so far as we know, visited or utilised by either pagans or stone circle enthusiasts aside from those who visit briefly and comment despairingly on forums such as the Stone e-list, the Megalithic portal, or the Modern Antiquarian forum. Arbor Low with its fallen (or flat) eroded stones is well known within the pagan and alternative spirituality community, and hosts or is subject to various kinds of ritual. Some leave their traces in offerings of flowers, even on one occasion a tiny circle of small stones placed amongst the huge limestones, or the symbols that puzzled tourists after Samhain 2004,

4.2   Arbor Low Henge, immediately after Samhain, looking across the flattened stones to the entrance to the henge and the landscape beyond. Symbols have been traced on the banks at cardinal points, one shown here.

set out in (apparently) a mixture of salt and flour around the banks of the circle. (Interestingly, several pagans who had never communicated with each other, from different areas of the Peaks and indeed some from other areas of Britain, reported recognising and celebrating the same goddess at Arbor Low.) These and other monuments are described by Barnatt (1978, 1990), Barnatt and Smith (2004) and, in possibly more poetic ways that integrate them with time and with present sensibilities, Edmonds and Seaborne (2001).

The protest

All in all, the situation at Stanton Moor is one that displays a number of relations and interactions between pagans, landscape, local people, and numerous others. Comments expressed to us range through concern about sound disturbance to the ambience, concern about wildlife habitat destruction, ideas of the landscape of the moor as a single unit, and the relationship of cairns and burials to the circles (not only the Nine Ladies). A constant strand in comments is that going ahead with quarrying based on the 1952 permission makes mockery of all the focus on environment and landscape, and environmental science and legislation, that has arisen since. One comment came from a building product supplier:

> Stanton Moor, the Nine Ladies, other sacred sites, moorland
> and archaeological finds in the area are under threat by plans
> to quarry for building material. While we need such work to be
> done, there are appropriate and inappropriate places to
> conduct quarrying. No guesses required where this falls!
> (Cam, 25 February 2004)

The situation, therefore, is complex, and informed all round by perceptions of landscape and 'heritage'. Pagan concern about quarrying has intensified, especially with the increase in stone planned to be extracted, and hence the quarry company's apparent disregard of representations from heritage and scientific organisations. Pagans, reading new protest camp leaflets, are raising questions online and in person, and through the medium of the press, about 'who benefits' from the quarrying. The landowner, Lord Edward Manners of Haddon Estates, has during the time of the protest agreed a new lease to the quarry company, and would gain a considerable sum (estimates differ – the protesters in 2004 suggested £100 million) if the Endcliffe/Lees Cross quarries were activated and stone taken out as per the new application. Media including Radio 4 (Seven Days, 24 March 2004) and the Guardian (6 March and 13 March 2004) found the story newsworthy.

Protestors listed the following problems with the proposals:

1   Further degradation of the hillside and setting of the Nine Ladies
     Stone Circle and Stanton Moor
3   The old 1952 consent is wholly inappropriate today and runs
     contrary to Peak Park policies
4   Dangers of quarrying on a geological landslip
5   Threat to the local water table including a spring supplying local
     residents
6   Dangerous lorry traffic and access to and from the sites
7   Decimation of wildlife habitats including badger setts, bat roosts,
     and rare plants such as heath cud-weed
8   Noise and dust pollution
9   Effect on visitors and tourism
                                      (<http://www.nineladies.uklinux.net/>)

     And, in their own words, they suggest:

> If this scheme goes ahead it will not only destroy a part of the
> world's second most popular National Park (the most popular
> is in Japan) including a Grade II Listed building (the Earl Grey
> Tower, a monument erected to commemorate the passing of
> the 1832 Reform Act) and threaten a sacred site, the Nine
> Ladies Stone Circle and the rich archaeological landscape of
> Stanton Moor
>
>   (<http://www.nineladies.uklinux.net/>)

The confused situation of Stanton Moor exemplifies a host of
issues arising elsewhere. Tensions exist between protestors and local
people, who initially welcomed the protest. Now, while some locals
still take food to the protest camp, others have said that they would
rather have a quarry than the camp, and there have been attempts by
some locals to have the camp evicted. At a 2004 public meeting in
Stanton-in-the-Peak, while several residents were attempting to raise
issues of meeting 'quarry lorries' on the narrow, steep roads, one
proclaimed that he had been almost run over by a protestor, and
stories have circulated such as those included in an article in *The
Daily Telegraph* (13 March 2004, shown to us by indignant camp
members) about protestors spitting on food in local shops and,
bizarrely, hijacking a bus.

Indeed, while these charges seem far-fetched, others may have
more substance, at least in the minds of some local people. The camp
was originally started by five people in October 1999. Their initiative
was reported in local papers, and *Private Eye* commented that:

> All that stands between the company and two gaping wounds
> on the historic moors are some dedicated tree huggers and

burrowers (facing a cold Christmas), a small but outraged local community and an uncertain and untested piece of 1995 legislation which is being enforced by the National Parks Authority.
(Christmas issue, 1999)

By May 2000, the camp was described in *The Guardian* as the largest on-going eco-protest in England at that time. Since then, numbers of protesters have hovered around 20–30, though at times when the threat appears greatest they can increase dramatically. In late September 2006, one of us met a protestor who joined the camp at Beltane 2000, and another who was approaching his first anniversary there. The Nine Ladies Anti-Quarry Campaign – to give the protest its formal name – attracts a fluctuating population, and not all have had the same care for the landscape as those who first started the campaign. Protestors have spoken to us of problems with particular individuals who, while they left some time ago, have made their mark on local opinion. Further, those who arrive for a day or a week may be seen by outsiders as part of the protesting group. The tents often seen around the Nine Ladies circle, with associated firepits and possible fire damage to archaeology, are not those of the protest camp.

Yet a walk up through the camp has its depressing side. There is what a casual visitor will note as 'rubbish' – bins overflowing with bottles, a child's plastic tricycle, an old sofa – seemingly strewn by the side of the path or within some of the recent ruins on the public right-of-way. The caravans look unkempt and the treehouses show signs of deterioration and constant mending, not surprisingly as these are very temporary dwellings which have to be rebuilt as their trees grow and change. Some of the ground-based tents and shacks show efforts to present a neat, cleared front (and one has a sign requesting passers by to not let their dogs foul in front of people's homes), but others appear, unsurprisingly, ramshackle. The life of a protestor is not easy: there is always fuel to be gathered from dead twigs and fallen wood, and in winter keeping warm is a major task. And, during the early years and at the periods of greatest threat, protestors were doing what they considered their proper 'work' – building tree-houses, networking ropes high above the old quarry, setting up barricades, and tunnelling into the rock; the objective being to make it as hard as possible, and as costly, for bailiffs to remove them.

Threats were two-fold: first, that the quarry company would attempt to start work, and second that the protestors would receive an injunction to vacate the land. Indeed in 2003 and 2005 attempts were made to use planning regulations to remove the 'unauthorised' protest camp. These are summarised in a report to the PDNPA plan-

ning committee of 17 June 2005, which contextualises the issue
thus:

> In 1999 the submission of the Environment Act scheme caused
> concern amongst local people and various groups and individ-
> uals who were concerned about the resumption of quarrying in
> this sensitive location close to local villages, Stanton Moor and
> the Nine Ladies Stone Circle. A Protest Camp was established
> at the site without the benefit of planning consent and
> without the permission of the landowner or leaseholder. This
> encampment has grown and become better established with
> the construction of tree houses and temporary structures. At
> first the existence of this site was generally accepted by local
> people since it was seen to be directly supporting the resistance
> to further quarrying. However this was followed by expressions
> of concern from some residents of the local community about
> the existence of the camp and the effect on the character of
> the area. Furthermore the Authority was criticised for not
> pursuing enforcement action against this unauthorised use
> whereas other unauthorised development is pursued.
>
> (PDNPA report 2005: 1)

The recommendation on the basis of this report was a repeat of the
previous recommendation of 2003,

> That no action to secure the removal of unauthorised struc-
> tures, the cessation of unauthorised use (including removal of
> caravans) and the reinstatement of the land at Lees Cross and
> Endcliffe Quarries be taken for a further period of 12 months,
> or sooner if a resolution of the quarrying issue at the site
> becomes clear.
>
> (p. 6: <http://peakdistrict.vianw.co.uk/ctte/
> planning/reports/2005/050617Item6-1.pdf>)

In making this recommendation, the committee took into account
the impermanent nature of tree-houses, and also the camp's attention
to the replacement or moving of otherwise more 'permanent' structures such as tents or caravans.

On several occasions 'yellow alerts' have gone out across the internet for people to stand ready, and to support the protest. These coin-
cided initially with the expected dates of (always postponed)
determination hearings, latterly with various 'scares' occasioned by
strangers identified as bailiffs or company officials within the camp.
A key period of anxiety and preparedness arose in early 2004, after
the submission of the second quarrying application based on the

supposition of 'active' working, but before the court ruling of the quarries as 'dormant'. At this time stories circulated of bailiffs gathering and of the company advertising for tree-climbers, and the expectation among protestors was that attempts would be made to remove them. The camp gained considerably in numbers and members of a telephone tree, previously put in place, were prepared to put out alerts for more personnel. As things were, no eviction attempts were made. Protestors have indicated their belief that at that time their efforts had indeed prevented the start of quarrying.

The camp has had its share of tragedy. A man was drowned swimming the Derwent river, and in June 2000 a young man, Andrew Harrop, was killed when he fell into an old quarry on the moor when attending an event described as a 'rave' to celebrate the Summer Solstice. Finally, on 7 March 2002 a protestor, Jo, died in a blaze that destroyed a two-storey hut known as 'The Tower'. Other camp members built a memorial garden for her on its site.

Representation and ritual

The protestors are few compared to the many who come to the moor, as tourists, walkers, local people seeking recreation or tranquillity, or pagans attending to make ritual. As at other sites, the categories are fluid, with a particular individual attending perhaps to see the landscape and the view, to meditate or talk with local wights or spirits, to investigate archaeology, to support the protest, to engage in a formal ritual, or all or any combination of these. Many site users will recognise only the Nine Ladies as archaeology or as a ritual site. New signage installed by English Heritage at entrances and at this circle attempts to indicate that the whole of the heathland is of importance, and makes a plea for care on the part of those visiting:

> Stanton Moor is a Scheduled Monument because of its national importance. You can help us to look after it by:
>
> - respecting these ancient sites and the beliefs of the people who built them
> - avoiding any damage or disturbance
> - keeping to the public rights of way shown on the map
> - keeping dogs on leads
>
> *It is an offence to damage a Scheduled monument. This include removing stonework, digging holes, lighting fires, felling trees, all of which would harm buried archaeological layers.*
>
> (Text of signage at Nine Ladies circle, 2005)

The notice adds that the moor is:

> a spiritual place, particularly for our ancestors, who built cere-
> monial monuments as well as burial mounds for their dead.
> (Text of signage at Nine Ladies circle, 2005)

This phrasing harks to the preservation ethos discussed in earlier chapters, with little indication that the place may be perceived as a site sacred for today's people as well as the rather vague 'ancestors' referred to. Yet the signs do notably emphasise sacredness as part of the importance of place.

Most obvious ritual use takes place, today, at the Nine Ladies, and it shows a huge variation in its styles and intents, and in the traces it leaves behind. In one of the more bizarre manifestations, on Boxing Day 2002, the site was found to be festooned with candles and tea-lights, and 'spiked' with over a hundred incense sticks. As one of us approached the circle, a friend said 'it feels like it's bristling'. Bristling indeed. At the circle, bemused tourists and walkers were gazing at the 'bristling' turf and whispering about the candles. These were at least in glass jars, and from the quantity of material present it seems that the ritualists had intended to return. Members of the protest campaign had earlier, via their website, given a reminder and some practical advice for others who would 'help':

> Try putting your tealights in glass jars. The ones sold with dips
> for tortilla chips are just right; they're about 9 cm. across, and
> shallow enough that the flame won't run out of air. And
> there's no danger of leaving molten wax behind. Of course,
> don't even think about this unless you are prepared to take
> your jars home with you. We can do without broken glass
> around the stones, thank you very much.
> (Sparky, 18 April 2002 on Nine Ladies website message board,
> now no longer accessible, quoted with permission)

The Nine Ladies attracts rituals to celebrate the seasons, the Wiccan 'wheel of the year', and various life-rites such as hand-fastings; we have also found human ashes scattered within the circle. A variety of objects appears in succession on a nearby oak-tree: most common are ribbons or rags (not all biodegradable), or on occasion pieces of plastic bag tied as if they were ribbons; but the objects have included dream-catchers or other items made from sticks and thread, small bunches of flowers or foliage, strips of bark, wooden tablets with symbols painted on them, a fork carefully tied on with yarn, and an assortment of trin-kets and stones, sometimes in offering-bags. Each, clearly, has meaning for those offering them. Within the circle it is common to find flowers, foliage and the ubiquitous tealights, sometimes with coins and other small items, and even decorations including tinsel

4.3 The Nine Ladies circle shows many moods through the seasons. People arrive even on a chill February day. Those here include walkers, pagans, and a journalist who interviewed one of the authors.

4.4 A banner above the path to the Nine Ladies shows protestors' opposition to the idea that 'it's OK'. Sound and structural damage travel to the stone circle. However, this reinforces the idea that the Nine Ladies is what matters. The boundary of the registered monument would be much closer, at its nearest just ten metres from the quarry permission area.

strands. The nearby circle of Doll Tor, west of the moor, receives similar attention as a known site though on a smaller scale.[3]

The Nine Ladies circle was a 'known' centre for ritual before the quarry applications hit the press, though it has grown in popularity since; hence the association of the protest with the circle. Yet this focus on the Nine Ladies, while attracting considerable attention, can also divert attention from issues of the landscape context: the circle as an example of a 'mysterious past' is photogenic but also outside the quarry area – 'two football pitches away' according to quarry spokespeople who used this phrase to detract from the protest campaign. The protest camp's cartoon banner displayed across the path in February 2004 attempts to show the proximity and reduce the impact: 'two pitches' is not a long distance for the sounds of blasting or of quarry lorries to carry. Earlier they used on their website the image of an apple 'core' remaining of the moor, holding the Nine Ladies and a single birch tree 'stalk', but with little else remaining, the quarries having taken their 'bites'. In this 'alternative' representation of Stanton Moor by the protest website, the circle becomes a metaphor for the moor, and pagans and others identify with the circle. However, this living landscape means different things to different groups of pagans: many treat the circle as a ritual focus, a place to meet spirits, deities or ancestors of the moor; others engage with spirit-lines or tracks, or leylines. Rituals are performed at the circle to give energy to stones and land. The Dragon Network, most notably, has suggested a ritual to awaken earth-energies of moor and stones – this being a ritual that people can perform elsewhere, imaging the landscape in order to strengthen the natural (or supernatural) defences of the moor. The 'Dragon bind-rune', a symbol created from north European rune shapes by members of the Dragon Network, has been found in use near the Nine Ladies. Whereas network members and protestors speak of tracing the shape with a finger, with chalk, with water, it is also scratched into a metal plaque at a stile leading to the Nine Ladies.

It is worthwhile re-stating here that most pagan engagements with site and landscape do not leave objects behind. We have participated in Druid, Wiccan and Heathen rites at the Nine Ladies which involved activities such as dancing, drumming, chanting or singing, and, as 'offerings', pouring drink or scattering crumbs – or indeed clearing up the remains of others' rituals or picnics as the offering. The 2001 ritual designed to strengthen the site and the protest, mentioned above, used drumming and chanting to give power and protection to the place. Heathen rites have focused on 'galdr' (Old Norse roughly translated as 'sung-spell') – in one case this involved rune-singing – and on making an offering of mead. Other events have used more of the landscape, as pagans adopt different means of calling on land spirits and/or deities to protect and guard the land: a Heathen ritual in 2004 involved singing and making a procession around areas of the moor, with offerings of ale and mead to land-wights, and calling the 'Lord of the Land', Freyr (a Norse god), to protect the integrity of the landscape, the hillsides, and the rock. The performance of paganism at this site therefore includes cleaning up litter, engaging in meditation or ritual, singing and playing instruments, talking to reporters and taking food to the protest camp, or indeed talking to local people who use the moor for recreation and dog-walking, and who are not always aware of the quarrying applications. Just as the moor – as part of the Peak District National Park – serves as a 'lung' for the surrounding communities of Sheffield, Derby, Nottingham, Stoke, Manchester and even Birmingham, Pagans from these areas are claiming the conflict as theirs. The 'site' for our fieldwork, therefore, extends from the moor into homes and workplaces, into internet sites and mail lists, to local group meetings and the Peak Park determination process, and to all the places where pagans or others constitute identity with respect to the moor; the boundaries of 'pagan identity', once again, become blurred. Just as not all protestors are pagan, paganism is not something 'done' at ritual sites; it is increasingly constituted in creations of worldview that may require its adherents to constantly evaluate their knowledge and understandings of place and self against dominant discourses of place, power and heritage.

Issues and tensions

It is noteworthy that the meanings or representations developed in talking to pagan friends or to sympathetic heritage managers (of whom we have met many) disappear when they – or indeed we – need to produce campaigning documents. In pagan circles, some will talk about wights on the moor and specific experiences and engagements, trying to understand these, trying to re-discover ways to relate to place, time and people. Yet the documents produced for purposes of liaising or negotiating with non-pagans talk about noise levels and sustainability, adopting the discourse of environmental science and heritage management even though this disallows agency to the landscape or to these beings whom pagans may meet within it.

Tensions within and between those groups who celebrate on the moor are many. There is no homogeneity – not among pagans, nor among protestors. While many of the 'regulars' at the camp will advise against tealights at the stones, they are themselves subject to critique for their own activities, especially tunnelling. A comment sent to us read:

> [Y]ou know the protesters have usually got less to do with a
> spiritual quest to defend a sacred landscape and more to do
> with acceptance and approval within a deeply conservative
> scene. The valued expressions of protest like tunneling and tree
> houses deliberately exclude many other protesters, forming an
> elite and failing to acknowledge their own rape of the land. . . .
> FIRSTLY the protest sites are about hanging about on the scene
> and LASTLY are they about defending the sacred.
>
> (Email from 'tinsel' to the Sacred Sites project)

This commentator told of how a tunneller at another site had
dreamed when in the tunnel that the earth goddess spoke to him,
asking 'why are you ripping apart my body'. Andy Letcher, post-
doctoral researcher for the project and veteran of other protest sites,
has a similar story of how a protestor met an elf, who told him to
leave the protest: which this protestor did (pc). While those protestors we have spoken with have seemed interested in others' contributions, and some have been very willing to work with local people
and indeed with heritage agencies, some conflicts have been evident.
Particularly at times of threat, when the numbers at the site have
been reinforced from elsewhere, it may be that some indeed have
little feeling for the site but identify with a protest lifestyle rather
than the sacredness of the land. It should be mentioned, though, that
of those whom we have spoken to at any length, two had university
degrees, one being an environmental biologist. Several spoke to us at
some length about watching wildlife, in particular the bats that roost
in or near the old workings, and the spring birdsong. People engage
with site and protest for many reasons, and at least two protestors
have hoped to record the passage of the year and the variety of its
wildlife within the quarry site, though whether they were able to,
given the pressures of protest life and the changeover of site personnel, we do not know.

Other kinds of protest have come from far and wide, notably envi-
ronmentalists and pagans. Examples include from those Birchover
residents out for a walk on the moor for health reasons, who told us
(having asked 'what is going on?') that 'We don't want any more
bloody quarries!' Typical of responses from further afield is a letter
sent to a councillor member of the PDNPA by a member of the
Modern Antiquarian web-forum, and posted also on that forum
(<http://www.themodernantiquarian.com/>), on 23 June 2004,
which read in part:

> I would like to point out that 'tourists' such as myself provide
> a large cash influx to the local economy. In September, I and
> my fiancé spent a weekend in Stanton in Peak (which is

when we learned of these plans). During our visit, we spent money on accommodation, eating out, petrol, photography equipment, entrance to local attractions, souvenirs and other sundries.

I will say categorically that if this development goes ahead, I shall never visit the Peak District again. There are plenty of other areas of the country that appreciate their heritage and do their best to preserve it, without the need to sacrifice either the landscape or the local economy . . .

It is my understanding that while you do not have the power to refuse permission for the quarry to re-open, you do at least have the power to impose highly restrictive conditions of operation on the site. I would urge you to follow this course of action, for the benefit of the economy, the local community, and the unique environment of the area.

As you are obviously aware, planning permission for a quarry in such an area would never be granted if the application were made today . . .

Chief among protests and reactions, though, must be those of local people, notably those liaising with the CPRE. Yet again, tensions are evident here: Stanton Lees is almost on the threshold of the Endcliffe and Lees Cross quarry sites, while Stanton-in-the-Peak is a short distance west, past the entrance to Dale View quarry. Initially there appeared a united front against the application, but later this changed as attitudes to the protest began to alter and ideas were circulating of 'trade-offs' between these applications and an extension to Dale View which might have a greater effect on Stanton-in-the-Peak. In early 2004, the quarry company employed a spokesperson in Stanton-in-the-Peak, who may have influenced thinking on this issue. A consultation event in February 2004 showed a divided population, though not on simply geographic grounds: as previously mentioned, when several people attempted to discuss the difficulties involved in meeting quarry lorries on the steep hill roads, this was used by one individual to emphasise the difficulties he had had with a protestor on the road. Around this time the Stanton Lees Action Group produced a set of statements about the issues they saw with the applications, relating to noise, lorries, loss of ambience, and potential problems to their water supply, but the threat of further expansion of Dale View has remained in the forefront of some others' perceptions. Members of the protest camp have, however, maintained that they will equally campaign against an expansion of Dale View. More recently, the trade-off indicated from 2005 has not happened, and so we, with the PDNPA, the protest camp, English Heritage, the CPRE and other nature-related trusts, the Stanton Lees and Stanton-in-the-Peak residents, and the quarry company, continue to wait.

Thornborough henges

The situation of 'dormant' quarries such as those at Stanton Moor has been summed up by Denton et al. (2004: 4.22, p. 42):

> [T]hey present a potential threat to the English National Parks. Although there may not be any serious intention to work the sites at the present time, they do have an extant permission which allows, in principle, development to take place once modern conditions are agreed. There is the possibility – sometimes remote, sometimes all too real – that someone may wish to re-work the site in the future. Dormant permissions can therefore be viewed as potential environmental 'time-bombs', quietly 'ticking away' in our finest landscapes.

In North Yorkshire, Thornborough Henges do not have even the protection afforded by being in a National Park. Indeed, until recently, few members of the general public (and relatively few pagans) had heard of Thornborough. Yet the site has been described by David Miles of English Heritage as 'the most important prehistoric site between Stonehenge and the Orkneys', according to publications and websites distributed by campaigning organisations such as Heritage Action and Timewatch (<http://www.timewatch.org/>), and the initial campaigning group Friends of Thornborough Henges (<http://www.friendsofthornborough.org.uk/>). Some information about the major monuments is given by Harding (2003) although recent fieldwork indicates more extensive archaeological material. The website prepared by the University of Newcastle (Thornborough 2003: <http://thornborough.ncl.ac.uk/>) gives at the time of writing the most up to date overview of the archaeology of the Vale of Mowbray, including the Thornborough area, describing the fieldwork led by Harding in two stages in the late 1990s to early 2000s and in 2003. Aerial photography mapping conducted in 2004-5 (English Heritage ALSF projects 2004) has indicated further material at a distance from the henges. This and other recent research has been funded by English Heritage from the Aggregate Levy Sustainability Fund, and there is indeed a sense of urgency to the research, as the issue at Thornborough is that of permissions granted in 1955 and now held by Tarmac to quarry for gravel in the vicinity of the henges and within their landscape.

Some introductory description of the site is required. The major Thornborough complex consists of three henges in an alignment which has been widely described as that of the three stars of Orion's belt. The henges are evenly spaced and almost identical, each around 240 metres in diameter with a separation of approximately 550 metres. The complex extends for almost 1.7 kilometres, running north-west/south-east, and is associated with several other features, some known only from excavation or from aerial photography: an earlier cursus in part underlies the central henge, later round barrows associated with a double pit alignment lie close to the southern henge, and other round barrows are scattered through the landscape (Thornborough 2003) <HYPERLINK "https://webmail.richmond.ac.uk/exchweb/bin/redir.asp? URL=http://thornborough.ncl.ac.uk/"\t"_blank" http://thornborough. ncl.ac.uk/>. The research of Goodrick and Harding (2000 and continuing, see <http://thornborough.ncl.ac.uk/vrml.htm>), using virtual reality modelling, has shown support for the Orion's belt hypothesis relating both to the orientation of the henges and that of the partly-destroyed underlying cursus. The three henges at Thornborough appear to each be replicated in the henge monuments at Cana Barn, Hotton Moor and Nunwick all within the Vale of Mowbray, which are down-river from Thornborough (the river being the Ure). The standing stones known as the Devil's Arrows (see Burl 1991), to the south of the Vale and close to the A1, are rather better known.

The central henge lies close to Thornborough village. Next to the monument is a landfill site, so that the calls of seagulls are a constant accompaniment to visiting, and this has attracted criticism. Earlier, parts of the southern henge were bulldozed, and ploughing has severely affected areas of the banks of the central and southern henges. During World War II, the central henge was used as the location for a munitions store. The current threat to Thornborough, perceived by archaeologists, activists and pagans alike, lies in the quarry plans from Tarmac, based on extensions of the permission first granted in 1955. When the magazine *British Archaeology* drew attention to Thornborough in 2004 (Harding and Johnson 2004), editor Mike Pitts commented that:

> When permission was granted for gravel extraction in 1955, archaeology was not considered. Now conservation interest focuses on wildlife, almost ignoring archaeology. By creating new habitats, it is believed, quarrying and restoration can add landscape value.
>
> (Pitts in editorial addendum, Harding and Johnson 2004)

The campaign to 'save Thornborough' is based on ideas of how the henges relate to their landscape. Until 2003, few people had heard of Thornborough unless they lived locally or were involved with the archaeology of the site. It hit headlines when archaeologist Mark Horton publicised its plight through an episode of the BBC series Time Fliers, filmed in 2004. Pagans had already discovered it, in part through the activities of campaigners, their websites and petitions, and pagan events have been taking place at Beltane (1 May) since 2003, publicised by local pagan groups, with smaller events on other occasions. While this is hardly 'old custom', pagans make no attempt to say that practices taking place there today are anything other than 'new'. Today, it is Druid groups, particularly, who hold festivals there, though we know of local heathens visiting and other pagan events since 2002. The North Yorkshire pagan group, Sacred Brigantia (<http://www. sacredbrigantia.com/>), have organised and coordinated Beltane celebrations at the henges with permission from the local landowner, using car parking available in a field adjacent to the central henge. Smaller events include private visiting, meditation or singing by small groups. The henges have also been used for hand-fastings: a spokesperson for Sacred Brigantia commented that the first pagan event he knew of was a small scale hand-fasting which his group held in late 2002.

Today activist George Chaplin, one of the initial members of Heritage Action and founder of Timewatch, addresses pagan conferences and gatherings to enlist support and 'get the word out' about the threats to Thornborough. These have included the Pagan Federation conference in London in 2004, and smaller events such as the first pagan conference local to Thornborough, held in Masham in September 2006, where a planned ritual at the henges had to be cancelled because of exceptionally heavy rain and sodden ground. Pagans comment on the 'feel' of the three henges, each very different. The wooded northern henge, with its high banks relatively well preserved, guards some uncommon plants and woodland wildlife.

Tarmac currently quarries at Nosterfield quarry, north and northeast of the henges, which is now almost worked out, employing local people (currently with 55 workers, of whom 15 are full-time). The company submitted an application for extraction of sand and gravels at Ladybridge Farm, east of the existing quarry, a half-mile from the nearest part of the henges, seeking to extract 2.2m tonnes from 45 hectares over four years. Tarmac have pointed out that the new plans relate to an area slightly further from the henges than was Nosterfield. Planning consent was refused in early 2006, after which Tarmac, though initially raising the possibility of an appeal, submitted a revised planning application, reducing the area to 31 hectares by omitting the south-western quarter, the nearest to the henges, because of archaeological sensitivity. All plans have included proposals for restoration of landscape as wetlands, and Tarmac points to the previously-quarried area west of the northern henge which is now Thornborough nature reserve, and to their current work on landscape after extraction at Nosterfield.

Indeed, one of the complexities of the Thornborough situation is a division between archaeological and wildlife interests. Plans show restored habitat and a small lake to the north-west of the henges. The area forms part of the remit of the Lower Ure Conservation Trust, part of the Swale and Ure Washlands project designed to turn former extraction sites into a series of linked nature reserves through public funding, grants and partnerships. This project has been much praised by wildlife organisations including the Royal Society for the Protection of Birds (RSPB), and indeed in 2003 the Swale and Ure Washlands project became the first winners of the RSPB/CIWEM (Chartered Institution of Water and Environmental Management) *Living Wetlands Award*, giving recognition to the efforts to increase wildlife habitat and biodiversity. According to the RSPB's website announcing awards, 'The Swale and Ure Washlands project was chosen as the winning project as it links industry, community and conservation groups to create a chain of nature reserves on former mineral workings in the Swale and Ure valleys of North Yorkshire' (<http://www.rspb.org.uk/policy/waterwetlands/livingwetlands/ 2003_award_winners.asp>). The nature reserves would offer tourism potential for the area, with landscape therefore moving from farming through quarrying to become a tourist attraction.

Activists such as Chaplin point to the previous and continuing destruction of existing habitat by the quarrying operations as a process that is not justified by the later creation of an 'artificial' habitat. These activists state that creation of heritage tourism through interpretation and provision of trails would also bring tourist revenues, and that while creation of wetlands habitat may be appropriate in some areas it is not appropriate in the rich archaeological landscape of the Vale of Mowbray. They point also to the longer-term plans of the quarry company, in addition to the issue of Ladybridge. Tarmac has earlier identified 'preferred areas' for quarrying on Thornborough Moor immediately adjacent to the central and southern henges on both east and west. The company has since (in 2005 and 2006) emphasised that currently they are not presenting applications for these areas, but they were awaiting production of a conservation plan from English Heritage (which is now available). Chaplin and others have emphasised that this does not mean that the company has abandoned plans for future quarrying and landscaping on Thornborough Moor. All agree that the henges themselves, as scheduled ancient monuments, are not under threat: but the Friends of Thornborough Henges campaign describes a future scenario of flooded artificial wetland with only the Henges and a strip of land connecting them remaining above water.

The arguments hinge on the importance and interpretation of archaeological finds, and the significance of landscape context, and so raise a familiar concept: the specific importance of particular archaeology as unique or special. The archaeological consultancy (Mike Griffiths and Associates) associated with the quarry company and investigating and monitoring finds during quarrying, points to the poor state of known monuments and artefacts, subject for centuries to ploughing in this farming landscape. Furthermore, the interim report on the consultancy's watching brief and that on sample excavations at Ladybridge has indicated that finds span a wide range of times (Mesolithic to Iron Age and Roman) and that while interesting, they are not of national significance. (See <http://www.archaeologicalplanningconsultancy.co.uk/> where reports and analyses are being made available including Copp and Toop [2005] relating to the Nosterfield watching brief, and Timms and Dickson [2005] on sample excavation at Ladybridge). The quarrying operations, in this view, provide an ideal opportunity to investigate the changing uses of an area over time. Jan Harding has taken issue with these views, maintaining that many of the identified monuments are connected; in particular, that evidence of settlement in the Ladybridge area is contemporaneous with the henges. Harding emphasises in his letter of submission to the NYCC Planning Committee that current theorising of this sacred landscape indicates areas of activity in all quarters – of which only Ladybridge now remains in the north (Harding, available <http://www.friendsofthornborough.org.uk/misc/Hardings_objection.html>). The Council for British Archaeology has likewise made representation to the Planning Committee on the importance and uniqueness of the Thornborough complex, as did English Heritage, in line with their pronouncement in early 2006 that the area of Thornborough Henges is indeed of national significance, naming it 'World Heritage Class' and 'One of the top ten prehistoric landscapes in the country' (EHAC 2006).

Increasingly, therefore, major archaeological concerns and analysis are coming to recognise the large-scale nature of the 'setting' of Thornborough henges. Planning Policy Guide note 16 (PPG16, Department of the Environment 1990, currently undergoing change but still operational), advises in clause 8: 'Where nationally important archaeological remains, whether scheduled or not, and their settings, are affected by proposed development there should be a presumption in favour of their physical preservation'. Activists and heritage archaeologists alike are claiming here that the visible monuments (the henges) are not the only important features, and that understanding the henges requires retaining the landscape, in so far as can be now attained given the previous quarry activity. Mike Heyworth, director of the Council for British Archaeology, commented on the CBA email list Britarch:

> A lot of people have worked very hard to get and keep Thornborough Henges in the public eye. They are to be congratulated. However, this isn't the last of the matter and we now need to work even harder through the proposed Conservation Plan to try and find a way to reduce the damage being caused by agriculture to the archaeology in the area around the Henges. It would be a hollow victory if we fought off the quarry only to find the site ploughed out and the archaeological knowledge lost for ever. But for now, it is well done to every one concerned.
>
> (Heyworth, used with permission)

The Conservation Plan (NYCC et al. 2006) is now available in its final form from North Yorkshire County Council, accessible at <http://www.northyorks.gov.uk/files/NYCC/Environment/Heritage/ Thornborough%20henges%20-%201030/Thornborough HengesConsPlanLR_v3.pdf>, and public consultation is underway regarding five strategies for management of the landscape around the henges indicated. The plan refers explicitly to 'spiritual and emotional involvement' and makes reference to Druid and other involvements with this landscape (4.53, p. 51); Sacred Brigantia has a voice on the Thornborough Henge Advisory Group relating to the plan and future conservation.

Contesting landscape

The instances of Stanton Moor and Thornborough illustrate several features of relationships between places and today's public, pagans included, and many processes by which landscapes are contested. The case of Thornborough, particularly, has also shown how archaeological emphases have changed even since the mid 1990s, with landscape archaeology coming to the fore, and the adoption of the term 'sacred landscape' along with understandings of the 'setting' of monuments that go beyond only what is visible today. Harding's investigations of the orientation of the Thornborough Henges, and the underlying earlier cursus (partly quarried away in the older extraction that created the landfill site) relate to what might be termed 'spiritual', or to use the preferred archaeological nomenclature, 'ritual' meanings. Are these however only in the past, or are today's pagans and others attempting to rediscover why this valley was so important, and apparently so highly regarded? And what of the previous overlooking of its importance? Did Thornborough escape public, pagan and tourist attention because it has no *stones*, or because it is in the north rather than the south of England (as Mike Pitts has speculated), or for some other reason? Did the threat to Thornborough seem insignificant because it had escaped the public eye and was not on the tourist route? Does the offer to create 'new' wildlife habitat counterbalance destruction of archaeology and disturbance to existing habitat – or are there ways to create some further wildlife habitat while retaining the key features of the *sacred landscape* to which Harding refers? And, can there really be a comparison between the contract-consultancy archaeology at Nosterfield which describes finds, and the interpretations of Harding and others at Thornborough Moor, which seek to theorise and not merely record? The Sacred Sites project is watching the case of the Thornborough complex as a contested landscape, where many groups present their own interest and involvement, where the meanings of Thornborough are intricate and convoluted, and where new relationships of people and landscape, new alliances and identities based in protection and sacredness, are in the forging.

CHAPTER 5

Spirits of Moor and Glen: Pagans and Rock Art Sites in Britain

Will our culture's 'museum-consciousness' never stop? Is the whole landscape of this country and this planet to be infected by our self-divided civilisation, turning it into an all-embracing, terminal museum? Turning us all into 'observers' and 'visitors' whether we like it or not? . . . I think we need to ask ourselves a big question: do we want to preserve these sites absolutely as long as possible, but experience them from a distance (unless you're a scientist); or do we want to accept a slightly increased rate of erosion and decay – and actually experience them? How does conservation and the acquirement of increasingly accurate scientific information weigh up against the right to experience ancient sites as they were actually intended – i.e., without a bloody great fence between you and them? . . . Do we value data *over* experience?
(Gyrus 1998b: 79–80).

These students came, with their professor, from somewhere. Edinburgh University, I remember it was. And they had something they painted on the cup-marks, so they could photograph them better. And we were all worried. They shouldna hae been doing this, we thought. But then the rain washed it all away. So that was all right then.
(A woman met at Poltalloch, from fieldnotes made by Blain in 1999.)

In the previous chapter we extended analysis away from such honey-pot sites as Avebury and Stonehenge in the south of England, to less well-known sites in central and northern England, focussing on the two examples of Stanton Moor in the Peak District of Derbyshire and the henges of Thornborough in North Yorkshire. These sites are threatened by quarrying, and efforts to protect them have heavily involved pagans, often in direct action. In this chapter, discussion will return to continue a focus on the north of England, with the case study of Ilkley Moor in West Yorkshire. First, though, it moves further north to consider the archaeology of the Kilmartin Valley in mid-Argyll on the West Coast of Scotland. Both locations are rich in archaeology, particularly rock art, and so our analysis concentrates on pagan engagements with this body of prehistoric visual culture just as pagans themselves have come to 'identify' with it in various ways. In so doing, the Kilmartin example, taking our discussion outside of England for the first time, demonstrates other modes of pagan interest in sites. A separate volume entirely would be required to do justice to the complexity of issues emerging in Scotland, as well as Wales, and more detailed analysis is certainly in order in the West Country and other parts of England not yet covered by the Sacred Sites Project. In expanding research in this way, it should be noted that the sacred sites of Britain attract not only British pagans who establish relationships with local sites and who may also travel extensively across the country on their 'pilgrimages' to sacred sites, but, in an increasingly globalised world, also attract pagans (amongst other 'visitors') from outside these islands. Often the connections formed between foreign pagans and British sites are based on notions of ancestry, and sites provide locales at which transnational identities are formed and reified. These issues are explored in the Kilmartin study. The Ilkley Moor study, by contrast, considers the contest that has arisen over pagan ritual and 'new' rock art as creative maintenance of a millennia-old practice, or as vandalism, particularly when it is on the same outcrop as Bronze Age art. At these two sites, away from the media gaze that focuses on the honey-pot sites, pagans and other site users develop their own ways of engaging with ancestors, which may be problematic for managers or other users of heritage.

The Kilmartin Valley, Argyll

The Kilmartin Valley in mid Argyll, on the west coast of Scotland looking towards the Western Isles, is, according to the Kilmartin House Museum, 'Scotland's richest prehistoric landscape', with 150 recorded prehistoric monuments within a six-mile radius of Kilmartin Village: 'This extraordinary concentration and diversity of monuments distinguishes the Kilmartin valley as an area of outstanding archaeological importance' (<http://www.kilmartin.org/>). The area is important in various ways to local people, not least to those supporting the tourism infrastructure, as well as an important part of identities based in Scottish history and prehistory, with these and other sites under the jurisdiction of Historic Scotland. This importance extends to pagans, particularly including West of Scotland pagans and Scottish pagans more generally, but also many from elsewhere in Britain and those visiting from outside Britain including those who are or claim to be of Scottish descent many of whom (particularly from North America and from Australia) have traced family lines to Argyll. Just as archaeological monuments in England have provided a resource from which to establish a pagan identity, so these sites in Scotland are similarly engaged. Groups arrive from Glasgow and elsewhere to make ritual, whether Druid, Heathen, or more generically pagan, at monuments in the valley, and may camp near Lochgilphead and drive to Kilmartin to explore the scenery as well as to conduct celebrations. Individuals or families arrive to explore the landscape and meditate or seek inspiration at stone settings or at outcrops covered in engravings. Earth Mysteries adherents attempt to dowse ley-lines or question the positioning of stones in the Temple Wood circles (which are among the oldest stone circles in the British Isles). Other 'stones' enthusiasts gather to experience the proximity of the many sites and to speculate on the meaning and uses of motifs in the rock art. However, this rock art for which Kilmartin is famed attracts a somewhat different, more 'shamanic', attention to the sacred glen.

5.1   Temple Wood, in the Kilmartin Glen, is the site of two circles including one of the oldest stone circles in the British Isles. Earth Mysteries adherents dowse for positions of missing stones, and many pagans visit. The south circle had many uses, and was eventually covered with stones of a cairn. The stone on the far right of this image bears two engraved spirals.

Reported experiences are many: they include personal meditations at outcrops, and events occurring within monuments such as, in particular, the Neolithic chambered cairn at Nether Largie South. Such events might include visions of people creating cups and rings, pecking designs, or encounters with deities and other wights or beings. These rich layers of experience have not been brought together into any volume that we yet know of, but they demonstrate the development of new sets of folklore, building on those of the past (which are told by at least some of the people who live in Kilmartin today). Our task in this chapter, though, is to illustrate contest within context, and Kilmartin Glen – the location of prehistoric tombs in a 'linear cemetary', one of the oldest stone circles in the British Isles, stone settings and a henge monument in addition to the plethora of carved outcrops – provides a study of appropriation, from many quarters.

To begin – not with archaeology, but with present-day shamanism[1]: Kaledon Naddair, founder of the Edinburgh-based 'College of Druidism' in 1982, suggests that 'Pictish and Keltic shamanism is the native initiatory system practised by the ancient Druids' (Naddair 1990: 94). He describes use of incenses formulated from native plants which revives the 'power smoke of the [Druid] Shamans' (1990: 97) without the use of entheogens.[2] He also recounts how 'just like a traditional Shaman I acted as a channel . . . and whilst I allowed a mighty Keltic God to speak through my body, my own higher consciousness was instantaneously teleported to a far-off steep hillside' (1990: 94). Attending to sacred sites, and rock art in particular, Naddair suggests (1990: 102) that shamanic rituals at cup-and-ring mark sites - 'of major importance to my Ancestors' spirituality' - facilitated communication with 'Rock Spirits' which revealed the 'essential [ritualistic] purpose' of the sites. These spirit helpers also improved Naddair's 'hand-dowsing' abilities, giving him an '"uncanny knack" of discovering new Cup and Ring mark sites long-buried' (1990: 103). Furthermore, he suggests (p. 104) that 'much of the knowledge previously experienced at Cup and Ring mark sites was encoded upon the later Pictish symbol stones', and that this was enacted by the 'Pictish Druids' at the time of and after the 'Roman threat'. A spirit being has revealed to him knowledge of some of the symbols of Pictish stones, and he says 'I have also been given the "lost" meaning to certain Pictish symbols through my Wildman-Teacher' (1990: 105).

These extracts indicate ways in which a 'Keltic' or 'Pictish' Druid identity, specific to Scotland, was discursively constructed by one practitioner in the 1980s and 1990s. Naddair's use of the terms 'Kelt', 'Pict', and 'Druid' are problematic in various ways, for example because this use of them extends the sense of an established, singular, enduring and *unchanging* modern Scottish identity back into prehistory (negating, thereby, the centuries in which Scottish identities, diversely understood and contextualised, have been formed). Furthermore, this unchanging Scottish-ness is presented as consistently being subject to 'threat' from outside, so that resistance to that which is perceived to be outside becomes for Naddair a resource for forming a pagan identity rooted in a nation which seems to owe more to imagining than to the nation of today's Scotland.[3] His comments also raise issues for archaeological conservation in that the 'buried' rock art sites, rather than being new discoveries, might have been covered by archaeologists for conservation purposes (an established practice in various parts of the world).

A further example of 'shamanic' experiences at rock art sites and how these contribute to the negotiation of a 'Celtic' pagan identity returns us directly to Kilmartin Glen. Writing for the magazine *Shaman's Drum*, MacEowen (1998), an American of 'Scots-Irish descent', tells how he is reclaiming, reviving or reinventing (depending on your viewpoint) the ancient shamanic traditions of his ancestors. MacEowen's own use of Lakota-based Native American shamanic traditions apparently ended during a Sundance ceremony in which the vision he received was not of Native American teacher spirits but, he says, his ancestral Scottish spirits. This prompted him to re-explore what he perceived as indigenous shamanism, which he calls both 'Pictish and 'Gaelic', saying: 'I believe it is possible to rekindle specific Gaelic shamanic methods and spiritual practices via a combination of deep remembrance and ancestral transmission' (MacEowen 1998: 36). His account describes a short visit to the Kilmartin Glen, as an area to which he traces ancestors. Arguing for the positive contribution of alternative engagements with the past, he asserts that academic researchers 'are able to accept the reality of ancestral transmission when it happens within indigenous tribes, yet they summarily discount this same possibility when it is within their own bloodlines – which were rooted in shamanic tribal cultures such as the Celts, Germans, and Norse' (MacEowen 1998: 35).

He is not, of course, alone in indicating and critiquing such concepts, pointed to by for example Wilson (1994) and Blain (2000) as part of a western Eurocentric slew of assumptions or expectations of difference in an exotic or romanticised *other*. Within such constructions of alterity, cultural concepts and understandings of 'tribal' people may be given a hearing, seen as interesting, indeed even glorified, but any such lack of 'rationalism' from a European is seen as at best misguided. Wilson, a Canadian anthropologist, found that his students were prepared to listen to the shamanic experiences and interpretations of Native experts but not of Wilson himself. To acknowledge the possibility (rather than 'reality') of ancestral transmission in indigenous cultures elsewhere, but derogate the possibility of such transmission in a European context or to a 'westerner', seems the obverse of the coin of Eurocentricity. MacEowen and others rein-venting forms of European shamanism – however termed – indicate a rather more even-handed approach, in attempting to explore possi-bilities of altered consciousness for creating knowledge. What we encourage, in this book and elsewhere, is a consideration of ideas from many 'ways of knowing' and the evaluation of these within their contexts and their own means of critique (see e.g. Schieffelin 1996, 1998; Blain and Wallis 2006a).

We have considerable sympathy, then, for what many shamanic practitioners are attempting: different epistemological frameworks are part of what this book is about. Nevertheless, it does seem rather problematic that particular ancestors, so distant in time, and only these, are 'channelled' in some of the ways pointed to. Chapter 7 further discusses issues of 'ancestors' and 'bloodlines', including a *discursive slippage* that we have indicated elsewhere (Blain and Wallis 2006d) in which ideas of honouring specific shamanic worldviews, or indeed specific individuals, may become a claim to speak for ances-tors as a bounded cultural, tribal or racial group. MacEowen asks: 'why shouldn't we expect descendants of these people to be prone to ancestral transmission?' (p. 35) and states, 'My path has been to connect with those aspects of primal Celtic spiritual consciousness that best mirror my genetic propensities' (p. 36). Surely such 'ances-tors' are shared widely by many people today in the West of Scotland and much further afield, not all of whom will identify as either Scottish or 'Celtic'. Biological determinism in spiritual and religious ability is not something most pagans generally entertain deliberately, but it is a construction that may arise unwittingly, in implications and suggestions, and in discursive constructions of 'the Celts' as mysterious and spiritually gifted, a people set apart, associated with the second sight and with mists on the highlands (see also Gallagher 1999; Bowman 2000; Blain 2001, 2006c). We are concerned, too, about the apparent conflation of the distant past of standing stones and rock art with historic families of the middle ages or later, from which this particular writer traces a descent. The understanding of 'Pict', like Naddair's, seems obscure and extremely vague, encompass-ing a span of at least five thousand years of Scottish history and prehistory, and emphasising the romantic notion of 'primal' eras. According to his article for *Shaman's Drum* (in which, we appreciate, he may have been simplifying for a particular audience with very little previous connection with Scottish landscapes or histories), all the Neolithic and Bronze Age monuments and medieval ruins in the Kilmartin Valley are 'Pictish', [4] and a caption to a photograph of the Neolithic chambered cairn at Nether Largie South reads 'One of the many ancient Pictish burial complexes found in Kilmartin Valley' (MacEowan 1998: 35).

MacEowen had apparently come to the Kilmartin area to facilitate contact with his ancestors of that landscape, and he associated the symbol of a cup-and-ring mark (which he terms a 'Pictish motif') with shamanic or altered consciousness work in quest of knowledge. The concept is in line with at least some speculation regarding 'abstract' rock art interpretation, the cup-mark as a way into another world or a way into the rock itself (or indeed out of the rock - Holtorf, pc). We question, though, how the link is made in this particular example between landscape and specific ancestral or 'bloodline' inheritance, and we wonder what might be enabled by a greater knowledge of the history, archaeology and socio-politics of the area. Many people have journeyed to Kilmartin, and a fair number will meditate on cup marks: are their experiences all driven by ancestral 'bloodlines'? At a somewhat later Bronze Age tomb nearby, he spent a night communicating with 'Pictish ancestors' which included hearing a troop of beings (human or *sidhe*) pass by, and experiencing the enlightenment of the great song which he terms *Oran Mor* (a term also used in bagpipe music).

Shamanic tourism: inspiration and appropriation

MacEowen's text becomes a useful introduction to issues involved with pagan engagements with rock art, and to the phenomenon which we might call 'shamanic tourism', mirroring some of the contradictions indicated for general pagan uses and appropriation of landscape and location. In particular these are romanticism, cultural appropriations and claims to 'truth' which, of course, pagans are not alone in making. The concepts of tradition, enchantment and authenticity, discussed in Chapter 1, appear in an interweaving of several strands, certainly not unique to this particular practitioner's account which may be unpacked here. One strand relates to the construction of Native North American 'shamanism' as basic, pure or essential (and, paradoxically, unitary); another to the construction of 'Celticity', and the Celts as an equally-oppressed population. The interweaving as a whole is reliant on the concept of 'cellular memory', the claim to authenticity based in an idea that people can be taught the shamanic traditions of their ancestors if they can find a way to 'remember', together with the idea (again, quite widely shared among those who propose systems of 'Celtic Shamanism') of being descended from a line of hereditary shamans. The symbols that will jog this memory become the stones, and the engravings on them, keys to re-enchantment, although (somewhat paradoxically) there is no mention of the expanses of rock art on the hillsides south of Kilmartin (the largest being at Achnabreck) or in other areas of the valley. Sleeping in the grave to 'recover other shamanic traditions through direct contact with my Pictish ancestors' (MacEowen 1998: 37) echoes quests of British practitioners who seek knowledge in cairns and longbarrows in Kilmartin, Avebury and elsewhere, making pilgrimages to sacred sites in order to undertake initiatory shamanic journeys.

MacEowen certainly does not claim to have discovered the only true form of 'celtic shamanism'.[5] There are many, he says, rooted in different 'bloodlines'. He does claim 'truth', and authenticity, within his own 'bloodline' or lineage, and as previously indicated we do find this concept problematic. How, for instance, may this difficult concept relate to population genetics, and how many people, descendants of those who pecked the cupmarks or, much later, were recorded as belonging to the clan system of the area, might also claim a shared 'cellular' inheritance? Most of those descendents, for the last thousand years and more, have practised a very different form of spirituality; and those shamanic practitioners elsewhere who look to ancestral teaching do so within a different context of an animistic culture. Yet the account relies on, and is interwoven with, material from anthropology, archaeology, and folklore, which its author brings to his *Shaman's Drum* readership. Thus, snippets of information appear in the account: as the mention of the derivation of 'shaman' from the Tungus word *sa:man*, though without reference to how or why. The concept of sleeping within a grave may be a conflation of tales (from both Nordic and Scottish/Irish folklore) of sitting out on the gravemound for wisdom, or spending a night in the 'hollow hills' of the *sidhe*. Indeed, the author indicates that he was following the idea of sleeping at the grave of an ancestral bard. He attempts to support the concept of what he calls 'ancestral transmission' by mentioning ethnographic accounts of Tungus, Inuit and other cultures, indicating that these 'show that shamanic initiates are often chosen and trained directly by ancestral or clan spirits... I now believe that ancestral transmission is an innate human phenomenon.' (footnote 1, p. 39)

Perhaps, though, the account of MacEowen best typifies one strand of pagan practice in its sense of isolation, its remoteness from cultural patterns or daily human activity.[6] Though he describes hearing a (perhaps otherworldy or sidhe) band passing, his vision is otherwise unpeopled, and his insights deal in 'ancient' knowledge (with claims that one of the 'Pictish' cup and ring marks represents a path to ancestral wisdom), but include little, apparently, about the landscape, its people whether human or otherwise, or the circumstances relating people and environment whether today or in the past. Despite the mention of ethnographic work and folklore, with a footnote referring to 'anthropological theories of shamanism', and despite the setting in the stones of the tombs which surely bear witness to human activity, organization and collective construction of meaning, the account shows little grounding in culture, history, work, change, movement or discovery, or, most specifically, community. This permits the identification of an ancestral shamanism that can be reclaimed, presumably unchanged, and used in the present, separate from community context. It permits, also, the collapse not only of centuries but of millennia, in the problematic identification of ancestors, shamanism, and monuments as 'Celtic' and 'Pictish'. Possamai (2003), discussing issues of appropriation within pagan and alternative spiritual practice, points to phenomena of cultural consumption, with people choosing spirituality though selecting pieces of history and esotericism with which to identify; many popular presentations of Scottish history and identity are easily accessed, and their simplifications may not encourage seekers, tourists and pilgrims to look for complexity and detail in stories of the near or far pasts.

Yet, the inclusion of folklore elements in MacEowen's account and the attempts to investigate concepts such as that of the 'co-walker' (a spirit-being discussed in this account as an ancestral helper) might form a basis for discovering contexts for these ancestors. There is scope, in the work and writings of shamanic practitioners, to make use of the changing, storied, landscape to link pasts and present, and in the work and writings of heritage and tourism personnel to produce accounts that fire the imaginations of those who arrive to 'visit' and may find themselves coming 'home'. Rather than a separation of otherworldly or spiritual/shamanic perception from that of archaeologists or management, we recommend further attempts to combine insights from 'shamanic' understanding with speculative archaeology. The story of Kilmartin Glen can be told in many ways, allowing room for alternative understandings; some starts at such tellings are made in presentations of the small museum at Kilmartin House. The ambiguity of prehistoric rock art, in particular, lends itself to presentations which display alternative understandings, not as *truth* but as *possibility*. Disputed interpretations of rock art may themselves form a basis for presentation, from the shamanistic interpretation (that some imagery is derived from the altered consciousness of shamans) to particular stones as ancestral persons themselves (Wallis in prep.). A first question that many tourists ask is 'what does it mean?' and often they – especially those coming to 'ancestral' lands – are interested in debating the answers they are given. In the Kilmartin area, there is no shortage of prehistoric rock art (Beckensall [2005] indicates over 100 'sites', small or large, of rock-art in the vicinity). At Kilmartin, many of the seekers after 'Celtic' or 'Pictish' ancestors may be surprised and immensely pleased to find a much greater depth of heritage than they had envisaged or even sought, if speculations and contested theories are presented to them: they can be drawn into the mysteries of the past and themselves contribute to the stories and interpretations.

The above has included a fairly extended discussion of one practitioner's published views and experiences. Today, numerous practitioners are constructing specific Scottish shamanisms, in some cases with considerable knowledge of local history and culture, creating their own relationships to urban or rural landscapes and working in ways that link communities with the flow of ancestry and time. Others such as American practitioner Tom Cowan (e.g. 1993) have sought to derive Celtic shamanism from an association of Core Shamanic practices (on which see Harner 1980, Ingerman 1991 and critique by Wallis 2003) with Irish and Welsh 'Celtic' literature,[7] but specific Scottish practitioners (not usually terming themselves 'shamans') have tended to look to folklore and to practices from, for instance, gypsy or travelling-people traditions. Practitioner Geo Trevarthen (formerly Cameron) explicitly draws on anthropological accounts from practitioners worldwide, and achieved a PhD from Edinburgh University in tracing 'shamanic' concepts through 'Celtic' literature; she also has a connection with Core Shamanism but says that in her particular form of 'Celtic' shamanism she is *'much more religious in my approach!'* (<http://www.celticshamanism.com/dec03printable.html>) She was given inspiration through hereditary tradition – relating to the environment in which she grew up; and her discourse appears to bridge between the North American focus on 'Celticity' and those contemporary Scottish practitioners who root their experiences in landscapes and in deities and spirits of the land. Argyll's sacred glen, though, retains a special status, contributes its own enchantment and works its transformations, increasingly part of the tourist trail despite its remoteness. Many pagan practitioners arrive in Kilmartin, their numbers increasing year by year, and often a goal is to spend time, or a night, in a tomb, variously described as sleeping, meditating, or keeping vigil. Usually (according to staff at the Kilmartin House Museum, pc) the chosen tomb is the Neolithic chambered cairn at Nether Largie South, and experiences there range greatly. Kilmartin, though, is only the centre of an area hugely rich in archaeology and history. Achnabreck has the largest expanse of rock art in Scotland, indeed in Britain. The glen holds at least 350 recognised monuments, over 150 of these being prehistoric. The rocky hill five miles south of Kilmartin village is known as Dunadd, the capital of the Scots kingdom of Dalriata for around 400 years, now known for its carved footprint, boar and ogham inscription; the history of the area since this time finds illustrations in the carvings of the mediaeval and early modern stones in the village churchyard, and in the neighbouring castles at Kilmartin and Carnasserie and the nearby

Poltalloch House. The area, almost crowded with its monuments, attests to the engagement of humans with landscape, and to issues of power, politics and indeed social class.

Today, the small hamlet of Kilmartin includes bed and breakfast accommodations, in addition to its parish church, the Kilmartin House museum, a hotel, some shops and the houses of those who work on the farms or in various industries, including heritage and tourism along with others such as quarrying. It is a 30-mile bus ride from Oban, and about eight miles from Lochgilphead. In an area in which cattle and sheep farming exist along with tourism, the village and the museum suffered hugely from the Foot and Mouth outbreaks in 2001 (although these did not reach Argyll) due to the lack of tourist revenue.

5.2
Achnabreck, south of the glen and approaching Dunnadd, has the largest expanse of rock art in Scotland. This photograph shows only part of it.

5.3 The landscape of Kilmartin Glen showing the Glebe Cairn, part of Kilmartin's linear cemetery, with the nearby village including its museum.

It is perhaps a pity that MacEowan could not spend sufficient time at the Kilmartin House museum and in other areas of the glen to talk with people about the area's richness. He would have discovered a wealth of material which might have been of use to him, also finding considerable interest and enthusiasm for the monuments among people in the area, who include those whose direct acquaintance with the landscape goes back over many generations. Speculation about meaning and use is not restricted to either pagans or archaeologists, and a feeling of belonging and indeed of 'ownership' of the monuments is not restricted to those who claim to be 'Pictish'. Near Poltalloch house, one of us (Blain) heard the concerns of local people (in chapter epigraph) who had been disturbed when students from Edinburgh University came on a field trip to study the two rock art panels in that vicinity. Apparently they had used 'something they painted on the cup-marks' to enable photography. Local people were worried and also felt they should have been consulted. While being relieved when the substance was washed away by rain, they were still telling this tale to a visiting anthropologist several years later.

What may not be evident to spiritual visitors is that the sacred glen and its archaeology are not free from threat. Recently, a sand and gravel quarry to the north-west of the village has removed all traces of a timber circle identified there in 1993. The timber circle has been described as 'the largest and rarest monument ever to be discovered in Kilmartin' (Kilmartin House 1998 p. 7). Preliminary excavation was conducted in 1993, and more extensive investigation in 1997 before the quarrying operation continued. *British Archaeology* summarised the initial findings in 1997, giving some context for this episode of what has been described as 'cultural vandalism'.

> [The quarry] has been worked for several years, but in the late 1980s the quarry operators, M&K MacLeod of Lochgilphead, applied for permission for a major extension. Both Historic Scotland and Strathclyde's regional archaeologist, Carol Swanson, advised against the development, because of the cultural sensitivity of the area. The regional council overruled their objections, because of the jobs the quarry would create.
> (British Archaeology News 1997, November)

Further developments resulted in the Museum personnel being told that they could not campaign against the quarrying, neither could they take visitors to the site, a few hundred metres from their door.

Further information from the excavation has indicated that the site was indeed incredibly important to prehistoric archaeology. A later *British Archaeology* news item (2002, April) has termed it a 'Sacred Pool ringed with totem poles in Scotland's ritual glen' and comments that 'post-excavation analysis of the pits and postholes ... has concluded that the timber circle was far more unusual than was initially thought.' Seemingly, the early Bronze Age timber circle, 47 metres across, surrounded what has been described as a votive pool. Amongst and around the timbers of the circle were burials. The monument, however, seems to have stood upon one end of a Neolithic cursus demarcated by 'hundreds of close-set oak posts', and there are even earlier traces of Mesolithic occupation.

The remoteness of Kilmartin from the immediate focus of most British pagans – or at least the media to which they have access – has meant that during the period of time when the timber circle at Holme-next-the-Sea ('Seahenge') was hotly contested, traces of the circle at Kilmartin were silently quarried away. Kilmartin illustrates, therefore, an area where alliances could have been developed, and serves as a reminder that major threats to sacred sites do not necessarily arise from pagan uses or interpretations – indeed, as demonstrated in previous chapters, pagan involvement can be an aid to the interests of heritage management.

Ilkley Moor, Yorkshire

Pagan engagements with rock art sites also take place in England and in this regard we have focussed our attentions on Ilkley Moor. The *Ilkley Moor Management Plan 2003–2012* (City of Bradford Metropolitan District Council 2003) describes Ilkley Moor as comprised of 'an area of 676 hectares (1670 acres) on the southern slope of Wharfedale (which) forms part of the upland watershed between Wharfedale to the north and Airedale to the south - collectively known as Rombalds Moor' (p. 3, part 3.2). The moor carries the official designations of Urban Common, Site of Special Scientific Interest, and Special Protection Area.

Commenting on the archaeology, the plan draws particular attention to the abundance of Bronze Age rock art and its unique importance:

> Of the field monuments that are still to be found above ground, the most important group are on the boulders and outcrops of natural rock which are commonly known as 'carved rocks'. These have been carved with a range of simple motifs to formal designs of various complexity and Ilkley Moor is one of only a few areas where they are to be found in such concentrations. As sites of national importance they have recently been granted Scheduled Monument status which provides statutory protection for the rocks themselves and their immediate environs up to a distance of 10 metres. In addition, where they occur in close proximity to other settlement features, such as low lying stone 'walling', the area of scheduling has been extended to take in much larger areas.
>
> (p. 56, 6.3)

What the management plan neglects is a rich history of folklore (old and new) associated with the moor and which has been enthusiastically picked up by today's pagans. 'White Wells' cottage, for instance, is the location of springs associated with healing properties since the eighteenth century, and it was here that the keeper of the cottage, William Butterfield, witnessed a sighting of 'little creatures dressed in green', or fairies – recorded in the *Folklore Record* of 1878:

> William Butterfield . . . always opened the door the first thing in the morning, and he did this without ever noticing anything out of the common until one beautiful, quiet, midsummer morning. As he ascended the brow of the hill he noticed rather particularly how the birds sang so sweetly, and cheerily, and vociferously, making the valley echo with the

music of their voices. And in thinking it over afterwards he remembered noticing them, and considered this sign attributable to the after incident. As he drew near the wells he took out of his pocket the massive iron key, and placed it in the lock; but there was something 'canny' about it, and instead of the key lifting the lever it only turned round and round in the lock. He drew the key back to see that it was alright, and declared, 'it was the same that he had on the previous night hung up behind his own door down at home.' Then he endeavoured to push the door open, and no sooner did he push it slightly ajar than it was as quickly pushed back again. At last, with one supreme effort, he forced it perfectly open, and back it flew with a great bang! Then 'whirr, whirr, whirr', such a noise and sight! [A]ll over the water and dipping into it was a lot of little creatures, all dressed in green from head to foot, none of them more than eighteen inches high, and making a chatter and jabber thoroughly unintelligible. They seemed to be taking a bath, only they bathed with all their clothes on. Soon, however, one or two of them began to make off, bounding over the walls like squirrels. Finding they were all making ready for decamping, and wanting to have a word with them, he shouted at the top of his voice – indeed, he declared afterwards, he couldn't find anything else to say or do – 'Hallo there!' Then away the whole tribe went, helter skelter, toppling and tumbling, heads over heels, heels over heads, and all the while making a noise not unlike that of a disturbed nest of young partridges. The sight was so unusual, that he declared he either couldn't or daren't attempt to rush after them. He stood as still and confounded, he said, as old Jeremiah Lister down there at Wheatley did, half a century previous, when a witch from Ilkley put an ash riddle upon the side of the River Wharfe, and sailed across in it to where he was standing. When the well had got quite clear of these strange beings he ran to the door and looked to see where they had fled, but nothing was to be seen. He ran back into the bath to see if they had left anything behind; but there was nothing; the water lay still and clear just as he had left it the previous night. He thought they might perhaps have left some of their clothing behind in their haste, but he could find none, and so he gave up looking, and commenced his usual routine of preparing the baths; not, however, without trotting to the door once or twice to see if they might be coming back; but he saw them no more.

(Smith 1878: 229–30. Available online: <http://www.the modernantiquarian.com/site/6342>; see also Crook 1998)

The region is indeed infamous for fairy sightings, but while the Cottingley Fairy phenomenon and its photographic 'evidence' of the early twentieth century is largely regarded as a 'hoax', various folklore is associated, intriguingly, with the cup-and-ring engravings in nearby Cottingley Woods, south of the moor (as such, this previously little-examined rock art was named the 'fairy stone' by Crook [1998]). More recently, the discourse on 'little green men' as fairies has been updated as the aliens of UFOlogy, with one of the most dramatic accounts being from a policeman who, just near to the original source of the White Wells spring in 1989, experienced an alien abduction (Crook 1998).

The rock art and other archaeology of Ilkley Moor clearly has a rich folklore associated with it, and this provides a fecund resource for pagans engaged in re-enchanting their lives. Not all alternative direct engagements with rock art have been cognisant of conservation, however. Willy Hall's Wood Stone, for example, is a huge slab of mill-stone grit situated between two stream tributaries, on the northern edge of the moor. It is engraved with impressive cup-and-ring images – but these have attracted vandalism, with two recorded instances, noted on the 'Megalithic Portal' webpages (FIGURE 5.6):

> Almost a year ago, someone traced the cup and ring design in red paint and scrawled runic characters on the north face of the stone. Further graffiti has also appeared on the stone recently [April 2004]. [T]he paint on the Willy Hall's Wood Stone has [been] allowed to dry to a matt, rock hard finish that will take decades to weather away. Grafitti is a growing problem on Ilkley Moor and a very real threat to the delicate rock art on these moors. Many of the designs are unique to the Ilkley area and are of international importance.
>
> (<http://www.megalithic.co.uk/article.php?thold= 1&mode=flat&order=0&sid=2146411589>)

The recent red paint tracing on the ancient engravings is reminiscent of the intentional painting-in with red paint of many rock engravings in Scandinavia, where the heritage bodies undertook such action based in part on the evidence that some rock art there was painted in the past. There is no such evidence for painted rock engravings in Britain, but the similarity in use of red paint is striking; in addition, a series of rune staves in the same red paint has been depicted elsewhere on the slab, again recalling Scandinavian heritage as well as referencing the use of runes for magic and divination by pagans (in Britain and elsewhere; in some traditions there is a concept of colouring runes carved on wood with one's own blood). While a pagan connection is not demonstrable, the use of runes makes it likely, and this instance among others draws attention to the nonordinary ways in which people are engaging with rock art on the moor.

Other engagements inspired by the moor's archaeology and rock art are similarly problematic, particularly the production of contemporary rock art, some of it juxtaposed with prehistoric imagery. Some of this imagery draws on rock art traditions elsewhere, such as the image of a 'Pictish' deer (FIGURE 5.4). Other images are inspired by 'pagan' themes, such as an engraving of a Gorgon's head: enclosed in the alchemical-like triangle is a pendant depicting a fish-tailed and winged goat (the astrological/astronomical Capricorn image) with the word 'Capricorn' underneath (FIGURE 5.5). Elsewhere on the moor there is also an engraved antlered human head, perhaps a representation of the 'Celtic' horned god Cernunnos – popular as a deity among many pagans. In another example, a spiral maze is associated with a serpent. Given the prevalence of modern 'graffiti' on the (much-visited) 'Hanging Stones', ranging from the late nineteenth-century inscriptions to those from the current time, it might be argued that this new 'rock art' is part of an ongoing 'tradition' of image-making established in prehistory. That some of the new rock art has been intentionally defaced indicates a critical response from some locals, however.

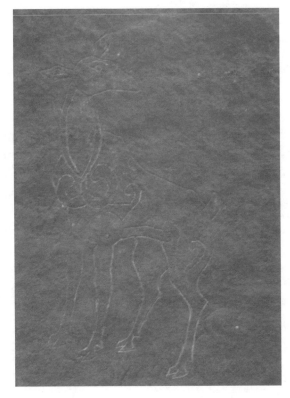

5.4 Contemporary rock art on Ilkley Moor: A 'Pictish' style deer.

5.5 Contemporary rock art on Ilkley Moor: a carved Gorgon's head is accompanied by a triangle, both coloured red, with a Capricorn symbol in silver fixed into the rock inside the triangle.

5.6 Runic graffiti at the Willy Hall's Wood Stone, Ilkley Moor.

The journal *Northern Earth*, dedicated to '"earth mysteries", appealing to all those with an inquiring interest in historical landscapes, folk lore and custom, the unexplained, earth-based consciousness and spirituality or a "Gaia" vision of the Earth' <http://www.northernearth.co.uk/> has kept close tabs on the incidents on Ilkley Moor. In a letter to the journal, the local artist and archaeologist Paul Bowers comments on the contemporary rock art:

> With regards to the vandalism of ancient stones (NE79, p. 3, 26–7), I feel attention should be paid to vandalism on Ilkley Moor in the name of art – a series of carvings inspired by Scandinavian rock art, carried out by a local artist apparently with official approval. The artist's signature even appears on one of the rocks, the famous Idol Rock. Though the work does not impinge on any cup and ring marks, that it should appear close to well-known examples of ancient rock art is outrageous, especially if colluded to by persons in authority. Consequently, many carvings have been defaced and others added by copyists, leaving the stones in an abused state. Recent graffiti on the Haystack Stone above the Cow and Calf is also a matter of great concern. I would urge readers who live locally or regularly visit the moor to keep a sharp eye out for any such damage being perpetrated and try to prevent it; report it to West Yorkshire Archaeology Service at Wakefield and to the readers of this magazine! Disfigurement of these rocks cannot go unchallenged – too much has been lost already of our common heritage – let's protect it if we can.
> (Northern Earth 80 [September 1999] <http://www.northern-earth.co.uk/80/ilkley.htm >)

A local pagan also commented:

> There's the continuous alteration and destruction of the Twelve Apostles circle. And the vandalism of the Willy Halls Wood rock art with red paint. And the regular appearance of new carvings on stones with rock art – not all just mindless graffiti, some is quite considered attempts at 'new art'.
> (DR, 6 November 2006)

Heightened awareness of Ilkley Moor's archaeology – in part as a result of local tourism initiatives such as guided tours or even the management plan itself – inevitably leads to increased visitor pressures and other impacts including those of graffiti. The presence of some modern graffiti on various rocks encourages yet further graffiti, and even the ancient art may inspire some visitors to add their own contributions, though there may be no obvious connection in meaning. The Twelve Apostles stone circle on the moor has been subject to vandalism. On one of our visits, in July 1998, fires had been lit directly next to some of the stones and others had been pushed over. And in March 2005 one of the stones of the Twelve Apostles stone circle had been split in two, probably in an act of 'vandalism' that intended the stone to crack. In response to the 1998 impact, it was clear that other people had made attempts to rectify this damage, and re-erected other stones. Such well-meant reconstructions might not be the most 'authentic' ones. We have already noted similar events at the Doll Tor circle in Derbyshire, with both deliberate vandalism and attempted restoration involving moving stones, the latter apparently based on dowsing (Barnatt 1997). Such damage is clearly regrettable and, fortunately, uncommon: the graffiti is rather more prevalent.

As elsewhere, and as demonstrated by discussions thus far, pagans can be seen as allies to the efforts of archaeologists and heritage management. Important works on the history and prehistory of Ilkley Moor have resulted from pagan engagements, for instance in the works of Gyrus (1998a, 1998b) and Bennett (1998). This alternative discourse has helped to raise awareness of the important archaeological (as well as folkloric and other) value of the area, as well as attending to evidence which has otherwise been neglected by archaeologists (such as Gyrus' discussion of the Romano-Celtic goddess of the River Wharfe, Verbeia). Conversations with 'Gyrus' (originally working and living in the city of Leeds nearby, in interviews with Wallis) revealed numerous instances of visionary experiences induced at the rock art sites of the moor. Gyrus commented that many Chaos Magickians use the monuments on the moor in their rituals. Chaos Magickians might be described as the mages of postmodernity and their magical practices interface with those of pagans. Interestingly, Leeds was the birthplace of Chaos Magick in the works of Phil Hine and Peter Carroll, among others (for example Carroll 1987). In his online and other publications, including the sumptuous 'DreamFlesh' journal, Gyrus classifies his approach to rock art and ancient sites as 'personal': 'I have to experience the place I'm involved in. I spend time there and immerse myself in it, meditate and do rituals, note dreams and synchronicities' (<http://dreamflesh. com/essays/wharfedalegoddess/>). He describes a first visit to the Badger Stone rock art site at which:

> I was too wet to care about the rain, a state which alters
> consciousness into a more receptive mode. . . . I did some
> spontaneous chanting and whirling . . . my intuitive offerings
> to the Badger Stone consisted of pouring some of my drink

(water or whiskey) into the cups and watching it stream down the grooves.

A torrent of hailstones at another time,

> was blowing hard from behind me, hurting my head, and coming in at an almost horizontal angle, creating a tunnel-like effect before me – and an extremely conducive state of mind.
> <http://dreamflesh.com/essays/wharfedalegoddess/>

Gyrus also mentioned an occasion where he experienced visions at the Badger Stone after ingesting an entheogen. While chanting into the rock he perceived that changes in tone affected the frequency of vision patterns, something he feels would be useful in determining how original creators of the engravings perceived them. He likened the experience to synaesthesia, a state often reported by shamans in which the senses blur into one another; the subject may see a taste, hear a smell or feel a sound. We find Gyrus' practices and experiences fascinating because by interacting with the Rombald's Moor rock art and megalithic sites, he – among others such as pagans and Chaos Magickians – is engaging in alternative activities which directly affect archaeological interpretation, with his experiences prompting and inspiring him to write interpretative archaeological works (e.g. Gyrus 1998) about the region. Furthermore, his sustained alternative research involves critical appraisal of the heritage industry and its 'museumification' of the landscape, as illustrated by the epigraph opening this chapter.

Such modern engagements re-establish rituals with rock art sites, such as the leaving of offerings (of various fluids) in cup-and-ring engravings, that appear to have been operating until recently, certainly until the end of the nineteenth century. In effect a new psychic geography is emerging that implicates the spirituality of landscape in contestations of ancient site use and custodianship. This revival of tradition re-engages pagans with ancient sites in an active accomplishment of meaning, with experiences that challenge passive and normative archaeological approaches to the sites. Scholarly work on rock art by archaeologists, art historians and anthropologists has tended to consider the meaning of the imagery as passive records of 'art-for-art's-sake', territorial markers, hunting magic and scenes of daily life; but to pagans, cup-and-ring marked rocks are actively constituted, alive with spiritual meanings today.

Other local pagans know the area well. There are concerns about what will happen when an area under plantation at High Moor by Rivock Edge is cleared, and concerns that the local council's plan will not provide adequate protection for what pagans feel are unmapped sites; nor will it give people information that might prevent some of the more casual graffiti.

> Bradford Council seem intent on improving access to the moor for visitors, but all the money seems to be being spent on better footpaths and park benches. There's nothing to tell people about the environmental or historical treasures up there. Prominent features like the Haystack rock are always being defaced and clambered on, because people don't know what it is.
>
> (DR, pc 6 November 2006)

Contesting polarisation

Given the extent of pagan interest in the archaeology of Ilkley moor, as evinced here, as well as instances of deliberate vandalism – linked in some instances to pagans – it seems more than remiss for the Ilkley Moor Management Plan 2003–2012 to not engage with pagan discourse at any point, particularly since dialogue between pagans and heritage managers (as well as other) interest groups has produced productive dialogue and other collaborations at Avebury and Stonehenge (as discussed in chapters 2 and 3). Clearly, such dialogue is also not in the ascendant at Kilmartin where we see the threats of quarrying – precisely the same threat which has brought pagans and heritage managers into largely successful collaboration at Stanton Moor and Thornborough, as examined in chapter 4 – but where sharing of knowledge has potential to result in imaginative and artic-ulate presentations to inspire tourists, spiritual pilgrims and rock art researchers alike. From our analysis hitherto, it is clear that pagan engagements with the past – particularly in terms of direct impacts on sacred sites – can not be polarised in any simplistic way into 'good'/'bad'; rather, there are diverse actions which affect each site in different ways and have various implications for heritage manage-ment which may be viewed as allied or problematic. In the following chapter, in an effort to represent a case study which might usefully and positively exemplify pagan–heritage collaboration and its successes in action, we explore the example of the Rollright Stones in Oxfordshire.

CHAPTER 6

The Rollright Stones and the Rollright Trust

[A] little river . . . speedeth him into Isis: which riveret on the very border of the shire passeth by an ancient Monument standing not farre from his bank, to wit, certaine large stones placed in a round circle (the common people usually call them Rolle-rich stones, and dreameth that they were sometimes men by a wonderfull Metamorphosis turned into hard stones) . . . For, without all form and shape they bee, unequall, and by long continuance of time much impaired. The highest of them all, which without the circle looketh into the earth, they use to call the King, because hee should have beene King of England (forsooth) if hee had once seene Long Compton, a little towne so called lying beneath and which a man if he goe some few paces forward may see: other five standing on the other side, touching as it were one another, they imagine to have been knights mounted on horsebacke and the rest the Army. . . . These would I verily thinke to have beene the Monument of some Victory and haply erected by Rollo the Dane who afterwards conquered Normandy.
(Camden 1586 *Britannia*, trans. P. Holland 1637, in Evans 1895)

Discussion thus far indicates that on the one hand there is an ongoing tension and climate of distrust between pagans (and other alternative interest groups) and heritage managers (as well as archae-ologists, etc). On the other hand, there are, increasingly, examples of fruitful interaction: from the round table discussions leading to managed open access for the summer solstice and other pagan cele-brations at Stonehenge, to a Guardianship scheme at Avebury and dialogue at Stanton Moor. Each site offers its own problems and, in many instances, reconciliations – there is no single way of under-standing sites, contests, rites and rights. A different set of circum-stances is evident, yet again, at the Rollright Stones, the final site studied. Here, some pagans and some archaeologists appear to have made common cause, in part by drawing actively on the diversity of discursive interpretations and positionings evident at the site. A climate of inclusivity and multivocality has resulted, quite simply, in fruitful negotiation, although events have not been without their problems.

The Rollrights: The King's Men, The Whispering Knights and The King Stone

The Rollright Stones, or simply 'the Rollrights', near the village of Little Rollright on the border of Oxfordshire and Warwickshire, consists of a complex archaeological arrangement including prehistoric monuments from the Neolithic and Bronze Age, as well as Iron Age, Roman and Anglo-Saxon remains. The site is described by Lambrick (1988) and in a booklet by Burl (2000), and attracts visitors to see what is visible – the prehistoric material represented by the 'Kings Men' (c.2500–2000 BCE), a stone circle, as well as related features including the 'Whispering Knights' (c.3800–3000 BCE), a megalithic dolmen (the easternmost example of a portal dolmen in England), and the 'King Stone' (c.1500 BCE), a single standing stone. The King's Men comprise a stone circle some 30 metres across with, unusually, many small stones clustered together to form a continuous, jagged wall. These stones, of heavily weathered oolitic limestone, now number 77 but are impossible to count according to the folklore (e.g. Bennett and Wilson 1999:45). Certainly the current number is recent since late nineteenth-century illustrations show only around 25 stones; and the account of the history of the stone circle on the Rollright Stones website quotes an anonymous nineteenth-century author as revealing, 'In the year 1882 the proprietor of Little Rollright replaced all the fallen stones in their original foundation' (<http://www.rollrightstones.co.uk/history3.shtml>). A process of re-erection is evinced by the drawings made on three successive occasions in the latter part of the nineteenth century by Sir Norman Lockyer, the Astronomer Royal. The antiquarian William Stukeley described the stones of this circle as 'corroded like worm eaten wood, by the harsh Jaws of Time', which offered to him 'a very noble, rustic, sight, and strike an odd terror upon the spectators, and admiration at the design of 'em', and they attracted attention from other, earlier, antiquarians including Aubrey and Camden, quoted in the chapter beginning epigraph. The circle is located on a prehistoric trackway at the edge of a ridge which descends steeply northwards, looking towards the village of Long Compton. The Whispering Knights, standing some 365 metres east from the stone circle, form a chamber thought to be part of an early Neolithic long barrow. The King Stone stands 45 metres to the north of the stone circle and is severed from the circle and dolmen by a minor road; this megalith may have been part of a Neolithic long barrow, although Lambrick (<http://easyweb. easynet.co.uk/aburnham/eng/rolltalk.htm> and <http://www. rollrightstones.co.uk/tour/king-stone.mp3>) argues it is a monument to the Bronze Age burial ground (including two round barrows) excavated here. Lambrick's mp3 guided tour of the monument (downloadable from the website) includes instructions to find other sites such as bronze age cairns close to the King Stone, and locates the Rollright complex within changing landscapes defined by geographical and political, as well as archaeological, features.

Folklore of the Rollrights

Local folklore pertaining to the names of the monuments is first referred to in published form (the oral legend may be much older) by Camden in 1586. A king from Europe, so the story goes, was marching his soldiers near Long Compton when a witch – sometimes said to be Mother Shipton of Shipton-under-Wychwood[1] – appeared and challenged the king:

> Seven long strides shalt thou take
> And if Long Compton thou canst see,
> King of England thou shalt be.

Certain of his destiny, the king strode off claiming 'Stick, stock, stone, As King of England I shall be known.' But while his view had been clear, on his seventh stride the ground rose up in a long mound (sometimes known as the Arch-Druid's barrow), shielding his view of the village. The witch laughed, declaring:

> As Long Compton thou canst not see
> King of England thou shalt not be.
> Rise up, stick and stand still stone
> For King of England thou shalt be none;
> Thou and thy men hoar stones shall be
> And I myself an eldern tree.

Thus, the King became the King Stone, his men the King's Men stone circle, and his knights the Whispering Knights – who, as they lean towards one another, might be plotting against the king or in prayer. According to some retellings of the legend, the spell will be broken one day with the king and his men continuing their quest to conquer England. Meanwhile, the 'eldern tree' is said to be in the hedge between the King Stone and King's Men, and if it is cut when in blossom, it will bleed. According to other lore, Mother Shipton's spell is temporarily broken at midnight when the King's Men come back to life and, joining hands, they dance in a circle. Also at the witching hour the Stones go down the hill to drink at a spring at Little Rollright spinney, although the King only goes when he hears the Long Compton clock striking twelve. Anyone witnessing these scenes will either go mad or die, just as three successful attempts to count the stones will result in madness, death – or one's heart's desire fulfilled. Simpson and Roud (2000) mention a baker placing a loaf on each stone in order to count them, unsuccessfully; and stones dancing in the air. Folklore abounds at the Rollrights, with other tales involving fairies living beneath the stones, who dance around them by the light of the full moon, as well as further stories of witches. And recently, a whole new set of stories of Witches, pagans and the stones has been added to their history and, one imagines, future folklores.

The Rollright Trust

The site, though open to the public, is not curated by English Heritage or the National Trust. A campaign beginning in 1997 resulted in eventual purchase of the land by a private charity, the Rollright Trust. The purchase has its own history. The site was in private ownership when the previous owner, Pauline Flick, put it up for sale. She was already working with local pagans, in addition to archaeologists and others, to discuss issues relating to site management. In 1991 she had given an interview to *The Independent* (Roe 1991) relating to problems of managing a prehistoric monument which had become attractive as a place for pagan use.

At this time the Trust came into being. Initially its attempt to buy the land was not successful. Trustee Karin Attwood tells the story, during an interview conducted in 2001.

> In May 97 this place was put on the open market. And I'd only got into stone circles six months before. . . . And I'd been to Stonehenge, I'd been to Cornwall: I'd seen the sites in Cornwall, on to Stonehenge – I saw the car parks, coaches, and we'd come to here. After I'd been to the sites in Cornwall, I used to come up here, once or twice a month for healing, charging, to connect, to connect with my ancestors. I'd been a witch for quite a long time, I'd been a pagan for *less*, but here I felt that I was connecting with everything that was behind me, that I was connecting with nature, and I was worried about what this place could become. And I'd heard rumours of commercial interest. I was worried that the place would either

be bought by somebody very rich to keep it as a private play-ground to stop people visiting, or that it could be commer-cialised like 'Rollrightland with Witch-go-rounds', that sort of thing! I mean I knew nothing at the time about things like scheduled monuments and historic protection, that sort of stuff. And, I was concerned. I rang a couple of people like Andy Norfolk . . . in my naiveté I actually rang them, 'cos he was involved with earth mysteries and has been for years, not knowing at the time that this place was famous. 'I live in Oxfordshire near a stone circle, the Rollrights, have you ever heard of it? It's up for sale, erm, and I'm a bit concerned; have you got any ideas of whom I could contact?' And I wanted – I had this vague idea in mind that somehow it could be looked after in a way that was sympathetic to the spiritual nature of the place, the tourist nature of the place and everything else, but without exploiting or commercialising it. Well, Andy put me on to various other people . . . [which led to these people saying to Karin and her husband] 'You're local people, start an appeal!'

So, Karin and her husband led an appeal, 'so that the land will never again have to be sold' (Attwood, pc) and she comments that 'It was never intended – I was only looking to find somebody else that I could maybe help out to support who might be trying to buy it.' The appeal attracted immediate money and pledges, 80 per cent from pagans, according to Attwood:

> Within less than one week we had the support of the Pagan Federation, of the Druid orders, the Fellowship of Isis, Odinshof, the lot. . . . But we also had the backing of the Church of England – all in less than a week. And I found out afterwards that the Stones are supposed to be the most power-ful six days after the new moon, which is when I made my first phone call. By the time of the full moon, we had everybody including the – (laughs) – archbishop of Canterbury for the Sacred Land project. Not bad for a couple of rank amateurs!

The initial attempt to buy the land was not successful, possibly due to the caution of the site-owner who looked for a purchaser who could take immediate financial responsibility while facilitating a tran-sition to the Trust: and this is what happened. The purchasers, 'a couple of City gentlemen', worked with the Trust, with Attwood becoming a volunteer site manager, and eventually, in 2001 after further appeals and, crucially, a grant from the Hanson Environment Fund, the Trust was able to buy the land from them, marking the change of ownership with an event for National Archaeology Days in 2001. The Trust is a Registered Charity with a board including archaeologists, a biologist, a landscape architect and others including Attwood. 'There's an out Pagan, there's an out Christian', she says. That is, the land does not belong to any one religion, and the monuments are curated by the Trust in a 'guardianship' relationship with English Heritage in order to enable and balance conservation, research, and cultural and spiritual use.

Objectives of the Trust are:

- to protect and conserve the Rollright Stones and their environment in a manner that promotes their long term physical preservation.
- to facilitate and ensure public access for quiet enjoyment of the site in a manner which seeks to avoid inappropriate commercialisation and development.
- to facilitate and promote research and educational activities relating to the Rollright Stones and their environment.
- to acquire, or seek agreement on the management of land adjacent to the Rollright Stones, so as to facilitate conservation and access and to improve the environment of the site.
- to permit the reasonable use of the site for small private gatherings (religious, cultural or otherwise), provided that such gatherings do not conflict with the objectives of the Trust, and in particular do not cause a nuisance to others or damage to the site.
- to promote the conservation of megalithic and other sites and monuments adjacent to the Rollright Stones or elsewhere and of their environment, by acquisition or otherwise; and to facilitate and promote research and educational activities relating to such sites and monuments and their environment.
- to make donations of surplus revenue for other charitable purposes, priority to be given to charitable causes with a long-standing connection with the Rollright Stones.

< http://www.rollrightstones.co.uk/trust.shtml>

The site attracts visitors with interests in prehistory or religion, earth mysteries adherents, dowsers, spiritual tourists and others, worldwide. The Trust charges a small admission fee for entry to the King's Men and pagans are frequent, and returning, visitors. ASLaN, the Ancient Sacred Landscape Network, can be seen as a development from the efforts of the Rollright Trust, encouraging people to 'adopt' sites and care for them. As a recent entity, therefore, the Trust has engaged with pagan interests from the start; it has hosted its own open pagan rituals by, for instance, asking known Druid, Heathen or Wiccan groups to develop and perform these, and the King's Men can be 'booked' for special events such as the celebrations of specific groups, hand-fastings, child-blessings, and so on. Visitors can join a support group, the Friends of the Stones, which produces a newsletter and organises fund-raising events and activities. According to the Rollright Stones website, funds raised by the Friends have gone towards 'helping with the cost of the much needed erosion work, helping with the purchase of the Whispering Knights field, printing pamphlets, paying for new gates, refurbishing the warden's lodge, and anything else that needs doing to promote the long-term care and conservation of the Stones'.

The management stance is that it is important to avoid 'imposing a context' on the Rollright Stones complex. The Stones and associated sites are not perceived as pagan in that they do not relate to pagan groups or practices of today, nor do they have any other religious or cultural affiliation, but they are 'sacred' in the usual heritage sense of the term: they are ancient, part of our heritage and should be protected. Yet, endeavouring not to impose a context on the site is in itself a location which implies context nonetheless. This context, as exemplified in the Trust's stated 'objectives', does seem to centre around the emergent heritage discourse of sacredness built on the preservation ethos. As made clear in the discussion of understandings of 'sacred site' in Chapter 1, the discourse of the preservation ethos raises various issues and concerns which impact pagan interests in such sites. This chapter will display some of the tensions inherent in the objectives of the Trust and some of their emergent or attempted solutions.

Plurality and multivocality: a context of inclusiveness

In terms of (re)presentation, where other heritage bodies (principally English Heritage and the National Trust), marginalise alternative discourses with their emphasis on 'scientific archaeological facts', the Rollright Trust has attempted to embrace plurality of interpretation. The rich folklore of the site is detailed on the Rollright Trust website and in on-site literature; pagan interests are represented on a subtle level here, where the folklore of witches is tied positively to historical references to the same, clearly offering a perceived tangible link between witches of the past and pagan witches of the present. The website and on-site literature also details abundant anomalous activity at the site which is of interest to Earth Mystics, and visitors are encouraged to send accounts of their 'experiences'.

Indeed the Rollright monuments have been the subject of intense alternative analysis. Most obviously, Ley Hunters associate three leys with the site:

1   The first was discovered by Alfred Watkins and runs through Long
    Compton church, the Rollright Stones, Chipping Norton church
    and a tumulus near Charlbury before ending at another (un-named)
    church.
2   The second was suggested by Devereux and Thomson in 1979(8)
    and follows a route from Arbury Banks in Northamptonshire, across
    Cropredy Bridge to All Saints church, Wroxton. To the south-west of
    the church the ley crosses Castle Bank camp and Madmarston Hill
    camp before reaching the Rollrights.
3   The third runs from the Rollright Stone Circle on the Cotswold
    ridgeway to the Uffington White Horse in a perfect north–south
    orientation.
                            <http://www.rollrightstones.co.uk/history2.shtml>

The Rollright Trust website also provides more recent interpretations of leys, drawing on the work of Paul Devereux (whose findings have been published in such reputable archaeological
journals as *Antiquity*: see Devereux 1991, 2001; Devereux and Jahn
1996), stating 'A fresh analysis of leys has started to emerge over
the last few years. These views see leys not so much as prehistoric
trackways but as spirit paths, corpse or death roads, dream tracks
or flight paths for the faerie folk, which can be found in ceremonial landscapes all over the world'. Devereux's work is also referred
to in his capacity as Director of the Dragon Project[2] which, in the
late 1970s, scientifically examined anomalous activities at sacred
sites, beginning with the Rollrights:

> Ultrasonic pulsing has been detected at the King Stone at
> sunrise, although the levels varied with the seasons. During the
> Summer Solstice it was observed that there were no ultrasound
> readings within the Circle, almost as if the Stones were acting
> as a shield from the low background levels of ultrasound that
> are normally present in the landscape . . . [Furthermore] a
> steady hot spot of beta and gamma radiation has been
> recorded a few feet from the northern edge of the Circle,
> underneath the road. There has been a solitary, unexplained
> alpha radiation reading at the Whispering Knights.
>   <http://www.rollrightstones.co.uk/history2.shtml>

In terms of (re)presentation and interpretation, then, the Rollright
Trust is liberal and accommodating, interweaving 'scientific' archaeology with folklore and Earth Mysteries. The same section of the
website also discusses – in a non-judgemental way – UFOlogy.
    More explicitly pagan descriptions include encounters with ances-
tors, with a goddess of the place, with wights of the land, with the

dead, with the Anglo-Saxon god Woden, and with a Guardian woman (described by several speakers independently). A visitor from the United States, Diana Paxson, has discussed possibilities of using techniques of seidr (North European shamanic practice – see Blain 2002) to gain experiential perceptions of the history of the stones, and indeed pagan visitors will often spend time in meditation and other work using deliberate alteration of consciousness to commune with wights and stones. An article on the website, reprinted from *Wood and Water* magazine (Asphodel 1997), indicates tensions and contradictions: the writer had spent the night communing with a goddess of the place, but was disturbed in the morning by a shouting crew who had come, with various forms of electric equipment, to test 'psychic' energies and ordered her out!

Site management on a day-to-day basis involves a paid manager and volunteer wardens who staff the site. Until an episode of vandalism in early 2006, staffing was based at a wardens hut at the King's Men stone circle. Staff have a variety of materials for sale including information about the site such as Burl's (2000) booklet on the archaeology of the Rollrights complex, earth mysteries material, pagan interpretations, and of course the legends and folklore associated with the landscape. A CD available from the wardens gives a guided tour with interpretations and history, with brief accounts from folklore from archaeologist George Lambrick (chair of the Trust) together with a story-teller's re-telling of the tale of the Witch and the King, these being also downloadable from the Rollright Stones website.

Damage and preservation

Despite these concessions to pagans and others with alternative interests, in terms of (re)presentation/interpretation, not all is smooth-running, of course: disputes occur, some pagans and others feel marginalized, perhaps because of the Rollright Trust's monopoly over how the site is managed, and there are even incidents of deliberate vandalism: a piece of one megalith was chipped off, probably as a souvenir, in the summer of 2001, yellow gloss paint was spattered over stones of the King's men circle early in the morning on the 1st of April 2004 (also partly over the oldest measured lichen colony in the UK), and visitors ask why the 'pink stone' has not been 'cleaned' to restore it to the colour of the others, since it was discoloured by a fire set against it some years ago (Attwood, pc. This stone was found to be cracked by the fire). Not all of these events can be reliably linked to pagans; and indeed some might be protests at pagan interests in the site. As might be expected, the Rollright Trust labours hard against wilful and unintentional damage to the site. In the discussion of the King's Stone on the Trust website, we learn that:

> The strange shape (likened to a seal balancing a ball on its nose) . . . has less to do with the weathering effects of nature than with the destructive habit of 19th century drovers who chipped off small pieces to act as lucky charms and keep the Devil at bay. Thankfully this superstitious vandalism no longer goes on.
>
> <http://www.rollrightstones.co.uk/history3.shtml>

Explicit in the Trust's discourse here (and in line with that of site custodians elsewhere such as English Heritage and the National Trust) is the preservation ethos. The efforts to establish the Rollright Trust are well known among pagans, and many pagans support the Trust and its aims. But other, alternative interest groups experience marginalisation and there is considerable debate over what is acceptable use of the stones, and what can be done there. The most obvious issues with site-use are those of erosion, and the leaving of offerings or other material, as noted for other places. The Trust has attempted to cope with erosion through reinforcing paths both within and outside the King's Men (and indeed has created a reinforced walkway that is wheelchair accessible to facilitate access to the Whispering Knights dolmen); ongoing attempts are made to deal with material offerings through education. These tensions are made clear in a series of articles in the Trust's journal *The Right Times* in the late 1990s, in which various authors, mainly pagans such as Claire Prout (now Slaney) and Sam Fleming, railed against damage to this site (and others) occasioned by votive offerings. A coin wedged into a crack in the rock might draw inspiration from Rollrights folklore advising that a coin left for the fairies brings luck, but it is damaging to the stone in which it is inserted, and its removal may cause further problems. Unauthorised fires have damaged site flora temporarily, as well as colouring the 'pink' stone referred to above. Excavations at the centre of the circle in the summer of 2003 revealed a (modern) deposit of two large crystals. Of less obvious impact are offerings which are left to rot, such as flowers and fruit. These, along with tea lights, candle wax and incense sticks, might be termed 'ritual litter', with Fleming declaring 'I am one of those who remove your rubbish' and expressing concern with damage to rare lichens and other flora (Fleming, n.d.c).

We return here, then to problems in 'imposing a context'. Ritual litter, here or elsewhere, most obviously intrudes into the perception of others, so imposing both immediate context and implied interpretation. Yet, disallowing physical signs of ritual in itself creates context, and comparisons have been made with, for instance, shrines in Japan where there are places or areas where the authorised leaving of offerings is facilitated. A particular issue at the Rollrights has been the deposition of human ashes, and the Trust is attempting to work with communities to ensure that personal wishes to have ashes scattered at the Stones can be fulfilled without this becoming obvious to other visitors to the site.

There are other issues here, including those of acceptable and unacceptable ritual use, variously defined. We have friends and acquaintances who are members and volunteers of the Trust, or who have been asked to perform public rituals at the Stones (as has Blain) – and others whose requests to use the Stones have been rejected (by a volunteer), seemingly because of involving ritual work. There are also issues of complaints from visitors when they arrive to find that a special event is in place or that the site has been booked by others. Indeed, rites are contested here. In an extreme instance, any ritual use may be problematic, even when it does not involve offerings or physical traces. Fleming, when a volunteer at the Rollrights, considered that abuse of sites took place on a 'spiritual' level, as well as in physical traces, suggesting that to meddle with a site's energies is 'psychic vandalism' (Fleming 1999) – and, indeed, that most forms of pagan ritual constitute site damage:

> I find it unnecessary to perform any ritual at a prehistoric site unless the site is actively involved in the ritual . . . [I]f the ritual could be performed in exactly the same way in any other location then the site is providing no more than an atmospheric backdrop and that is insufficient reason to expose a delicate and unique monument to the risk of damage.
>
> (Fleming n.d.a; see also n.d.b)

The terms 'delicate' and 'unique' here are reminiscent of those used by the heritage bodies, but in presenting the primary concern that ritual at a site 'will . . . change its character' (n.d.a), the writer merges ideas of 'wrong' spiritual use with those of the preservationist ethos, reinforcing the latter. Equally problematic, in a similar vein, are pagan practitioners we have encountered who visit sites in order to psychically 'clean-up' or 're-tune' the stones. Others have voiced similar concerns at the Rollrights and elsewhere, though usually with less extreme effect: if as we have suggested much pagan practice (particularly within eclectic Paganism, Wicca and Goddess spirituality) tends to treat ancient places as temples in which one or more goddess or god can be honoured or greeted, there are senses in which sites do become interchangeable rather than recognised for their distinctiveness. However, it is becoming more common for the practitioners to in some way include local deities or spirits in their ritual, or at least to ask their permission before 'taking over' the site for a particular event: and some (particularly animist) pagan practices explicitly focus on beings located in site. Pagans will often say that they have 'come to know' local entities and local landscapes through spiritual practice which originally had different intent, so that there is a gradient of practice rather than easily defined categories. Yet how such issues could be adjudicated by a site manager is problematic, to say the least.

Rather than erecting further physical and metaphorical fences around the Rollright Stones (the nineteenth-century railings around the King's Stone and Whispering Knights notwithstanding – now a part of the context and, indeed, perhaps ironically, preserved as part of the scheduled monuments) the Trust attempts to negotiate practices and interpretation with pagans and others, facilitating alternative forms of engagement to foster inclusivity. Yet the lack of physical protection of the site has its probems. In January 2006, the warden's hut was broken into and a fire started, leaving the wooden building damaged beyond repair. Currently a series of benefit gigs are being run by 'The Rollright Project' <http://www.rollrightproject.org/> to enable construction of a new, more secure, hut, pointing out that 'The Rollright Trust do not have the money to fund this, as they are a hand to mouth organization' – a reminder that indeed the Trust, as a small volunteer-based charitable organisation, does not have the resources of the large heritage organisations, though it does have to deal with similar political and community issues and tensions.

Facilitating engagement

What we identify of major interest here, and of consequence for other sites, not only of similar size but with implications in terms of negotiation for elsewhere, is less the Rollright Trust's discourse on how a site should be interpreted and (re)presented, or even engaged with, but more its attempted inclusive approach in terms of management. In contrast to other site management plans, the Rollright plan goes some way to assuming that active engagement with the site, including pagan rituals and other practices, is possible. We mean by this not only acknowledgments that pagans may consider they develop insights through practices including meditation and deliberate connection with landscape and deities, but the recognition that these produce meaningful interpretations which may be of assistance to others. Indeed, management discourse blends some components of pagan and heritage narratives, with even the *Conservation and Management Plan* for the Rollright Stones (Lambrick 2001) including a section on implications of paganism, both in the present and inherent in the folklore surrounding the site. Plans are ongoing to foster interest in the stones and their setting in ways that permit use by pagans and others while setting and explaining limits, re-narrativising the stones within today's social and community contexts rather than only as 'timeless heritage'. The Rollrights provide an example of how pasts become part of present identities, and how 'guardians' can have their identities legitimated – occurring through the direct and intensive work of a number of people who have set out to accomplish shared meaning. Today's use, and yesterday's folklore, become simply a part of the ways that the monument can be viewed. The stones are not seen as sterile, to be 'preserved' behind a fence, without people engaging with them closely. Illustrating these points, the official – secular – handing over of deeds to the Rollright Trust in 2001 included a ceremony incorporating Morris Dancers and a play by the local primary school on the local story of the witch, the king and his men. The evening even saw a notable sacred 'party' in celebration.

6.1   Visitors to the King's Men stone circle try their hand at dowsing.

6.2   The Whispering Knights, a dolmen, with project members Robert Wallis and Andy Letcher. There is now a wheelchair-accessible path which connects the Knights with the King's Men circle.

6.3   The stones are reflected in the sculpture by Kapoor, in a temporary installation in 2003, as are all who attempt to view or photograph them!

Local pagans often attempt to keep a careful watch on the activities of 'outsiders' at the site in order to ensure as little damage as possible. This is suitably demonstrated by reactions to a notification in spring 2002 that a 'Prophets' Conference' (organised by groups in the United States but with links to one or more 'Mayan Elders' who were encouraged to attend) was to be held in Oxford with trips to Avebury, Stonehenge and the Rollrights, with the goal of 'awakening the stones' through ritual. Numerous representations from pagans (many local) and from the Rollright Trust pointed out that this event was an affront to local pagans and the site itself: the stones are not a 'resource' to be tapped into and the site may not itself require 'awakening', since many pagans have reported experiencing the place as 'alive' for many years. There is a clear difference here in what might be best described as 'New Age' rhetoric with its assumption that a sacred site is a resource to be used, and a pagan perspective which encourages dialogue with place. These protests, combined with others (including an exchange of emails between one of the authors and Starhawk, a well-known Wiccan in the United States, billed as a speaker at this proposed event), resulted in the postponement of the conference and we have not seen plans for a revival. In this instance at the Rollrights, among others, it is clear that management and pagan concerns can align and that together heritage and pagan interests may result in a strong force for site welfare. While the situation of the Rollrights has its own problems in distancing some potential users (such as the Prophets' Conference), by and large collaborations are positive, and orthodox viewing from the 'tourist gaze' is not privileged over alternative engagements – as it may be at others of the sites we have discussed.

The Trust takes a similar, inclusive approach to alternative engagement and access in situ. The Rollrights were staffed until recently by volunteers, many of whom have been pagan, with the current site custodian/manager being 'pagan-friendly' or at least aware of why it is that pagans visit and what they want to do within this landscape. Pagans and other groups can 'book' the stones for ceremonies and events, and at major pagan festivals the site is open to all comers. At these events, fire-dishes are made available so that ad hoc fires – fire being essential to many pagan rituals – do not damage the flora and associated archaeology, and their provision is designed as both practical and educative. Even porta-loos are provided. Often an open pagan ritual is scheduled, with various groups or individuals asked to conduct this – just as other events, such as an annual Shakespeare performance, are scheduled. No particular difference is drawn (positively or negatively) over a pagan event and a non-pagan one. As a charitable organisation, the Trust provides for all, and does not favour any one religious, or secular, group.

The Rollrights complex is small yet much frequented: contained within a landscape, yet bounded by road and pathway, visually by topography and field fences and politically through negotiation for leases on specific pieces of land. This site is not a model for other sites – each with their unique attractions and problems – and we do not present it as such. Rather, we present it as an example of what can occur when archaeologists, pagans, and others listen to each other, attempting to learn each other's discourse and celebrate a multiplicity of understandings of a site, not as modernist museum fodder,[3] top-down 'education', or even as public display, but as living interpretation based on engagement which furthers identity. The installation of Anish Kapoor's sculpture 'Turning the World Inside out' (1996) inside the King's Men circle in the summer of 2003 demonstrates, for us, some of these issues, returning also to creative uses of sacred/prehistoric space and ways in which sites can be managed as 'living' and changing environments. This installation, to celebrate the centenary of the Art Fund, facilitated types of interpretations and engagements that would not otherwise have been experienced (see Wallis 2006 for a detailed discussion). More relevant to this discussion, the installation was negotiated by the manager and trustee group, which includes pagan members, and the Rollright Trust consulted with the Cotswold Order of Druids, the Pagan Federation and local people. Within such discussion it was agreed to be a good idea. The process of consultation here is, we argue, crucial to engaging with pagan, local, and indeed all interests *vis-à-vis* sacred sites. Comments from 'visitors' indicate a wide range of responses to the installation, as contributing to the ambience of the circle and as disrupting this (again, see Wallis 2006). As an 'incomer' the installation itself becomes an interpretation – fleeting (the installation was temporary) and, to most, fascinating, though some thought it did not 'belong', becoming intrusion rather than interpretation. To us it becomes a metaphor for the interpretation and reinterpretation of site and land, changing with sky and cloud, at once appearing a window into another circle while reflecting an altered landscape – and reflecting also the viewer/photographer who cannot escape the transformation. Here, at the Rollrights, our final case study, we indeed find ongoing attempts to create reflexive site management and custodianship, in contexts that facilitate discussion and dialogue. Yet, not even the Rollrights can escape the suspicions embedded within today's power politics, and the relationships of Rollrights management to paganisms are not at all simple.

CHAPTER 7

Reburial, Museums, Pagans and Respect

Then the Geat people began to construct
a mound on a headland, high and imposing,
a marker that sailors could see from afar,
and in ten days they had done the work.
It was their hero's memorial; what remained from the fire
they housed inside it, behind a wall
as worthy of him as their workmanship could make it.
And they buried torques in the barrow, and jewels
and a trove of such things as trespassing men
had once dared to drag from the hoard.
They let the ground keep that ancestral treasure,
gold under gravel, gone to earth,
as useless to men now as it ever was.
(Beowulf: Heaney trans. 1999: 99)

Pagans and ancestors

The examples given in earlier chapters display how pagan–heritage relations are complex. As indicated in Chapter 1, there is no single pagan voice: in 1999 there were pagans against the excavation of Seahenge, there were those for it; today at Avebury (Chapter 2) pagans side with villagers or with festival-goers, and perspectives and alliances change; and at the Rollright Stones (Chapter 6) pagans form part of management. A major challenge facing heritage managers is how to engage with a variety of pagan views, from those claiming 'rights' to or even 'spiritual ownership' of sacred sites, to those who are supportive of the preservation ethos, and all in between who combine stances and discourses in negotiating the specifics of 'their' landscapes. There is common ground that might prove useful for all interested parties – especially in the example with which we close our discussion, the emergence of a reburial issue in Britain, and its current status at the time of writing. 'Reburial' has been a central issue for archaeologists and anthropologists in Canada and the United States,

Australia and elsewhere where the lobbying of indigenous communities for the repatriation and/or reburial of human remains and artefacts held by museums (and other institutions) has met increasing successes (e.g. Biolsi and Zimmerman 1997; Dongoske and Anyon 1997). In the United States NAGPRA (Native American Graves Protection and Repatriation Act 1990), and in Australia the 1988 South Australian Aboriginal Heritage Act, mark examples of policy which have enabled some indigenous communities to make legal claims on 'their' pasts. For archaeologists and anthropologists the ramifications have been immense, with opinion varied: from those who largely support the indigenous claims (e.g. Biolsi and Zimmerman 1997), to those, particularly osteoarchaeologists and physical anthropologists, who argue vital scientific data is being irretrievably lost (e.g. Chatters in Radford 1998). A process of decolonising archaeology and anthropology has been crucial in order to negotiate these issues (see, for example, Layton; 1989a, 1989b; Swidler et al. 1997; Smith 1999; Mihesuah 2000; Watkins 2000; Kreps 2003; Peers and Brown 2003).

Within the United Kingdom, various sets of guidelines have been produced regarding human remains; Historic Scotland produced guidelines for respectful treatment in 1997, and in England and Wales a working group was set up in 2002 to examine issues of human remains within museum collections and make recommendations for proposals 'which might form the basis of a consultative document'.[1] Pressures for these guidelines have arisen from indigenous communities as indicated above, but also from museum personnel and archaeologists, and from Christian organisations within Britain (regarding the status of Christian-era burials). Such issues are not only controversial in indigenous contexts: the reburial issue is now on the agenda in Britain, although so far with little reference to pre-Christian remains[2]. It is commonly argued, and seen as a matter of common sense, that there are no indigenous communities remaining in Britain, the current multicultural milieu, largely an after-effect of colonialism, being only the most recent result of a diversity of ethnic groups choosing the British Isles as 'home'. Processes of immigration are commonly thought of as in action since prehistory, from the so-called Bronze age 'beaker people' who were thought to have 'conquered' Neolithic peoples, to more recent Anglo-Saxon 'invaders' who, it has been claimed, pushed the Iron Age 'Celts' to the fringes of these Isles. Archaeologists now approach such ethnic engagements in more subtle ways, and the focus on 'invasions' no longer predominates, but still 'indigeneity' in the political sense claimed by peoples of Australia or the Americas would be misplaced and misguided. Tooth enamel analysis reveals far more movement, on a personal and family basis, than fits with a conventional understanding of 'peoples' related to geography. Today we are all, says a pagan informant, 'mongrels' with diverse heritages and personal ancestries indicating a wide set of 'origins'. Contemporary Britain is a postmodern melting pot of cultures and traditions (and some, especially on the political left, might argue this makes Britain a truly cosmopolitan nation). To claim indigeneity here would at the very least be suspect and certainly politically and/or religiously motivated.

Nonetheless, increasing numbers of people feel they are 'native' to the British Isles. They may claim to be 'Celtic' even if they have no immediate Scots, Irish, Welsh, Cornish or Manx parentage, relating this concept to having great-grandparents from these nations (e.g. MacEowen 1998).[3] Just as there are 'wannabe' Indians (Green 1988), these are wannabe 'Celts,' whom Bowman (1995) terms 'cardiac celts', as they 'know in their hearts' they are Celtic (see also Bowman 2000). Some may indeed go to considerable lengths to study cultures and languages, so that their involvement becomes cultural rather than merely 'cardiac'. Heathens may make ceremonies to honour Anglo-Saxon or Norse 'ancestors' (see e.g. Blain 2002). Others (including both 'Celtic' and Heathen practitioners) feel they can relate more directly with prehistoric peoples whose monuments are extant in the landscape, particularly of the Neolithic and Bronze age, but also Iron Age Romano-British, or later, even mediaeval periods, up to present-day cemeteries where known ancestors are buried (Blain 2006c). And it is at these monuments, as we have seen in previous chapters, that Pagan understandings and engagements with place may confront those of heritage managers: Pagans not only make ritual (formal or informal) at sacred sites but also and increasingly they identify themselves as spiritually allied with the prehistoric peoples who built the monuments.

Rites at megalithic tombs and related sites – from Mesolithic pits (in the Stonehenge car park) to Neolithic Henges at Thornborough and Bronze Age cairns in Argyll or Round Barrows along parts of the Ridgeway – involving (perceived) direct communication with prehistoric 'ancestors' in particular, prompt many pagans to feel a responsibility to ancient peoples and the 'sacred sites' themselves. Pagans who return again and again to a place learn about the landscape, feel 'at home' there: they are not 'visitors', though they may be framed as such in management discourse. While they may never have engaged with excavation or even fieldwalking, they know the land through seasons as if it were part of or adjoining their own back gardens (which sometimes, of course, it may well be).[4] Practices such as collaboration with site managers in 'site' welfare, picking up litter and removing chalk graffiti are not necessarily undertaken as part of a 'preservation ethos' but may be because they are what one does in one's own home – to clean up a place, to remove traces of the last visitor in order not only to prepare for the next but to care for the space and enable one's own comfort there and that of one's household or kin. But as the spaces are shared with (or memorials to) other, earlier, inhabitants, pagans have also begun to address issues of 'ancestor' welfare, with concerns over the disturbance of rest caused not only by quarrying activities but by archaeological excavation and storage of human remains and artefacts, even challenging the excavation process itself. Pagans at Thornborough or Stanton Moor speak of disruption of landscape as an insult to ancestors: archaeologists excavating at Avebury in recent field seasons have had to deal with interest – some of it negative with regard to the excavation, some of it positive (there is no singular voice) – from local and other Druids.

The example of Kennewick Man in the United States illustrates how the claims of contemporary Pagans – however controversial – have been included alongside those of archaeologists and indigenous groups (see e.g. Wallis 2003: 190; also Radford 1998; Thorpe 2000/2001). In this somewhat infamous case, not only were claims made on prehistoric remains by both local Native American communities and a local pagan organisation, the *Asatru Folk Assembly*, but also both groups were granted access to the remains to perform ceremonies which honoured the 'ancestor', while the scientific analyses of the physical anthropologists were halted by law (Chatters 2000). This was a complicated and divisive case, which relates to constructions of identity, ethnicity and pasts in the United States, not in Britain, but it certainly evinces ways in which indigenous groups and, now, contemporary pagans, are making claims to the past which may include 'ownership' and reburial – with ramifications for archaeologists in Britain.

On the one hand there are many examples of 'repatriation' to indigenous communities: for instance, a Ghost Dance shirt brought to the United Kingdom by Buffalo Bill was returned in 2000 to the Lakota (Sioux) by Glasgow's Kelvingrove Museum, to the accompaniment of considerable publicity. Then, in 2001 the Royal College of Surgeons revised its policy on considering the return of human remains following requests from indigenous groups. As previously mentioned, a working group was set up in 2002 by the Department of Culture, Media and Sport to examine 'the current legal status of human remains within the collections of publicly funded Museums and Galleries in the United Kingdom'. This group produced a 'Human Remains Report' (DCMS, November 2003) which made recommendations for dealing with requests for the return of human remains, notably the assessment of claims by an independent expert panel – greeted with approval by the World Archaeological Council. The working group did not, however, make explicit recommendations with regard to British prehistoric material. More recently, a second working group with representation from the Church of England has produced a report on *Guidance for Best Practice for Treatment of Human Remains Excavated from Christian Burial Grounds in England* (Church of England and English Heritage, 2005). This report emphasises the need for treating any remains found with 'dignity and respect', but very obviously works within a Christian worldview – such was its remit; and an Advisory Panel sponsored by the Church of England, English Heritage and the Department for Constitutional Affairs has been set up to give specific advice. Importantly, this document sites treatment of remains within a theological as well as a secular ethical context:

> 21. The great majority of archaeological excavations, however, deal with the remains of long-dead individuals of unknown identity. Under these circumstances it is clearly impossible to trace living relatives or to determine the individual wishes of the dead (beyond the general ethos of the Christian theology under whose rites they were buried). It is therefore suggested that decisions regarding human remains should be guided by ethical criteria derived from Christian theology, from current secular attitudes to the dead, and from secular concepts of ethics.
>
> (CoE and EH 2005, p. 8)

On the other hand, British pagans, drawing on the examples of indigenous claims and the language used in these, and, now, the response of the working groups, have been calling for the 'return to the earth' or reburial of some (not all) prehistoric remains. They are not alone in this call, nor is their voice a 'fringe' one: on a British archaeology email list, archaeologists and museum curators discussed unease among members of the public when seeing prehistoric human remains, and some revealed considerable sympathy for the call for (at least) their removal from public view. Earlier, a British Archaeology news article (*British Archaeology*, November 1997: 5) discussed the 'Public Disquiet Over Digging of Graves', referring specifically to an excavation at an Anglo-Saxon cemetery in Suffolk. One remark is rather striking:

> How short a time do we have to be buried before it is permissible, even acceptable, for grinning archaeologists to dig out our bones, prod among our teeth, disperse our possessions, take the head off our horse and lay us, not to rest, in boxes in museums?

Indeed, 'When does sanctity, afforded to graves, cease to be an issue?'. In the article this criticism is levied at 'Britain's planning culture which appears to treat cemeteries, especially out-of-use non-Christian cemeteries, with little respect' (*British Archaeology* November 1997: 5). It seems people other than pagans express a sense of responsibility to these 'ancestors'. Pagan calls, though, go further, regarding context and philosophy of reburial as well as a need to 'remove' the remains from public view, with reports in the national press and pagan magazines (e.g. 'Pagans Angry at Christian Burial' in *The Times* [24 October 1999], 'Druid campaign for sacred sites' on BBC news [23 September 2006, <http://news.bbc.co.uk/1/hi/wales/south_west/5372598.stm>] and articles by Davies and Shallcrass in *The Druid's Voice* in recent years, discussed below).

Druid voices

Pagans have framed their approaches to British reburial in language similar to that of Native Americans and other indigenous communities. The words of British Druid Order member Davies are particularly striking in this regard:

> Every day in Britain, sacred Druid sites are surveyed and excavated, with associated finds being catalogued and stored for the archaeological record. Many of these sites include the sacred burials of our ancestors. Their places of rest are opened during the excavation, their bones removed and placed in museums for the voyeur to gaze upon, or stored in cardboard boxes in archaeological archives. . . . I believe we, as Druids, should be saying 'Stop this now. These actions are disrespectful to our ancestors.' When archaeologists desecrate a site through excavation and steal our ancestors and their guardians. . . . It is a theft...We should assert our authority as the physical guardians of esoteric lore. We should reclaim our past.
>
> (Davies 1997: 12–13)

Davies's words have an indigenous-inspired tone. Given that many pagans, shamanic practitioners (or neo-shamans) in particular, actively engage with indigenous spiritual practices, such rhetoric is not surprising. The new-indigenes of Britain include those who deliberately reflect indigenous discourses and those who attempt to adopt worldviews and practices of earlier people within the landscape. Davies' view also compares with New Traveller opinions that archaeologists are contemporary society's 'looters of graves' (Bender 1993: 271) – just as contemporary archaeologists see some early antiquarians. For Davies, the reburial of prehistoric human remains in Britain 'makes perfect sense; bones are living people and should therefore be respected and ceremonially reburied' (Davies 1998/9: 11), and he outlines how pagans can get directly involved in this issue:

> I speak for the ancestors and guardians of the land, those spirits not currently represented in the archaeological record. . . The Druid or Pagan shaman can use their gifts as 'harmonic bridges' to communicate between the realities of archaeology, land developers and Pagan Druids. . . . Druids should join together and encourage debate between archaeologists and museums in the reburial issue.
>
> (Davies 1998/9: 10–12)

As maintained throughout this volume, individual pagans and pagan groups do not have agreed core beliefs or practices, let alone centralised spiritual beliefs concerning disposal of the dead. Nor is their discourse on 'ancestors', within today's multicultural Britain, clear-cut. Issues of a 'slippage' between asserting pagan identities and implying ethnic inheritance and nationalist claims have been commented on by Gallagher (e.g. 1999) and by ourselves (e.g. Blain and Wallis 2006d). Yet the majority of pagans appear to attempt to walk a liberal line of ethnic tolerance and intercultural dialogue.

There are, though, many understandings of 'ancestors' to be considered, and these do include implicit and explicit constructions of ethnicity and 'race'. Pagan understandings of ancestors range from 'those previously living on the land', through 'family members' to ideas of bounded, identifiable 'peoples' who may be 'Celt' or 'Saxon'. 'Ancestors' therefore become another contested category within pagan relationships with place: how do the new-indigenes understand their relation to 'ancestors' and 'heritage'. When is 'protection of heritage' an offering both to ancestors and to those - all those - with an interest in Britain today, and when does it become exclusionary and even racist? And for at least some of today's pagans, a focus on 'ancestors' of the distant past, ancestors within place, may be seen as legitimated or even necessitated by the emphasis on culture and history that seems apparent for other – often marginalised and disprivileged – religious and cultural groups.

Within late modernity/post-modernity, paganisms may offer choices of alliances and identities. In this 'time of the tribes' (whether these be specific identifications of 'the tribes' by pagan groups, or the more fragmentary, fluid identities theorised by Maffesoli [1996] or Bauman [2000]) the reburial issue is gathering momentum and coherency. The heightened awareness of excavations forced by road workings or quarrying may be a factor here, as the idea of impious disturbance of the relationship between ancestors and place increases. Examples include the quarry threats mentioned in this book, and instances such as Prittlewell (Southend-on-Sea), where a Saxon cemetery is under threat from road construction. Stonehenge, within the context of the Management Plan and proposals for a tunnel to replace part of the A303, has become a focus for the reburial issue in the South-West of England, in part due to the site's iconic prominence for Britain more generally; the issue has been raised at Stonehenge Project meetings (the liaison group established to discuss the future of the Stonehenge environs).

As a result of her involvement with the Stonehenge Project, Druid priestess Emma Restall Orr formed the organisation *Honouring the Ancient Dead* (<http://www.honour.org.uk>, had@druidnetwork.org), encompassing a range of professionals such as academics, museum specialists, and field archaeologists as well as pagans (and including pagans professionally involved in academia, museums and archaeology) with aims to 'ensure respect for ancient pagan remains' through 'clear interactions between archaeologists, historians, landowners, site caretakers, museums and collectors...and the pagan community':

> The purpose of this interaction is clear and positive communication that will inspire a broader and deeper understanding of the sanctity of all artefacts (notably those connected with ritual, sacrifice, burial and human remains) sourced from the Pagan eras of the British Isles. HAD will be seeking assurances that there will be communication and consultation on matters relating to such artefacts and remains. (pc)

Although Restall Orr now manages a pagan cemetery in the Cotswolds where remains could be reburied, indicating that some of the logistics of reburial could be managed effectively within at least a localised South-West England area, HAD is not calling for mandatory reburial and is more concerned with furthering dialogue between the interest groups and in particular establishing consultation between these groups during excavations as well as creating the opportunity for pagans to 'make ritual in appropriate ways, honouring the spirits involved' (pc). There are issues here of how 'appropriate ritual' is constituted, since we do not know what sorts of rituals, if any, were associated with specific remains. It is however evident from ethnographic analogy, from Roman and other early writings, and from archaeological speculation based in specific contexts that original burial rituals would bear little resemblance to most 'generic' (that is, Wiccan-style) pagan practice today. Indeed, evidence for practices such as secondary burial following excarnation indicates meanings and distinctions that are rather far from most understandings in present day Britain (for instance dealing in symbolism of bones and flesh, and changes and developments in social practices relating to these over time, as pointed to by Thomas [1999, 2000]). Such issues of 'appropriate ritual' are also seen as problematic in some quarters of the pagan community, as discussed on the 'Association of Polytheist Traditions' (APT) and 'BritPoly' (British Polytheist) email lists. HAD has produced a document of guidance for construction of reburial ceremonies, requested initially by Leicester Museums, that takes into account at least some of the critiques from pagan and archaeological communities and specifies a need to state that the ceremony proceeds from a basis of 'not knowing' either the forms or the specifics of relationship with which the individual was first interred. Clearly 'the pagan community', or the diversity of groups and traditions adopting pagan worldviews in today's Britain, is not in its entirety represented by HAD. Restall Orr agrees: 'the Pagan community, considering its extremely diverse beliefs, CANNOT be entirely represented by HAD, and this HAD acknowledges. HAD does aim to represent a good proportion of Pagan perspectives, however' (Restall Orr, pc). Towards this end, HAD has some collaboration with the Public Bodies Liaison Committee for British Paganism (PBLCBP, usually known as PEBBLE), an organisation attempting to liaise between pagans and government in order to foster official recognition of pagan interests (there has been some challenge to PEBBLE's aims to represent all pagans, however, and as yet it is unclear how effective the organisation is). The aims of HAD to promote dialogue and respect have resulted most recently in collaboration with Manchester Museum (University of Manchester) and the Museums Association in a conference entitled 'Respect for Ancient British Human Remains: Philosophy and Practice' (November 2006), bringing archaeological and museum professionals and pagans further into dialogue.

Other pagans are pushing for more than respect for 'ancestors', the possibility of ritual, and dialogue on reburial. In 2004, the *Western Daily Press* (Bristol) reported that 'Druid leaders' had 'called for the creation of a sacred site at Stonehenge for the re-burial of human remains' (unearthed during the implementation of the Stonehenge Management Plan). 'They want a parcel of land near the site to be set aside as a ceremonial shrine for the Pagan and Druid communities' (*Western Daily Press*, 2 March 2004). Proposed changes to the landscape will inevitably detrimentally affect the archaeology. In 2000, when a 'cut and cover' tunnel was then proposed, initial field surveys showed that tunnelling work would be likely to damage or destroy 16 archaeological sites and that while 11 of these were already ploughed out (virtually nothing remaining), only two retained visible traces above ground, and an estimated four burials would be disturbed. Concerned about this disturbance, during discussions with English Heritage and the National Trust, Philip Shallcrass, a colleague of Restall Orr and Chief of the British Druid Order, asked a National Trust representative:

... if there was any possibility that priests used to working with the spirits of our ancestors could get access when such burials were uncovered and could make ritual for the spirits of the dead. He said that he knew re-burial was an issue in Australia and the US, but didn't know it was over here. I told him that it is a 'live' issue amongst the pagan community and was likely to become increasingly so. He expressed his personal sympathy to the idea. Inspired by this initial contact, I wrote a letter to some appropriate folk in English Heritage and the National Trust. In it, I expressed my concern that any burials found might simply end up in boxes in a museum basement. I asked for access to burials on site when they were uncovered, for permission to make ritual before burials were removed, and also whether it would be possible to re-bury the ancestral remains after a suitable period of study, preferably within the Stonehenge area. The latter seems important since our ancestors clearly didn't select their burial places at random and I felt they should be returned to the earth as close to the original grave sites as possible. Both English Heritage and the National Trust replied very promptly and favourably. The National Trust are putting my letter forward to the next meeting of the Stonehenge Archaeology Group and I'm awaiting developments. (pc)

After these favourable discussions Shallcrass attended, in March 2001, the first meeting of a liaison group consisting of representatives from the Stonehenge interest groups. He told us:

I'm hoping to see sympathetic noises translating into action and will keep plugging away until it happens. From [this involvement] and from making ritual and spirit journeys in and around the site, I've come to focus on respect and reburial as my primary reasons for being in the talks. I don't like the idea of any remains that may be uncovered during the work ending up either in a museum display or filed away in a cardboard box in a storeroom.

I have been, and will continue asking for any remains that are found to be treated with respect and then returned to the earth preferably with any accompanying grave goods and with suitable ritual as near as possible to their original burial sites. (pc)

He explicitly states that respect *and* reburial is his main reason for involvement with the Stonehenge Project. While some archaeologists, especially osteoarchaeologists, might react with outrage, and while private landowners may find themselves in a difficult position on this issue (perhaps erring on the side of being against reburial on their land), pagans have had some success in their campaigns. In *The Druid's Voice*, Shallcrass (2003) reports on the reburial of an early Saxon woman in the Woodford Valley, near Stonehenge. Following excavations by Wessex Archaeology, and a period of scientific analysis, the Home Office agreed to a reburial. The District Council's Director of Housing and Health sanctioned the burial site in the near vicinity of the original excavations, after which Wessex Archaeology (who had legal and moral responsibility over what they had excavated) reburied the woman's remains. McKinley (2003), of Wessex Archaeology, stated that 'in the rare cases of reburial which may occur it is necessary to ensure an appropriate location is used . . . and that any attendant rites and rituals followed during the reburial are appropriate to the date and probable beliefs of those being reburied as deduced from their archaeological context. In the latter, the probable beliefs of the dead are tantamount and should take precedence over those of the living who may not share the same beliefs.' Clearly, not only are calls for and negotiations over reburial in evidence, but reburial itself (though not here instigated by pagans) is now in effect, and the issue of the appropriateness of associated rites has not been neglected. The nature of the attendant rite, if any, at Woodford, is not raised by McKinley, and while Shallcrass offers an imaginative illustration of how it might have looked (FIGURE 7.1) it is not explicit whether or not this is meant to align with the 'probable beliefs' of the deceased.

Though Greywolf was unable to attend the second meeting (7 September 2001) of the Stonehenge liaison group he corresponded with other members, and was told that customarily there are different practices for burials not 'in consecrated ground' or those for which it is not evident what rites accompanied burial. He is now addressing these issues.

Such attempts at promoting respect and reburial do not stem only from pagan or new-indigenous susceptibilities: Within archaeological practice, as previously noted (in discussing emails on the Britarch list) there is an increasing tendency to demand respect from excavators for human remains, whatever their age. Student texts include codes of practice encouraging respect and reverence and debates involving the ethics of dealing with those long dead (see e.g. Parker-Pearson 1999: 199, who emphasises 'an atmosphere of respect and dignity' during excavation). More challenging and more difficult to engage with, however, are pagan voices which make authoritative claims, demanding the immediate reburial of high-profile remains. A Swansea Druid group naming themselves 'Dead to Rights' have asked for the reburial of the 'Red Lady of Paviland', a young man buried approximately 26 thousand years ago on the Gower peninsula, receiving publicity from regional BBC News (see <http://news.bbc.co.uk/1/hi/wales/south_west/

5372598.stm>). The Druid Paul Davies, cited earlier, has recently advanced his project beyond stating his opinion in Druid magazines by adopting an activist approach. In the summer of 2006, Davies made direct contact with the National Trust at Avebury and Devizes Museum

7.1   An imaginative reconstruction of the original Woodford burial, by Philip Shallcrass, 2003, previously printed in *Druid's Voice*. Copyright P. Shallcrass, reproduced here with permission.

in Wiltshire which holds much of the excavated material from the site, calling for the reburial of 'our sister' (pc), a female child excavated by Harold Grey in the early twentieth century from the southern ditch of the Henge. More recently, the Council of British Druid Orders produced a document, submitted to heritage organisations, entitled 'Guidance and Request for the Reburial of Druid Ancestral Remains at Avebury'; this was apparently shown or 'leaked' before public transmission to a pagan archaeologist, an employee of a heritage organisation, who published an online counter-response:

> I largely agree with the COBDO aims of reburial of human remains, and am not content with the current different treatment of Christian and non-Christian human remains that exists in the current laws. However, I encountered your 'Guidance and Request' while at work and had to respond as it claimed to represent my views. I, unfortunately, had to say I found it embarrassing to be associated with as I am openly pagan at work. It is badly written, and poorly argued, which largely defeats its noble objectives. . . . It was a great disappointment to see such an opportunity wasted. My reading and commenting on this document may break confidentiality, but I could not let the matter lie. I do not think such an important document, intending to set such a precedent, should be confidential.
> ('Obbyoss' 2006: <http://obbyoss.livejournal.com/869.html>)

Other pagans, knowing of our interest in this area, have contacted the Sacred Sites project through the internet to discuss the COBDO statement in similar terms. In this rebuttal, 'Obbyoss' is particularly concerned with the way in which COBDO did not consult with other Druids and Pagans in order to gauge wider opinion, before submitting their document to the heritage bodies. Pagan politics, and Druid politics particularly, are complex, so those engaging with such alternative views should expect a diversity of voices. How these voices are negotiated, however, presents a challenging problem for all others dealing in the area, including heritage and museum management and other pagans.

Negotiating the issues

The Human Remains Report (DCMS, November 2003) has met with its detractors. Views expressed include, at an extreme, those expressed online by Jenkins (2003), who points out that 'the affiliation of remains, as defined by the committee, extends 'beyond families' ties' to someone from the same 'country, culture or belief group' – in sum, anyone who might fall into the category of 'cultural descendants' (quoting from p. 7 of the report). For Jenkins, this is a serious problem, denying the claims of scientists for the study of skeletal material. Similarly, this online critique suggests that according to the report, 'Every molecule, hair and fingernail is seen as sacred until proved otherwise'. In a similar vein, some osteoarchaeologists have already noted pagan interests as a 'threat' to their research. In their 'Response to the DCMS Consultation Document "Care of Historic Human Remains"' the British Association for Biological Anthropology and Osteoarchaeology (BABAO) states:

> Guidelines for determining the legitimacy of claims on behalf of a religious community, in the absence of direct family relationship to the deceased, must address the question of how frivolous claims are to be discerned and rebutted. As one example, in the UK there are already new-Age and neo-Druid claims for the reburial of prehistoric remains, but no demonstrable continuity across the intervening millennia in terms either of genealogical descent or of recognition and care of the original burial location.
>
> (Steele n.d. 8)

Of particular interest here is the discursive construction of what is 'frivolous' (seemingly here pagan interests) and what is 'legitimate' (scientific research), with the *a priori* assumption that the former can be dismissed as wrong while the latter is common sense; indeed the issue of 'demonstrable continuity' raises, again, the concept of 'authenticity' as discussed in Chapter 1. Yet pagans, for their part, have also considered these issues: Restall Orr states:

> In terms of reburial, there is no sense of reaching for some authentic ancient rite, or even some ritual that is close to what would have been done in the past. The connection to the dead, to the ancestors, is what is important. Nor is this some special relationship with the ancient dead that Pagans claim: it is simply a religious obligation, integral to Pagan reverence for nature, for spirit, for life (past, present, future) (pc).

Archaeologists' reactions to pagan interests in reburial are themselves of interest in understanding tensions between the interest groups and how these might be addressed. After our article on pagans and reburial in the Council for British Archaeology's journal *British Archaeology* (Wallis and Blain 2004), the Curator of Archaeology at Guildford Museum replied in the letters column:

It is irritating to be told how to do one's job, by people who know little about it. . . . Careful excavation and study reveal a great deal about burial and ritual, and an understanding of what prehistoric people were doing, and why they did it. Archaeological method, by its very nature, involves respect for whatever is being dug up. It is archaeologists who discover the sites and suggest possible ritual landscapes, not 'pagans'. There is no tradition in this country that human remains should never be removed. They are far safer in museums than in the ground. By excavating human remains (only done when the site is to be destroyed) we are giving the individuals concerned a form of immortality. Who could object to that? When I am dead I will have better things to think about: whatever happens, I am happy to be dug up after a decent interval, and put in a museum.

(Alexander, 2004)

In contrast, another reader wrote:

'Pagan mysticism' may have 'no place in serious archaeology' (Letters, September) but pagans (like every other interest group) certainly have a role to play in the management of the archaeological resource. As a community heritage officer for a local authority, I work on many heritage and archaeology-related projects. There are as many outlooks, prejudices and hidden agendas as there are groups, but all are passionate about their heritage and committed to working for the benefit of the archaeology. They all have something of value to bring to the table and all deserve the common courtesy of respecting their views – even if we do not agree with them.

(Olding, 2004)

Respect, reburial and repatriation

Meanings inscribed in ancient 'sacred' sites are complex; sites have meanings for people which are spiritual, emotional, and political; and construction of meaning cannot be separated from political or pragmatic circumstances surrounding sites. Pagan claims to the past, particularly those which deploy such terms as 'ancestors' and which call for the 'reburial' of human remains and artefacts, are as much politically motivated as they are spiritually so. But archaeologists cannot claim scientific immunity here: their interpretations of the past are also constructions stemming from political, professional and scientific discursive practices. Ucko, with indigenous claims on the past in mind, suggests that a challenge for archaeologists today is to avoid being seen as the enemy by insisting 'they have the right to disturb and desecrate burial sites and to make decisions about the disposal of other people's dead' (Ucko 1990: xvi). In this light, we think it imperative that the reburial issue in Britain, voiced primarily with respect to prehistoric remains by pagans, is examined, and guidelines offered which move from the currently promoted issues of reverence to pragmatically address issues of the adjudication of respect and reburial *vis-à-vis* conservation and academic study.

Respect and dialogue are key issues, as evinced by improved relationships between curators and indigenous communities in museums. For example, on a number of occasions, most recently in October 2006 for the *Power and Taboo* exhibition of Pacific 'art', curators in the British Museum facilitated the ritual re-engagement of a London-based Maori community (Ngati Ranana) with various *taonga* – 'living treasures' (what many in the west would misleadingly and too simply term 'artefacts') – including those collected during the Cook voyages. Members of this indigenous diaspora left greenery in the display cases in order to engage respectfully in their 'traditional' way with the *taonga*, and these 'artefacts' were also used in performances during the opening of the exhibition. Similar protocols were facilitated in the same year at the Museum of Archaeology and Anthropology at the University of Cambridge (for the *Pasifika Styles* exhibition), and the Sainsbury Centre for Visual Studies at the University of Norwich (for the exhibition *Pacific Encounters*). These cases exemplify how a dialogic relationship between indigenous peoples and the current curators of such 'sacred' artefacts can be successfully established. The issue of human remains presents other problems, however. Indigenous communities may be able to (and are compelled to by, for example, Federal legislation in the United States) demonstrate genetic or cultural links to satisfy the law when calling for the reburial of ancestral human remains. Yet attempting to address the extent to which pagans can claim British prehistoric human remains are 'theirs' is to miss the point. First, the issue here is one of respect and reburial rather than repatriation. Most pagans, whatever their claims on the past, generally do not claim an exclusive relationship to 'the ancestors'. Second, the issue is whether archaeologists, heritage managers and so on are prepared to address such pluralities and engage with them dialogically, rather than dismiss them as 'fringe' and 'eccentric'. Previous chapters indicate ways in which dialogue between heritage management and new-indigenous pagans is already in action at several sites including Stanton Moor, the Rollright Stones, and most noticeably, Stonehenge. Recent pagan-heritage negotiations over the British 'reburial issue' at sites of prehistoric burial and their associated artefacts, too, suggest similar –

respectful – processes are already in effect. In the concluding chapter, we suggest 'stepping stones to common ground' which might also positively benefit pagan–heritage relations in this regard.

The Human Remains Report opened up a considerable debate, with room on all sides to explore the contested territory of what is 'sacred' and how 'science' may negotiate with the sacred. Indeed, pagans, indigenous peoples, and many British people today – including some archaeologists – indicate that 'sacredness' rather than perceived 'objective' and universally applicable scientific knowledges should be the default position. Prehistoric burials involve the deliberate placing of a 'person' (however constituted) within a landscape (also culturally constructed in some way). Today's pagans, policymakers, or archaeologists cannot know the particular interpretations of that landscape, or the person's relation to it pertaining at the time of interment of skeletal or cremated material, or even the meanings and symbolism behind the burial or of prehistoric personhoods, although theoretical speculations may be drawn. What is evident, however, is that there was, as shown by burials and mortuary practices, an intention which, from comparison with ethnographic records and indigenous accounts today, suggests a consistent 'sacred' relationship. By interrupting the association of person, land, and grave-goods, archaeologists and others are intervening in that relationship. We do not negate claims of scientific knowledge, nor do we automatically support the case for reburial put by the Druid voices expressed in this chapter. We do, however, suggest that the 'spiritual' evaluation of respect for British prehistoric remains is every bit as pressing as that for overseas indigenous claims, and we posit that science should have to make a particular case for the retention, in the private or public eye, of such material. In the Church of England report, attention is drawn to current and past Christian theology regarding remains, with the implication that where the specific wishes of the deceased are not known but remains are found in Christian consecrated ground, current Christian concepts should be part of decisions surrounding the remains. By analogy, where pre-Christian remains are found, it would seem appropriate to consider theologies and understandings of person and landscape that stem from polytheist and indigenous thinking, including the understandings of current British pagan traditions. The HAD website describes negotiations relating to production of the current *Draft Code of Practice for The Care of Human Remains in Museums* (DCMS 2005), where such differences in understanding were discussed, and comments:

> During a meeting between HAD and the Drafting Group, the Chair expressed a lack of understanding as how or why bones or other remains retained their significance even when the

'spirit left the body'. It was only when the non-dualistic world view of many animists and other Pagans was explained, together with notions of tribal song and the webs of land and ancestry, that he grasped the relevance, validity and importance not only of British Pagan sensitivities but those of Pagan traditions around the world . . .

<http://www.honour.org.uk/projects/care-museums.html>

While one would hesitate to claim that pagan theologies in today's Britain were all similar, or that any group of pagans today could speak authoritatively for past understandings, the point here is that many pagans are explicitly trying to move away from binary dualisms in their theologies and in their spiritual practices, so that a consideration of today's pagan philosophies (as many, not as one) can inform understandings of past and hence practices of respect which relate to these 'ancestors'. On this note it is important to state that HAD, in producing a draft 'rite of committal of human remains' (<http://www. honour.org.uk/articles/reburial_rite.html>) for potential use by museum personnel or others, is taking pains to specify how much is 'not known' of either the persons committed or their theology and ritual.

The position advocated by the Sacred Sites project is that a default assumption of 'sacredness' be applied and that, under most circumstances, after a suitable period of study, reburial as close as possible to the original association of person/artefact and land be encouraged, conducted with respect for the possible beliefs of the group who initially interred the person or persons concerned. Recent reburials conducted by the Church of England have occasioned pagan protests because of extreme differences in philosophy (referred to above) between most Christian and most indigenous perspectives on landscape. While a formal 'pagan ritual' of the types most commonly found today would likewise be inappropriate, a respectful statement of returning the person to its original relation to the landscape, whether conducted by pagans or archaeologists, would seem more fitting. Reburial cannot occur in every circumstance (and most remains are excavated today under 'rescue' conditions), but the same deliberations and weighing of theological, ethical and practical considerations should occur with pre-Christian burials or remains as with Christian interments. With regard to museum material, again reburial may not always be possible as the context of interment has been changed, either by roadbuilding or by past 'restorations' such as at West Kennet Long Barrow. If bones found there were collected and replaced (some were of course destroyed), what should happen to the monument? Currently visitors go past the great blocking slabs and into the chambers of the tomb. Replacing remains is not beyond the realms of possibility, together with removal of the concrete and the roof window, and re-sealing the tomb, and we have heard pagans advocate this course of action. But for other pagans the monument is currently a 'temple' where they make ritual, for instance taking advantage of the interesting acoustic properties of the (reconstructed) chambers, or a place of ancestors where they engage with shamanic journeying or 'vision quests'. In the extended period in which the barrow was in use it was not sealed, and there are indications of ritual having taken place within it and in the forecourt of the tomb – what is possible in today's climate of opinion? These are hugely complex issues and refer back to the differences in practices and sensibilities between Neolithic and modern periods, as previously discussed.

7.2   The chambered cairn at Nether Largie South is the oldest in the Kilmartin 'linear cemetery' and is where many pagans attempt to meet deities or local or ancestral spirits. Should places such as this – now a ritual site – be infilled to cover returned remains?

We commend the report on Human Remains, and anticipate seeing similar recommendations for indigenous British material in the near future. The concept of repatriation, however, deserves a further mention. In general, this has been taken as meaning the return of remains and artefacts when requests are made by cultural groups or nations outside Britain. However, there is considerable feeling about the centralised collections, at (for instance) the Museum of London, the British Museum and the Museum of Scotland, where regional or 'tribal' material has been taken out of context (for instance, the distribution of the Lewis Chess Pieces between the British Museum and Edinburgh). This topic, though, goes beyond the scope of the present volume.

CHAPTER 8

Towards a Conclusion: Strategies for Dialogic Interaction and Future Directions

Any final discussion of 'sacred sites' must return to issues of how 'sacredness' is constituted within discourse and in the interplay of humans and landscape, within time as within place. Meanings and interpretations change, as do the landscapes themselves, through erosion, farming and other land management, quarrying, landscaping or development. People change landscape. Landscape, in turn, affects those who work within or upon it. Animist pagan theologies are moving towards understandings of landscape as 'living', as changing those who live and work or make ritual within an environment, in short seeing landscape and all its components as having *agency*.

The rise of landscape archaeology (e.g. Bender 1992; Thomas 1993; Bradley 2000; Tilley 2004) would seem to give scope to some of these understandings, and indeed draws on indigenous theorising to assist in interpreting how past peoples moved within place, and how sacredness may be expressed in particular locations and drawn on by people in shaping their monuments or depositing their offerings. (See Bradley's [e.g. 2000] discussion of 'Cumbrian axes' or Thomas' [e.g. 1999] phenomenological analysis of the deliberate structuring of Neolithic monuments.) While specular interpretations are still privileged on the level of narration for 'visitors', archaeologists are addressing issues such as how sacredness informs all aspects of life, not only 'ritual' (see e.g. Hill 1995; Bradley 2005). There is considerable scope here for dialogue: but it requires all 'sides' in the issues addressed in this book to give up ideas of a single 'truth' – as expressed also by Edmonds and Seaborne in the epigraph which opened Chapter 4.

All approaches to sites – from the extreme hard-line preservationist angle of some site managers, to complex theorisings of landscape archaeology, to campaigning for access or campaigning for conservation, to the hands-on engagements of some pagans and even to the few instances of deliberate, and many more of non-deliberate vandalism – arise from *situated knowledges*, understandings derived discursively from social and theoretical location through specific structures of power; in turn, the approaches re-create or modify these knowledges and power structures. In short, they 'impose a context' which is social and political as well as geographic. Examples in this book, from across the spectrum of approaches, have emphasised the variety of engagements with the past, the plurality of voices and the diversity of the issues raised by these. To state that issues affecting sites are site-specific, with needs for management according to situated pragmatism,[1] might be to state the obvious. But this is especially important in the case of pagan interests, since there is such a diversity of paganisms and often their engagements with sites are very much site-specific. Furthermore, the situation and history of events at each site have implications for all sites and it is clear from the Sacred Sites project study that pagan activity will increasingly affect how sites are managed.

It is vital that the term 'sacred' continues to be theorised, contested and negotiated, so that a single meaning is not 'set in stone'. Pagans are, of course, only one issue on the heritage agenda, and we are not suggesting that they should be privileged over other interest groups. At the very least, it is timely that heritage managers are now taking pagan interests seriously and in many cases approaching them sensitively. The Rollright Stones marks an example of these points in action; but other examples discussed, be they Stonehenge or Seahenge, indicate there is some way to go before heritage managers, archaeologists and others with direct influence in how sites are managed and represented are prepared to debate these issues. Still other examples point to different alignments and negotiation over quarrying or development issues. To move forward, it is vital that the interest groups continue to meet and negotiate, developing ways of understanding each others' perspectives and reaching pragmatic solutions.

'Stepping stones to common ground'

Improving relations between indigenous communities and heritage managers elsewhere, particularly in North America, provide an example from which to imagine communication, negotiation and reciprocal empowerment between pagans and site custodians in the United Kingdom. We are not making inflated attempts here to resolve complex, sensitive political tensions, but we are venturing some practical guidelines. We are not comparing archaeologists in the United States or Canada with those in Britain, nor are we making a direct comparison between the perspectives of pagans as new-indigenes with Native North American struggles for self-determination and the repatriation of human remains and artefacts. There are of course huge differences. But, the territory of their 'common ground' may have something to tell us about how to avoid such problematic, protracted situations as at Stonehenge, or this exaggerated in the shorter-term as with the Seahenge fiasco. Simply put, we might consider five 'stepping stones to common ground' (see Swidler et al. 1997) and we applaud those attempts already in existence towards such rapprochement.

1 We must take each other seriously, and deconstruct stereotypes, by
2 embarking on productive, collaborative dialogues, involving
3 research ethics and rights, as well as
4 joint stewardship programmes, and
5 informed consent protocols.

Taking each other seriously, tolerantly, and deconstructing negative stereotypes

In the past, pagan views have tended to be dismissed as fringe, eccentric, inauthentic or harmless. This was made obvious in the *Time Team* programme on Seahenge, in which archaeologists and pagans (mainly druids) almost literally came to blows. Following this broadcast (29 December 1999), comments on the BritArch (British Archaeology) email discussion list were as follows:

> 'these people are not druids, nor are they the remnants of any aboriginal populations of this country any more than we are'

> 'the druids know nothing of druidism'

> 'it seems strange that a bunch of potheads can be taken quite so seriously'

> 'modern druids have as much to with Iron Age Druids as the Wombles'

It is easy to laugh – and of course all self-respecting archaeologists and pagans require a healthy sense of humour – but the significant issue that emerges is one of intolerance. Yet, the voices of some archaeologists expressed views similar to those of some Druids (as shown in Chapter 1). Discussion in this volume has indicated that as an increasing voice and pressure group, pagans can no longer be viewed as fringe. While Druidry might be seen as eccentric in the best of British eccentricity, its practices, and those of other paganisms, are by no means inauthentic – authenticity is born from working practice and newly established 'tradition', as well as an emergent maturity which eschews perceived 'unbroken tradition' in favour of contemporary relevance. Nor are pagans 'harmless' though indeed some (specifically Wiccans) hold to a principle of 'an it harm none'; engagements with sites have been problematic in terms of fire damage, ritual litter, and so on.[2] More generally, pagans occupying a wide variety of roles in today's society are capable, as individuals or through organisations, of lobbying for causes and engaging with public policy, in addition to the campaigns indicated in this book. In order to address such issues, it is imperative that site custodians take pagans seriously and engage with them sensitively. Such tolerance and a commitment to deconstructing negative stereotypes (pagans as Satanists, travellers as a nuisance, etc.) of course must work both ways. It is therefore incumbent upon pagans and associated alternative interest groups to similarly be tolerant, revising such stereotypes as archaeologists as 'grave-robbers' and heritage personnel as atheistic bureaucrats. Simply voicing marginalisation, as has been the case, can mistakenly provide the comforting solidarity of an us-and-them situation which obviates the need for a real dialogue.

To those opining on the Britarch list quoted above, Druidry is inauthentic, an invented religion, and nothing like 'real' Iron Age Druidry. In developing tolerance, it is worth noting that archaeology and Druidry are not so distant. Both share their origins in the Archdruid 'Chyndonax' for instance; that is, the eighteenth-century antiquarian William Stukeley. Furthermore, as Hutton suggests, 'Modern Druidry has a recorded history of over two hundred years. By contrast, the discipline of scientific archaeology...[has] been in existence for only about a century' (Hutton 1996: 17). By engaging with pagans and coming to understand their alternative histories, archaeologists and heritage personnel may move toward developing ways of transforming populist stereotypes and looking towards common ground.

Productive collaborative dialogues

To be productive, collaborative dialogues should look towards mutual benefit and understanding. The events at Avebury, Stonehenge, and other monuments, demonstrably require archaeologists to engage in dialogue with pagans. Pagans need, similarly, to be prepared to engage in this dialogue. Negotiation implies listening and compromise, and some will refuse to compromise; but at least attempts at dialogue are a step in a useful direction. This is the sort of negotiation we see in action in some instances at Stonehenge and Avebury, and more consistently at the Rollright Stones; and now emerging at Thornborough with the inclusion of pagan voices on the Thornborough Henges Advisory Group. An issue in some of these instances, however, is that consultation and dialogue are grounded in discourse: and *whose* discourse forms the basis of dialogue both stems from and constitutes relationships of power. If heritage personnel want to understand the basis of pagan engagement with sacredness and place, then at least some negotiation will be required to adopt discourses that can convey these engagements. This has happened elsewhere, where there are indigenous interpretations to be articulated within contested landscapes.

It is very necessary, here, to acknowledge the diversity of paganisms. While 'leaders' do exist, they are specific to different traditions or paths. Pagans do not speak with one voice, no more so than archaeologists. While the media may focus on the more colourful pagan characters – 'media tarts' as some pagans call them – it is vital that dialogue between heritage management and pagans includes strategies which engage with a multiplicity of voices rather than those who simply shout the loudest. We see the Round Table forum at Stonehenge as a forward-looking if not always successful example of this in action.

Research ethics and rights

'Who owns the past?' is a question which has been raised, now, many times. This book has given many examples in which ownership claims are made, implicitly or explicitly, by heritage personnel, archaeologists, pagans, local people, landowners and local councils, and indeed the All Party Parliamentary Archaeology Group; some being more willing to negotiate their claims than others. These are issues about where decisions are made and whose interpretations are valid. As the 'repatriation issue' and indeed the emerging reburial issue in Britain shows, archaeologists and other professional custodians of the past do not have exclusive rights to that past. Nor can any single group – archaeologists or pagans – be privileged over another. At sacred sites pagan interpretations of the past have been neglected in favour of the official, heritage discourse: indeed 20th century discourses of rationalism made this inevitable. But the example of literature available at the Rollright Stones, as well as pagan-friendly events, indicates how alternative views can be accommodated and indeed represented alongside more conventional discourse. Issues here include those of voice, appropriation, and interpretation, and of stewardship and consent – discussed below.

Joint stewardship programmes

The previous National Trust Guardianship Scheme at Avebury discussed in Chapter 2 marks an official example of how heritage bodies and pagans can join forces in joint stewardship. Local and visiting pagans watched over various sites during pagan festivals, tidied up afterwards, and generally kept a watchful eye. Pagan volunteers also helped to dissuade visitors from climbing Silbury Hill at festival times after the emergence of Silbury Hole. Although the current 'Avebury Guardians' initiative has yet to prove itself, this sort of co-operation between managers and alternative interest groups can reap many benefits. While some of the negotiations around Stonehenge solstices can be acrimonious (and power is not equal), pagan members of the Round Table participate very actively at managed access events by acting and recruiting others as Peace Stewards, providing information to a broad-based community, and assisting in leading other celebrants out of the field at 'closing time'. Meanwhile, in an unofficial capacity, many pagans act as site stewards of their local sacred sites. We would like to see more official recognition of this important work, and greater collaboration between heritage managers and pagans. At the Rollright Stones, this sort of joint stewardship is manifest in the composition of the Trustees of the Rollright Trust which includes heritage managers and pagans among other interest groups. It may extend, there and elsewhere (including we hope Thornborough), to the sharing of interpretation and perspective about sites to indicate to others how and why these are sacred, and hence how they may be treated with respect.

There is another issue with respect to stewardship: pagans have emerged as campaigners at threatened sites, whether in association with local people or management personnel, or through separate initiatives. The plurality of voices here adds immeasurably to the knowledge and appreciation of sacred landscapes, as more people are debating sacredness and site, and in more forums. Furthermore, on occasion there are things that can only be done by those outside of officialdom, active protest being one of these.

Informed consent protocols

At Seahenge, English Heritage made the decision to damage the fragile timbers with a chainsaw (in order to date the site) without inquiring as to the views of interested parties outside heritage management. As a result, local people, pagans and a wider public, including some archaeologists, responded angrily. Subsequent excavation of the site also began with little consultation, especially with local people. An emotionally charged situation could have been alleviated, although not entirely averted, if dialogue had been established from the start. The suggestion here is not that archaeologists should have asked 'permission' from pagans (and others) before excavating; indeed, pagans are not the only issue here. The point is that a reflexive, community-orientated archaeology evident elsewhere (e.g. the Community Archaeology Project at Quseir al-Qadim in Egypt, conducted by Southampton University's Department of Archaeology) indicates how dialogue and informed consent can lead to a more reciprocal result. At Stanton Moor, attempts by archaeologists to provide maximum information, though meeting with some suspicion, led on balance to greater understanding of situations pertaining to the site and the issues involved even in their small excavation. And where excavation results from 'rescue archaeology', as at Thornborough, we see it imperative that local people, pagans, and all interested others have access to reasons, and true participation in the processes of consultation and inquiry which may lead to the need for that excavation.

All in all, this volume is intended to raise issues of listening, of the sharing of knowledges, of discourses and decisions, and of respect.

Future directions

This volume has offered a detailed, critically engaged discussion of contemporary pagan engagements with the past, and also with the future, of some landscapes. Discussion is by no means comprehensive or exhaustive: paganisms are growing steadily, and sacred places of the British Isles are many. There is scope for substantial further investigation in a variety of areas. The Sacred Sites, Contested Rites/Rights project has conducted sustained research at certain sites focussing on England, with brief excursions to other parts of Britain and northwest Europe. Monitoring and interpretation even at the sites explored here is not complete, especially as issues regarding management develop over time and pagan involvements increase. The protracted history of the Stonehenge Management Plan and its implementation in coming years indicates how our research marks only a first step. The issues of anti-quarry campaigns and the emergent understandings of sacredness in threatened landscapes beg research, in a climate where both sites and spiritualities are contested.

Future research should certainly involve fieldwork where our project has yet to provide more than cursory analysis: such research fits well within developments in the history and sociology of 'new-indigenous' spiritualities, analyses of alternative histories and archaeologies, and the representation of the past in the present. In the archaeology-rich southwest of England a paganism specific to local identities in Kernow (Cornwall) is emerging, and long-term projects focused on Scotland and Wales, as well as Ireland, are also begging. In this volume our only excursion outside England related briefly to attempts to claim 'Celtic' identities at Kilmartin: we look however to the links now being forged between people and place, where local folklore and mythology are drawn upon by practitioners working with local and national histories and archaeologies. There is much scope for similar projects elsewhere in Europe,[3] possibly in Northern France, Scandinavia and Germany. Wherever paganisms are emerging and gaining coherence in the Western world, there are sacred sites for them to engage with, with significant ramifications for the heritage industry.

We look forward, therefore, to seeing the trans-disciplinary research areas of pagan studies and heritage studies turning their attentions to pagan engagements with sacred sites, as well as to this burgeoning issue being officially recognised as such not only by the implicated interest groups, but also by funding bodies that can move this first step in research, into its next phase. We sincerely hope that this volume becomes a stepping stone of its own, towards such a development.

Notes

Preface and Introduction

1   We have chosen to capitalise the various pagan paths and their practitioners
    (e.g. Druidry and Druid, Heathenry and Heathen) since this is nomenclature
    that pagans use to identify themselves (much as a Christian or Moslem would
    do). This use also helps distinguish between contemporary Druids, for
    example, and ancient 'druids'. We use 'pagan' and 'paganism' in lower case to
    indicate a generic term, the meaning of which is contested by different
    pagans. We also capitalise 'Pagan' and 'Paganism' in instances where the
    pagans in question identify their path as specifically 'Pagan' rather than
    Druid, Wiccan, etc. Where we discuss ancient paganism, we qualify the
    distinction in the text (e.g. using 'ancient paganism' rather than 'paganism',
    but avoid the term 'neo-pagan' (mostly a US usage) in order to avoid devalu-
    ing contemporary practice: the ancient and contemporary forms are not the
    same but the latter is not inauthentic as 'neo-' might imply.
2   Bender engages in 'Dialogues' with a variety of interviewees, but that entitled
    'The Dialogue that Never Happened' between Bender and an English Heritage
    representative is 'a one-sided conversation. . . . This dialogue is my invention'
    (Bender 1998: 174), because English Heritage refused to engage in such an
    interview on the politics of access to Stonehenge.
3   The separation of 'pagan' and 'new age' in the developing Pagan Studies may
    indicate the distaste of pagans for being subsumed into a category 'new age'
    which they consider bears little relation to themselves, their worldviews or
    practices. York (2005), however, in discussing permeability between 'pagan'
    and 'new age', has proposed a reversal of the common sociological usage, by
    considering 'new age' to be a sub-group within a larger category of 'pagan'.
4   We concur with Harvey's recent theorising of animism and shamanism, in
    which animism is the 'religion' (or rather religious framework or worldview)
    within which 'shamans' work, engaging with other-than-human people in
    order to maintain (or restore) harmony. For full discussion of the new
    animism see Harvey (2005). Many pagans use the term 'shaman' or
    'shamanic' in multifarious ways. Some Druids term themselves 'Druid
    Shamans' because they associate their 'spirit helpers' and use of 'altered
    consciousness' with what they perceive as 'shamanic'. Other practitioners,
    such as Gordon 'the toad' MacLellan, see the term as honorific and are termed
    'Shaman' by their community rather than adopting the title personally. Just
    as there are similarities and differences between ancient paganism and
    contemporary paganisms, so there are such regarding indigenous and modern
    western shamans. Issues of authenticity aside (examined elsewhere in this
    volume), it is the discourse that is of interest to us here.
5   Pagans are not Satanists, tending to distance themselves from people who
    claim to be Satanists as well as those of the Abrahamic religions, even if their

own upbringing has been monotheistic. During the spate of ritual abuse accusations which implicated pagans in the 1990s, most cases were dissolved in the courts.

6 The dating of rock art, particularly rock engravings, is in its infancy. The cup-and-ring art of Britain is conventionally dated according to its association with Neolithic and Bronze Age features, such as stone circles and chambered tombs which are more securely dated, as well as archaeological data excavated directly juxtaposed to panels of rock art (see e.g. Bradley 1997).

1 'Sacred Sites'? Paganisms, Representation and Imaginings of the Past

1 A famous example is the 'dialogue' instituted between archaeologist Ian Hodder and Anita Louise, a leading member of the Goddess movement: see the Chatalhöyük excavation webpages at <http://www.catalhoyuk.com/> and a view from the Goddess community at <http://www.awakenedwoman. com/goddess_in_Anatolia.htm>. For discussion of these issues see Rountree (2003a).

2 We have seen, for instance, a group leaving the Castlerigg stone circle in some dissension, having apparently realised that their attempted 'sacred fire' – made of self-igniting charcoal in a tin receptacle that resembled a baby bath – had caused very noticeable scorching to grass and earth in the centre of the circle and at its entrance. Concerned onlookers included a women's tour from Glasgow, who asked Blain, 'Should they be doing that?' and expressed dismay that people would be so naive as to think that a fire made in a thin metal receptacle would not cause damage.

3 Many Druids chant the 'Awen' during their ceremonies. One description of its meaning, though not necessarily definitive, is by Shallcrass (2000: 48): 'a feminine noun variously translated as 'muse', 'genius', 'inspiration', 'poetic furore', and 'poetic frenzy'. It is made up of two words: 'aw' meaning 'flowing', and 'en' meaning 'spirit'. So, literally, Awen is the 'flowing spirit'.

2 Avebury

1 Arguably, people of the Mesolithic must have had their own impact on the landscape, but there is very little evidence (and none to date for Upper Palaeolithic use). At Avebury, there are few examples of flint scatters from the Mesolithic, although nearby Cherhill registers more presence over time, which Whittle (1990) considers may reflect seasonal or transient exploitation. Such early use of the area is summarised by Pollard and Reynolds (2002) who point out the need for caution in assuming that because few tools or sites have been found the area, it held little importance, saying 'As a landscape it was not necessarily empty of significance. There is plentiful ethnographic evidence to show how hunter-gatherer communities invest landscapes with symbolic, mythical and narrative meanings' (p. 25). This is a caution that we bear in mind, and an analogy that we attempt to reflect in our work on the *Sacred Sites* project.

2 The division of the past into the discrete 'ages' of Stone, Bronze and Iron was devised by Christian Jürgensen Thomsen to organize Danish museum collections of archaeological finds. This was sub-divided further by the Swedish archaeologist Oscar Montelius and there have been further elaborations since. Useful as this 'seriation' method might be, it is discursively constructed based in ideas of technological 'progress': at the very least it is problematic to approach ancient people based simply on the materials from which they made their tools.

3 Singing a Rune-row refers to the runes of one of the Futharks, usually the Common Germanic Futhark, sung or chanted in order, and used by today's Heathens to focus energies in various ways. See Elliott (1987) for more on Runes and Futharks.

4 The sunrise can be seen twice, by moving down from the summit to the 'step' in the hill, an experience accentuated by the similarity in form of the horizon formed first by Waden Hill (seen from the step) and then the Ridgeway (seen from the summit). Once the double sunrise has happened, turning 180 degrees, it is possible to see a golden 'shadow' of light on the field below. This 'Silbury Glory' is caused by the refraction of sunlight in dew drops, and it is magnified and focused by one's own shadow when standing on the summit.

5 Phrases used to describe the documentary, on an email list discussing approaches to megaliths, include 'a spin document' and 'a con'.

6 This was certainly the case at 'Seahenge' (as indicated in Chapter 1).

3 Stonehenge

1 Stonehenge is also an iconic image worldwide, and is one of twenty-one finalists to be one of the 'New Seven Wonders of the World' (Ross 2006; <http://www.new7wonders.com/index.php?id=398&L=0>).

2 The Maori marae (wooden meeting house) named Hinemihi, located at Clandon Park (Surrey, England), provides one example of why this might be appropriate, albeit with an ethnographic analogy we have insufficient space to do adequate justice here. After sheltering members of a Maori community during a volcanic eruption in Aotearoa New Zealand, Hinemihi was brought to Clandon (now a National Trust property) and this act 'preserved' the site for use today (e.g. Gallop 1998): more than a National Trust 'artefact', Hinemihi is now used for traditional events by the Pacific diaspora in London, specifically the London Maori Club Ngati Ranana. The Maori understanding of Hinemihi might be interpreted as animistic: Hinemihi is a female ancestor, a living other-than-human person. Interestingly, recent pagan relations with members of Ngati Ranana have facilitated exchanges in discourse as well as discussions of common ground.

3 The terms 'drug', 'visionary plant', 'psychedelic', and 'hallucinogen' are value-laden and often too generalist or too specific: *drug* is vague and retains negative associations, *visionary plant* excludes a number of naturally occurring and synthesized substances and also unhelpfully privileges vision over other senses; *psychedelic* refers also to a specific, contentious era, and *hallucinogen* inevitably has connotations of mental aberration (illness) as does *psychoactive* in the prefix *psycho-*. 'Entheogen' (see, for example, Forte 1997, see also the

Council on Spiritual Practices: <http://www.csp.org>) less pejoratively describes substances with consciousness altering properties. Etymologically, *entheogen* derives from Greek *entheos*, 'possessed by a god' (which is related to the modern English *giddy* and Old English *gidig*, "possessed by a god/spirit") and *genous* "produced." Hence *entheogen* is literally 'generate god or spirit within'. While the term is increasingly accepted, it risks presuming a neuropsychological bias and monotheistic ontology, when in many indigenous contexts these substances are significant as other-than-human persons and for their purgative properties rather than for their active (visionary producing) chemical constituents (see Harvey and Wallis 2007).

4   See Worthington (2005) for accounts of the Beanfield; also NCCL 1986 report.
5   We have, however, seen an attempt to scale sarsens being shouted down by the crowd, with a celebrant next to one of us shouting loudly, 'get doon, ye fuil, ye'll *damage the lichens*'.
6   For 2007, the Glastonbury Festival is scheduled for the weekend of 22–24 June, and managed open access at Stonehenge for the night of 20–21 June, leaving one day between the events.
7   Lindauer (2006) contrasts the 'critical museum visitor' who unpacks the discourse of representation in collection displays, with the 'average' or 'ideal' visitor who is aimed at implicitly by the museum and addressed implicitly in the majority of such displays but is rarely identified explicitly. A similar contrast can be made in the instance of the Stonehenge 'visitor'.
8   Full details of this history are available online at <http://www.britarch. ac.uk/stonehenge/>.
9   Baxter and Chippindale 2002 state:

> Present plans for improving Stonehenge pursue an expensive solution with a new visitor centre in a greenfield development remote from the site.
>   Instead of a brief visit from an adjacent car-park with cramped visitor provisions, visitors will spend much longer in learning about the Stonehenge landscape and the inconspicuous but archaeologically important elements to it. One compelling benefit of that scheme, the promise that visitors would once more be able to walk freely amongst the Stones, has recently been cancelled. (p.1)

This information, apparently within the 2001 English Heritage publication, *The Stonehenge Project: Access to the Stonehenge Landscape*, comes from Chippindale's reading of the report, conveyed to us by Ian Baxter, to whom we are indebted for this information. And indeed current text of a FAQ on the Stonehenge Project Website reads:

> Will I be able to go into the Stone Circle?

> Access inside the stone circle has been stopped since 1978 because of erosion, vandalism and increased visitor numbers. However, it is possible to book private access outside opening hours. In the future, these arrangements will remain.
> <http://www.thestonehengeproject.org/news/faq7.shtml>

Baxter and Chippendale have endeavoured to promote a 'brownfield site' at the Stones themselves, pointing out that, despite ideas from landscape archaeology, what visitors (of all kinds) chiefly want to do is approach closely to and touch the stones.

10 Suggestions for a Grand Eisteddfod, initially mooted by Tim Sebastion in 2002, seem now to be bearing some fruit, according to minutes of Round Table negotiations (see e.g. <http://stonehenge.mercurymoon.co.uk/> for recent minutes). However this event, while around the time of the solstice, would be seen as 'separate', and will not occur until at least 2008. We look forward to this development.

11 For example, the theme of the Association of Polytheist Traditions conference (University of Central Lancashire, May 2006) on Polytheism and Animism.

4 Derbyshire and Yorkshire: Stanton Moor and Thornborough Henges

1 This is an 'older' version of the website. A more recent location was eventually abandoned by the protestors after it was, according to them, repeatedly 'hacked into' by persons unknown.

2 A pentacle is a five-pointed star much-used in ritual magic and adopted as a symbol of paganism by many, especially Wiccans.

3 We do not wish here to reduce the focus in this chapter on Stanton Moor itself. Dol Tor, however, to the west and across a road, accessed through farmland, is clearly a ritual centre for one or more groups today with items found after every seasonal celebration – see Figure 0.2, p. 10. Several years ago its stones were moved by, apparently, people who had decided through dowsing that they knew where the stones 'should' be. It has since been restored by archaeologists (Barnatt 1997). Similar events occurred at a circle closer to Sheffield, Barbrook II, which has also been restored and now presents a clear example of what some other Peak District embanked circles may have been like, although its moorland landscape will have changed considerably since the early Bronze Age. Doll Tor has suffered other fates – during excavation in 1931 archaeologists were startled when two of its stones were seriously damaged, apparently with a sledgehammer, overnight, and required reconstructing with concrete (Barnatt 1978).

5 Spirits of Moor and Glen: Pagans and Rock Art Sites in Britain

1 In this book we do not have space or scope to discuss the hotly-contested word 'Shamanism', which however bears considerable relation to our work both within academia (Wallis 1998, 1999a,b, 2003; Blain 2000, 2002, 2005; Blain and Wallis 2000, 2006a; Harvey and Wallis 2007) and as practitioners. The term is generally considered to come from an Evenki term for a specific practitioner, becoming generalised as a category for the West (see e.g. Flaherty 1992) and its application outside a Siberian, or indeed an Evenki context is today disputed. However it was adopted by Eliade (1964) and others as descriptive of a range of practices, and has made its way into popular discouse, as into ethnographic description.

Western Shamanic practice takes many forms, but the idea of shamanism as altered consciousness ritual work performed for or on behalf of a community, with transformatory effect, is inherent in some descriptions notably those of Maclellan (e.g. 1995, 1998; also Harvey 1998). 'Traditional' shamanism is not convenient or 'safe' practice; there are dangers to be faced and it is often hard to persuade potential shamans to take on a 'shaman' role (see e.g. Jakobsen 1999). Criticisms of some Western shamanistic practices are that these are 'safe' or 'fluffy' (examples of critiques include those of Jones 1998 and of many 'shamanic' pagans of our acquaintance). Issues of appropriation have been discussed by many (e.g. Johnson 1995; see also issues of 'indigeneity' in chapter 7) and the tendency is to see Western shamanisms as appropriating indigenous practices elsewhere. The discussion of 'Celtic' shamanism in the present chapter, however, indicates a thin line between reinvention of 'ancestral' practices and appropriation of history and culture within a specifically Scottish (or other) context.

2   See footnote to Chapter 3, and entry in Harvey and Wallis 2007 for our preference in using entheogen rather than 'hallucinogen' or other non-practitioner terms here and elsewhere in this chapter. Many shamanic practitioners do make use of entheogens. And some would however consider the 'power smoke' referred to by Naddair as entheogenic, treating constituents such as the native herbs mugwort or plantain as having their own plant spirits (indexed and addressed by the Old English *Nine Herbs Charm* [Pollington 2000; Blain and Wallis 2004b]) and able to engage with the practitioner to create or inform experiences of altered consciousness.

3   Let us be quite clear that we are in no sense denying Scottish identities or nationhood. What we find problematic is the romanticising of a single and simplistic identity (the persecuted but mysterious Scot with unchanging attributes or gifts from the past – another sort of 'noble savage') which to us not only appears ahistorical but also downplays understandings of regional variation within Scotland, and of Scottish importance and achievement within Europe and beyond.

4   The concept of all rock art in Scotland being 'Pictish' is one we have met with elsewhere, from visitors describing, for instance, the engravings in caves at Wemyss bay. These do include art dated to the fourth century C.E. and showing Pictish symbols, but there are also cupmarks which are very considerably older, and material from the middle ages and up to the present day. While Scotland's heritage most certainly includes 'Pictish' material it is not restricted to this.

5   The emergence of a practitioner-based 'Celtic shamanism' from the early 1990s can be chronicled by the publications and workshops of John and Caitlin Matthews (e.g. John Matthews 1991a,b,c; Caitlin Matthews 1995) in particular, as well as publications by Shallcrass (1995, 1997, 1998, 2000) and others. For critical discussion of Celtic shamanism in the context of contemporary Paganism see Wallis 2003. Specifically Scottish shamanisms are being developed independently by a number of practitioners, for example Geo Cameron or Trevarthen (see <http://www.celticshamanism.com/>), or the seidworker Malcolm who informed part of the work we have done on Heathen shamanic practice (Blain and Wallis 2000; Blain 2002; Wallis 2003).

6   Contrast with many indigenous shamanisms which are embedded in commu-

nity life, as well as accounts of the reclamation of various shamanic practices in Siberia (e.g. Fridman 1999) – or even some other forms of reclaimed western shamanic practice (Blain 2002; Wallis 2003).

7 Cowan teaches 'Celtic Faery Doctoring' as an 'indigenous shamanism' for the US-based Foundation of Shamanic Studies.

6   The Rollright Stones and the Rollright Trust

1 'It was the wrong witch, the wrong date and the wrong village', says Burl (2000, p. 25) of the attempt to associate 'Rollo the Dane' with the known Mother Shipton (1488-1561) of Yorkshire's Knaresborough – who might be much better linked, in this volume, with Thornborough Henges or Ilkley Moor! But it makes a good story, and has been retold and embellished at least since Camden's time . . .

2 For further information about the anomalies found by the Dragon Project at the Rollrights see *Circles of Silence* (Robins 1985).

3 Hooper-Greenhill (2000) theorises museum pedagogy and makes a distinction between the exclusivist teacher–pupil transmission-of-knowledge stance of the modernist museum and the relational, dialogic and multivocal interpretative approach of the postmodernist museum. The Rollrights management situation is exemplary of the latter.

7   Reburial, Museums, Pagans and Respect

1 From a Call for Contributions, Working Group on Human Remains, on the email list Britarch, 14 September 2001.

2 A session at the European Association of Archaeologists (EAA) meeting in 1999 (Ethics and the excavation and treatment of human remains: A European perspective) discussed the European reburial issue. Unsurprisingly, the 'alternative' voices of Pagans and others with spiritual concerns over the past were not discussed because the session organisers either hadn't heard of such concerns, or if they had, they were not seen as a serious issue for archaeology. A paper by Wallis did raise this issue, but in a different session, 'The archaeology of shamanism' (published as Wallis 2001), with specific reference to Britain.

3 See Chapter 5 and Blain (2001) for a deconstruction of this particular claim based on 'celtic' ancestry; also Wallis (2003: 146–8, 188).

4 And let us remember that while many pagans are urban, there are those who work on the rural landscape, including those who farm or are engaged with tourism or ecological management.

8   Towards a Conclusion: Strategies for Dialogic Interaction and Future Directions

1 Here we borrow Marilyn Strathern's term 'situational pragmatism' (Strathern 1998: 217).

2 'Not my little tealight!' said a celebrant at West Kennet Long Barrow, when a

pagan friend of the authors attempted to point out to her that the heat from her lit candle was contributing to sooting and potential cracking of an ortho-stat.

3   We think here on the work of Alves (2001) relating local historical and spiri-tual meanings in rock-art: she was not dealing with pagans, but certainly with local land-based spiritualities.

Bibliography

Alexander, M. 2004. Letter. *British Archaeology* 79, November 2004. Available online: <http://www.britarch.ac.uk/ba/ba79/letters.shtml>.

Alves, L. B. 2001. Rock art and enchanted moors: the significance of rock carvings in the folklore of north-west Iberia. In R. J. Wallis and K. J. Lymer (eds) *A Permeability of Boundaries? New Approaches to the Archaeology of Art, Religion and Folklore*, 71–8. BAR International Series 936. Oxford. British Archaeological Reports.

Alvesson, M. and K. Sköldberg 2000. *Reflexive Methodology: New Vistas for Qualitative Research*. London: Sage.

Antiquity 1996. Reports: The Future of Avebury, Again. *Antiquity* 70: 501–2.

APPAG (All-Party Parliamentary Archaeology Group) 2003. *The Current State of Archaeology in the United Kingdom*. Sevenoaks: The Caxton & Holmsdale Press Ltd.

Asphodel 1997. A Summer Solstice at the Rollright Stones. *Wood and Water* 77. Available online: <http://www.rollrightstones.co.uk/experiences/aspho.htm>.

Bakhtin, M. M. 1968. *Rabelais and His World*. Cambridge, MA: Massachusetts Institute of Technology Press.

Bannister, V. 2000. A Load of Old Rubbish. *Pagan Dawn* 134: 8–9.

Barnatt, J. 1978 *Stone Circles of the Peak: a search for natural harmony*. London: Turnstone Books.

Barnatt, J. 1990 *The Henges, Stone Circles and Ringcairns of the Peak District*. Sheffield: University of Sheffield.

Barnatt, J. 1997. Excavation and Restoration of the Doll Tor Stone Circle, Stanton, Derbyshire, 1994. *Derbyshire Archaeological Journal* 117: 81–5.

Barnatt, J. and K. Smith 2004. *The Peak District: landscapes through time*. Bollington, Macklesfield: Windgather.

Bauman, Z. 2000. *Liquid Modernity*. Cambridge: Polity Press.

Baxter, I. and C. Chippindale, 2002. A sustainable and green approach to Stonehenge visitation: the 'brownfield' option. Discussion paper circulated by I. Baxter, Moffat Centre, Glasgow Caledonian University and C. Chippindale, Museum of Archaeology and Anthropology, Cambridge University.

Baxter, I. and C. Chippindale, K. Fielden, W. Kennet and E. Young 2000. *The Stonehenge we don't deserve: responses to Geoffrey Wainwright's report, 'The Stonehenge we deserve'*. Available online: <http://www.savestonehenge.org.uk/deserve.html>.

Beckensall, S. 2005. *The Prehistoric Rock Art of Kilmartin*. Kilmartin: Kilmartin House Trust.

Bender, B. 1992. Theorising Landscapes and the Prehistoric Landscapes of Stonehenge. *Man* 27: 735–55.

Bender, B. 1993. Stonehenge – Contested Landscapes (Medieval to Present Day). In B. Bender (ed.) *Landscape: Politics and Perspectives*, 245–80. Oxford: Berg.

Bender, B. 1998. *Stonehenge: Making Space.* Oxford: Berg.

Bender, B. and M. Winer (eds) 2001. *Contested landscapes: Movement, Exile and Place.* Oxford: Berg.

Bennett, P. 1998. *The Twelve Apostles Stone Circle, Ilkley Moor.* Hebden Bridge: Fylfot.

Bennett, P. and T. Wilson 1999. *The Old Stones of Rollright and District.* Cockley Press: London.

Bhabha, H. 1994. *The Location of Culture.* London: Routledge.

Biolsi, T. and L. J. Zimmerman (eds) 1997. *Indians and Anthropologists: Vine Deloria Jr. and the Critique of Anthropology.* Arizona: The University of Arizona Press.

Blain, J. 1993. 'I can't come in today, the baby has chickenpox!' Gender and class processes in how parents in the labour force deal with the problem of sick children. *Canadian Journal of Sociology* 8(4): 407–31.

Blain, J. 1994. Discourses of Agency and Domestic Labour: Family discourse and gendered practice in dual-earner families. *Journal of Family Issues* 15(4): 515–49.

Blain, J. 1998. Presenting constructions of identity and divinity: Ásatrú and Oracular Seidhr, in S. Grills (ed.) *Fieldwork Methods: Accomplishing Ethnographic Research*, 203–27. Thousand Oaks: Sage.

Blain, J. 2000. Speaking Shamanistically: seidr, academia, and rationality. *DISKUS.* Available online: <http://www.uni-marburg.de/religionswis-senschaft/journal/diskus/blain.html>.

Blain, J. 2000 audio diary. Report on Summer Solstice 2000 at Stonehenge (sound recording). Available online: <http://easyweb.easynet.co.uk/aburn-ham/pers/sounds.htm>.

Blain, J. 2001. Shamans, Stones, Authenticity and Appropriation: Contestations of Invention and Meaning. In R. J. Wallis and K. J. Lymer (eds) *A Permeability of Boundaries? New Approaches to the Archaeology of Art, Religion and Folklore*, 47–55. BAR International Series 936. Oxford. British Archaeological Reports.

Blain, J. 2002. *Nine Worlds of Seid-Magic: Ecstasy and Neo-shamanism in North European Paganism.* London: Routledge.

Blain, J. 2004. Tracing the In/Authentic Seeress: from Seid-magic to Stone Circles. In J. Blain, D. Ezzy and G. Harvey (eds) *Researching Paganisms*, 217–40. Walnut Creek, CA: Altamira.

Blain, J. 2005. 'Now many of those things are shown to me which I was denied before': Seidr, shamanism, and journeying, past and present. *Studies in Religion/Sciences Religieuses* 34(1): 81–98.

Blain, J. 2006a. Heathenry, the past, and sacred sites in today's Britain. In M. Strmiska (ed.) *Modern Paganism in World Cultures*, 181–208. Santa Barbara: ABC-CLIO.

Blain, J. 2006b. Constructing identity and divinity: Creating community in an Elder religion within a postmodern world. In S. Reid (ed.) *Between the Worlds: Essays in Contemporary Neopaganism*, 241–65. CSPI / Women's Press.

Blain, J. 2006c. Ancestors? Which ancestors? Place, time and remembrance in living (and cultural) landscapes. *Association of Polytheist Traditions conference*, University of Central Lancashire, May 2006.

Blain, J., D. Ezzy and G. Harvey (eds) 2004. *Researching Paganisms.* Walnut Creek, CA: AltaMira.

Blain, J., A. Letcher and R. J. Wallis 2004. *Sacred Sites, Contested Rights: Heritage discourse, Pagan resistance*. Final report to ESRC. Available online: <http://www.esrcsocietytoday.ac.uk/>. Also available: <http://www.sacred-sites.org.uk/reports/esrc2003endreport.html>.

Blain, J. and R. J. Wallis 2000. The 'ergi' seidman: Contestations of gender, shamanism and sexuality in northern religion past and present. *Journal of Contemporary Religion* 15(3): 395–411.

Blain, J. and R. J. Wallis 2002. A living landscape? Pagans and archaeological discourse. *3rd Stone: Archaeology, Folklore and Myth – The Magazine for the New Antiquarian* 43 (Summer): 20–7.

Blain, J. and R. J. Wallis 2004a. Sacred Sites, Contested Rites/Rights: Contemporary Pagan Engagements with the Past. *Journal of Material Culture* 9(3): 237–61.

Blain, J. and R. J. Wallis 2004b. Sites, texts, contexts and inscriptions of meaning: investigating pagan 'authenticities' in a text-based society. *The Pomegranate: The International Journal of Pagan Studies* 6(2): 231–52.

Blain, J. and R. J. Wallis 2006a. Ritual reflections, practitioner meanings: Disputing the terminology of neo-shamanic 'performance'. *Journal of Ritual Studies* 20(1): 21–6.

Blain, J. and R. J. Wallis 2006b. Re-presenting spirit: Heathenry, new-indigenes, and the imaged past. In I. A. Russell (ed.) *Images, representations and Heritage: Moving beyond Modern Approaches to Archaeology*, 89–108. London and New York: Springer.

Blain, J. and R. J. Wallis 2006c. A Live Issue: Ancestors, Archaeologists and the 'Reburial Issue' in Britain. *White Dragon* 49 (Lughnasa): 15–19. Also available online: <http://manygods.org.uk/articles/essays/reburial.html>.

Blain, J. and R. J. Wallis 2006d. Pasts and pagan practices: moving beyond Stonehenge. *Public Archaeology 5(4)*: 3–16.

Blain, J. and R. J. Wallis 2007. Sacred, secular, or sacrilegious? Prehistoric sites, pagans and the Sacred Sites project in Britain. In J. Schachter and S. Brockman (eds) *(Im)permanence: Cultures In/Out of Time*, in press.

Boniface, P. and P. Fowler 1993. *Heritage and Tourism in the 'Global Village'*. London: Routledge.

Bowman, M. 1995. Cardiac Celts: Images of the Celts in Paganism. In G. Harvey and C. Hardman (eds) *Paganism Today: Wiccans, Druids, the Goddess and Ancient Earth Traditions for the Twenty-First Century*: 242–51. London: Thorsons.

Bowman, M. 2000. Contemporary Celtic Spirituality. In A. Hale and P. Payton (eds) *New Directions in Celtic Studies*: 69–91. Exeter: University of Exeter Press.

Bradley, R. 1997. *Signing the Land: Rock Art and the Prehistory of Atlantic Europe*. London: Routledge.

Bradley, R. 2000. *An Archaeology of Natural Places*. London: Routledge.

Bradley, R. 2005. *Ritual and Domestic Life in Prehistoric Europe*. London: Routledge.

British Archaeology News 1997. Public Disquiet Over Digging of Graves; and Timber circle in Argyll's ritual valley. *British Archaeology* 29 (November): 5. Available online: <http://www.britarch.ac.uk/ba/ba29/ba29news.html>.

British Archaeology News 2002. Sacred pool ringed by totem poles in Scotland's sacred glen. *British Archaeology* 64. Available online: <http://www.britarch.ac.uk/BA/ba64/news.shtml>.

Burl, A. 1986 [1979] *Prehistoric Avebury*. New Haven and London: Yale University Press (in association with the National Trust).

Burl, A. 1991. The Devil's Arrows, Boroughbridge, North Yorkshire: the archaeology of a stone row. *Yorkshire Archaeological Journal* 63, 1–24.

Burl, A. 2000. *The Rollright Stones*. Banbury, Oxfordshire: Tattooed Kitten Publications.

Calver, S. 1998. *Avebury Visitor Research 1996–1998*. Bournemouth University Report on Behalf of the National Trust.

Carmichael, D.L., J. Hubert, B. Reeves and A. Schanche 1994. *Sacred Sites, Sacred Places*. London: Routledge.

Carpenter, D. 1998. Symbolic Stupidity. *The Right Times* 2 (Summer Solstice): 24.

Carroll, P. 1987. *Liber Null and Psychonaut: An Introduction to Chaos Magic* (two complete volumes). York Beach, Maine: Samuel Weiser Inc.

Chadburn, A., F. McAvoy and G. Campbell; D. Field; R. Harding, A. Chadburn, F. McAvoy and G. Campbell 2005. A Green Hill Long Ago. *British Archaeology* 80. Available online: <http://www.britarch.ac.uk/ba/ba80/feat1.shtml>.

Champion, M. 2000. *Seahenge: a Contemporary Chronicle*. Aylsham, Norfolk: Barnwell's Timescape.

Chandler, J. 2001. *Marlborough and Eastern Wiltshire*. Salisbury: Hobnob Press.

Chandler, J. 2003 *Devizes and Central Wiltshire*. Salisbury: Hobnob Press.

Chandler, J. n.d. *Avebury Concise History*. Available online: <http://www.wiltshire.gov.uk/community/getconcise.php?id=11>.

Chatters, J. C. 2000. The Recovery and First Analysis of an Early Holocene Human Skeleton from Kennewick, Washington. *American Antiquity* 65(2): 291–316.

Chippindale, C. 1986. Stoned Henge: Events and Issues at the Summer Solstice, 1985. *World Archaeology* 18(1): 38–58.

Chippindale, C. 1994. *Stonehenge Complete*. Revised Edition. London: Thames and Hudson.

Chippindale, C. and B. Davison 2001. *The one million and the one hundred thousand: the people of Stonehenge's future*. Discussion document circulated to interested parties by the Wiltshire Archaeological and Natural History Society, available online: <http://www.savestonehenge.org.uk/million.html>.

Chippindale, C., P. Devereux, P. Fowler, R. Jones and T. Sebastion. 1990. *Who Owns Stonehenge?* London: Batsford.

Church of England and English Heritage Working Group on Human Remains 2005. *Guidance for Best Practice for Treatment of Human Remains Excavated from Christian Burial Grounds in England*. Available online: <http://www.english-heritage.org.uk/upload/pdf/16602_HumanRemains1.pdf>.

City of Bradford Metropolitan District Council 2003 *Ilkley Moor Management Plan 2003–2012*. Available online: <http://www.bradford.gov.uk/environment/land_and_premises/countryside_rights_of_way/> and directly at <http://www.bradford.gov.uk/NR/rdonlyres/3A5A0C6B-CB84-4AE3-8F13-5481F0BCAAA5/0/ilkley_moor_management_plan.pdf>.

Cleere, H. F. 1989. (ed.). *Archaeological Heritage Management in the Modern World*. London: Routledge.

Clifton, C. and G. Harvey (eds) 2004. *The Paganism Reader*. London: Routledge.

Cohen, M. 2004. *Methods of Enquiry: Theoretical and Conceptual Issues in Educational Research*. Lecture for the Doctor in Education (EdD) International Programme, Institute of Education, University of London, 2004.

Coleman, S. and J. Elsner 1998. Performing pilgrimage: Walsingham and the ritual construction of irony. In F. Hughes-Freeland (ed.) *Ritual, Performance, Media*, 46–65. London: Routledge.

Cooney, G. 2001. Bringing Contemporary Baggage to Neolithic Landscapes. In B. Bender and M. Winer (eds) 2001. *Contested landscapes: Movement, Exile and Place*, 165–80. Oxford: Berg.

Cope, J. 1998. *The Modern Antiquarian: A Pre-Millennial Odyssey Through Megalithic Britain*. London: Thorsons.

Cope, J. 2004. *The Megalithic European: The Twenty-First Century Traveller in Prehistoric Europe*. London: Harper, Thorsons, Element.

Copp, A. and N. Toop, 2005. Watching Brief, Nosterfield Quarry, North Yorkshire: Interim Report March 2005. Field Archaeology Specialists Ltd. On behalf of Mike Griffiths and Associates, client Tarmac Northern Ltd. Available online: <http://www.archaeologicalplanningconsultancy.co.uk/ mga/projects/noster/speciali/nost_pdf.html>.

Cork, T. 2006. Stone Circle Village Goes to War over Pagans in the Car Park. *Western Daily Press*, 12th October 2006. Available online: <http://www. westpress.co.uk/displayNode.jsp?nodeId=145809&command=display Content&sourceNode=145792&contentPK=15660289&moduleName= InternalSearch&formname=sidebarsearch>.

Cornwell, B. 1999. *Stonehenge: A Novel of 2000 BC*. London, HarperCollins.

Coughlan, S. 1999. Letter. *Pagan Dawn* 132: 46.

Council for the Protection of Rural England and Stanton Lees Action Group, 2003. *An evaluation of proposals to re-open Endcliffe and Lees Cross Quarries Stanton Lees, Matlock, Derbyshire under the provisions of the 1995 Environment Act*. Davis Planning Partnership on behalf of CPRE and SLAG.

Cowan, T. 1993. *Fire in the Head: Shamanism and the Celtic Spirit*. San Francisco: HarperSanFrancisco.

Craig, S. (ed.). 1986. *Stonehenge '85: Souvenir Issue – A Collection of Material to Commemorate 'The Battle of the Beanfield' June 1st 1985*. Glastonbury: Unique Publications.

Crook, S. 1998. *Away with the Fairies: Rock Art and Psychic Geography in West Yorkshire*. MA Dissertation, Department of Archaeology, University of Southampton.

Dames, M. 1976. *The Silbury Treasure*. London: Thames and Hudson.

Dames, M. 1977. *The Avebury Cycle*. London: Thames and Hudson.

Davies, P. 1997. Respect and Reburial. *The Druid's Voice: The Magazine of Contemporary Druidry* 8 (Summer): 12–13.

Davies, P. 1998/9. Speaking for the Ancestors: The Reburial Issue in Britain and Ireland. *The Druid's Voice: The Magazine of Contemporary Druidry* 9 (Winter): 10–12.

DCMS (Department of Culture, Media and Sport) 2003. Report of the Working Group on Human Remains. Available online: <http://www.culture.gov.uk/ Reference_library/Publications/archive_2003/wgur_report2003.htm>.

DCMS 2005. Guidance for the Care of Human Remains in Museums.

Available online: <http://www.culture.gov.uk/NR/rdonlyres/0017476B-3B86-46F3-BAB3-11E5A5F7F0A1/0/GuidanceHumanRemains11Oct.pdf>.

Denison, S. 2000. Issues: One step to the left, two steps back. *British Archaeology* 52 (April): 28.

Denning, K. 1999a. Archaeology and Alterity. Unpublished paper presented in the 'Method and Theory 2000' session at the Society for American Archaeology Annual Meeting, Chicago.

Denning, K. 1999b. Apocalypse Past/Future: Archaeology and Folklore, Writ Large. In C. Holtorf and A. Gazin-Schwartz (eds) *Archaeology and Folklore*, 90–105. London: Routledge.

Denton, N., R. Bate, R. Reeves and A. Tickle 2004. Old Mineral Permissions and National Parks. With additional contributions by Robert McCracken QC. Council for National Parks/Friends of the Peak District, June 2004.

Department of the Environment 1990. PPG16. Planning Policy Guidance: Archaeology and Planning. November 1990. Available online: <http://www.molas.org.uk/downloads/ppg16.pdf>.

Devereux, P. 1991. Three-dimensional aspects of apparent relationships between selected natural and artificial features within the topography of the Avebury complex. *Antiquity* 65: 249.

Devereux, P. 1992. *Symbolic Landscapes: The Dreamtime Earth and Avebury's Open Secrets*. Glastonbury: Gothic Image.

Devereux, P. 2001. Did ancient shamanism leave a monumental record on the land as well as in rock art? In R. J. Wallis and K. J. Lymer (eds) *A Permeability of Boundaries? New Approaches to the Archaeology of Art, Religion and Folklore*, 1–7. BAR International Series 936. Oxford: British Archaeological Reports.

Devereux, P. and R. G. Jahn. 1996. Preliminary investigations and cognitive considerations of the acoustic resonances of selected archaeological sites. *Antiquity* 70: 665–6.

Dongoske, K. E. and R. Anyon. 1997. Federal Archaeology: Tribes, Diatribes and Tribulations. In N. Swidler et al. (eds) *Native Americans and Archaeologists: Stepping Stones to Common Ground*, 197–206. Walnut Creek, CA: AltaMira Press.

Dowson, T.A. 2001. Afterword: Permeating Boundaries. In R.J Wallis and K.J Lymer (eds) *A permeability of boundaries: new approaches to the archaeology of art, religion and folklore*, 137–8. BAR International Series 936. Oxford: British Archaeological Reports.

Durkheim, E. [1912] 1964. *The Elementary Forms of Religious Lif*e. London: Allen and Unwin.

Edmonds, M. and T. Seaborne, 2001. *Prehistory in the Peak*. Stroud: Tempus.

Edwards, B. 2000. Avebury and not-so-ancient places: the making of the English heritage landscape. In H. Kean, P. Martin and S. J. Morgan (eds) *Seeing History: Public History in Britain Now*, 65–79. London: Francis Boutle.

EHAC 2006. Minutes, English Heritage Advisory Committee Feb 2006 Available online: <http://www.english-heritage.org.uk/upload/pdf/EHAC_Minutes_Feb06.pdf>.

Eliade, M. 1964. *Shamanism: Archaic Techniques of Ecstasy*. New York: Pantheon.

Elliott, R. W. V. 1989. *Runes: An Introduction*. London: St Martin's Press, 2nd edition.

English Heritage 1997. *Sustaining the Historic Environment: New Perspectives on the Future.* London: English Heritage.

English Heritage 2000a. *Power of Place. The Future of the Historic Environment.* London: English Heritage.

English Heritage 2000b. *Stonehenge World Heritage Site Management Plan.* London: English Heritage.

English Heritage 2002. *State of the Historic Environment Report 2002.* London: English Heritage.

English Heritage 2006. *Heritage Counts: The State of England's Historic Environment 2006.* London: English Heritage.

English Heritage (ALSF projects) 2004. Thornborough Henges: Air Photo Mapping. Summary 2004–05. Available online: <http://www.english-heritage.org.uk/server/show/ConWebDoc.5536>.

English Heritage News Release 2002. £57 Million Scheme brings a new Dawn for Stonehenge. Wednesday 31 July 2002.

Evans, A.J. 1895. The Rollright Stones and their Folklore, *Folk-Lore* VI(I): 6–51.

Fabian, J. 1983. *Time and The Other: How Anthropology Makes its Object.* New York: Columbia University Press.

Fairclough, N., P. Graham, J. Lemke and R. Wodak 2004. Introduction. *Critical Discourse Studies* 1(1): 1–7.

Fielden, K. 2006. Stonehenge Update for Rescue News No.100 (Autumn 2006). Available online: <http://www.savestonehenge.org.uk/rescueautumn06.html>.

Finn, C. 1997. Leaving More Than Footprints: Modern Votive Offerings At Chaco Canyon Prehistoric Site. *Antiquity* 71: 169–78.

Flaherty, G. 1992. *Shamanism and the Eighteenth Century.* Princeton, NJ: Princeton University Press.

Fleming, S. 1999. Psychic Vandalism. *The Right Times* 5 (Spring Equinox): 12–14.

Fleming, S. n.d.a. Organising Ritual at Prehistoric Sites. Available online: <http://www.ravenfamily.org/sam/pag/ritualmeths.html>.

Fleming, S. n.d.b. The effects of Physical Damage to Sites. Available online: <http://www.ravenfamily.org/sam/pag/site_dam.html>.

Fleming, S. n.d.c. A Plea to Practising Pagans. Available online: <http://www.ravenfamily.org/sam/pag/rrtart1.htm>.

Forte, R. (ed.) 1997. *Entheogens and the Future of Religion.* San Francisco: Council on Spiritual Practices.

Foucault, M. 1972. *The Archaeology of Knowledge.* London: Tavistock.

Fridman, E. J. N. 1999. Buryat shamanism: home and hearth – a territorialism of the spirit. *Anthropology of Consciousness* 10 (4): 45–56.

Gallagher, A-M. 1999. 'Weaving a Tangled Web? Pagan ethics and issues of history, 'race' and ethnicity in Pagan identity'. *The Pomegranate* 10: 19–29.

Gallop, A. 1998. *The House with the Golden Eyes: Unlocking the Secret History of 'Hinemihi' – the Maori Meeting House from Te Wairoa (New Zealand) and Clandon Park (Surrey, England).* Sunbury-on-Thames, Middlesex: Running Horse Books.

Gell, A. 1992. *The Anthropology of Time: Cultural Constructions of Temporal Maps.* Oxford: Berg.

Giddens, A. 1991. *Modernity and Self-Identity.* Cambridge: Polity Press.

Giddens, A. 1994. Living in a Post-traditional Society. In U. Beck, A. Giddens and S. Lash, *Reflexive Modernization: Politics, Tradition and Aesthetics in the Modern Social Order*, 56–109. Cambridge: Polity Press,

Gillings, M., J. Pollard, D. Wheatley and R. Peterson, n.d. Negotiating Avebury Project. Available Online: <http://www.le.ac.uk/archaeology/research/projects/avebury/index.html>; <http://www.arch.soton.ac.uk/Projects/projects.asp?ProjectID=7>.

Gingell, C. 1998 National Trust Guardianship Scheme. Letter in *Pagan Dawn*, 128 (Imbolc): 8.

Gingell, C. 1996. Avebury: Striking a Balance. *Antiquity* 70: 507–11.

Glastonbury, P. 2004. *Avebury CD1 – Panoramic Tour*. Devizes: Pete and Alison Glastonbury.

Glentoal Associates for Stancliffe Stone Ltd. 2003. Town and Country Planning (Environmental Impact Assessment) (England and Wales) Regulations 1999: Endcliffe and Lees Cross Quarries Non-Technical Summary. December 2003.

Goodrick, G. T. and J. Harding, 2000. Virtual Reality at the Neolithic Monument Complex of Thornborough, North Yorkshire. In J. A. Barceló., M. Forte and D. H. Sanders (eds) *Virtual Reality in Archaeology*, 115–19. Oxford: British Archaeological Reports (International series) 5843.

Green, D. 2001. 'Modernity, Magickal Cosmologies and Science: A New Cauldron for a New Age?', *Pomegranate: a New Journal of Neo-Pagan Thought*, 15: 22–35.

Green, D. 2003 Re-enchanting Modernity: Imagining Tradition as a Psycho-Social Concept, *Journal for Psycho-Social Studies*, 2 (2). Available online: <http://www.btinternet.com/~psycho_social/Vol3/JPSS3-DG1.html>.

Green, R. 1988. The Tribe Called Wannabee. *Folklore* 99(1): 30–55.

Green, S. 2006. Trust Committed to the Stones. Letter to *Western Daily Press*, 16 October 2006. Available online: <http://www.westpress.co.uk/displayNode.jsp?nodeId=145809&command=displayContent&sourceNode=145792&contentPK=15688450&moduleName=InternalSearch&formname=sidebarsearch>.

Greene, S. 1998. The Shaman's Needle: Development, Shamanic Agency and Intermedicality in Aguarina Lands, Peru. *American Ethnologist* 25(4): 634–58.

Greenwood, S. 2000. *Magic, Witchcraft and the Otherworld*. Oxford: Berg.

Greenwood, S. 2005. *The Nature of Magic: An Anthropology of Consciousness*. Oxford: Berg.

Griffin, W. 1995. The Embodied Goddess – Feminist Witchcraft and Female Divinity. *Sociology of Religion* 56(1): 35–48.

Griffin, W. 2000. *Daughters of the Goddess: Studies of Healing, Identity and Empowerment*. Walnut Creek, CA: Altamira.

Gross, D. 1992. *The Past in Ruins: Tradition and the Critique of Modernity*. Amherst, MA: University of Massachusetts Press.

Gyrus Orbitalis. 1998a. *The Goddess in Wharfedale*. Available Online: <http://dreamflesh.com/essays/wharfedalegoddess/>. Previously published as: G.T. Oakley, 1998. *Verbeia: Goddess of Wharfedale*. Leeds: Rooted Media.

Gyrus. 1998b. The Last Museum. *Towards 2012* IV 'paganism': 77–80.

Haraway, D. 1988. Situated Knowledges: The Science Question in Feminism and the Privilege of Partial Perspective. *Feminist Studies* 14(3): 575–99.

Harding, J. 2003. *Henge Monuments of the British Isles*. Stroud: Tempus.

Harding, J. and B. Johnson 2004. Yorkshire's Holy Secret. *British Archaeology* 75 (March 2004). Available online: <http://www.britarch.ac.uk/BA/ba75/feat5.shtml>.

Harner, M. 1980. *The Way of the Shaman*. London: Harper Collins.

Harvey, G. 1997. *Listening People, Speaking Earth: Contemporary Paganism*. London: Hurst, Adelaide: Wakefield, New York: New York University Press (under the title *Contemporary Paganism: Listening People, Speaking Earth*).

Harvey, G. 1998. Shamanism in Britain Today. *Performance Research* 3(3) ('On Ritual'): 16–24.

Harvey, G. 2001. News: Winter Solstice at Stonehenge. Available online, A. Burnham (ed.) Megalithic Portal pages: <http://www.megalithic.co.uk/article.php?sid=2146410508>.

Harvey, G. 2004. Pagan Studies or the Study of Paganisms? A Case Study in the Study of Religions. In J. Blain, G. Harvey and D. Ezzy, *Researching Paganisms*, 241–68 .

Harvey, G. 2005. *Animism: Respecting the Living World*. London: Hurst.

Harvey, G. and C. Hardman (eds) 1995. *Paganism Today: Wiccans, Druids, the Goddess and Ancient Earth Traditions for the Twenty-First Century*. London: Thorsons.

Harvey, G. and R. J Wallis. 2007. *A Historical Dictionary of Shamanism*. Lanham, Maryland: Scarecrow Press.

Hassan, F. A. 1997. Beyond the Surface: Comments on Hodder's 'Reflexive excavation Methodology'. *Antiquity* 71: 1020–1025.

Hawkes, J. 1967. God in the Machine. *Antiquity* XLI: 174–180.

Heaney, S. (trans.) 1999. *Beowulf*. London: Faber and Faber.

Heelas, P. 1996. Introduction: Detraditionalization and its Rivals. In P. Heelas, S. Lash and P. Morris (eds) *Detraditionalization*, 1–20. Oxford: Blackwell.

Heelas, P., S. Lash and P. Morris (eds) 1996. *Detraditionalization*, 1–20. Oxford: Blackwell.

Heselton, P. 2001. *Wiccan Roots: Gerald Gardner and the Modern Witchcraft Revival*. Milverton, Somerset: Capall Bann.

Heselton, P. 2003. *Gerald Gardner and the Cauldron of Inspiration: An Investigation into the Sources of Gardnerian Witchcraft*. Teaneck, New Jersey: Holmes Publishing.

Hetherington, K. 1992. Place, Space and Power: Stonehenge and the Travellers. *Here and Now* 12: 25–28.

Hetherington, K. 2000. *New Age Travellers: Vanloads of Uproarious Humanity*. London: Cassell.

Hill, J. D. 1995. *Ritual and Rubbish in the Iron Age of Wessex*. British Archaeological Reports 242. Oxford: BAR.

Hill, R. 2006. Short Cuts. *London Review of Books* 28(13) 6 July 2006. Available online: <http://www.lrb.co.uk/v28/n13/hill01_.html>.

Hobsbawm, E. 1983. Inventing Traditions. In E. Hobsbawm and T. Ranger (eds) *The Invention of Tradition*, 1–14. Cambridge: Cambridge University Press.

Hobsbawm, E. and T. Ranger (eds) 1983. *The Invention of Tradition*. Cambridge: Cambridge University Press.

Hodder, I. 1997. 'Always momentary, fluid and flexible': towards a reflexive excavation methodology. *Antiquity* 71: 691–700.

Hodder, I. 2000. Developing a reflexive method in archaeology. In I. Hodder (ed.) *Towards Reflexive Method in Archaeology: the example at Çatalhöyük*, 3–14. Cambridge: McDonald Institute for Archaeological Research and British Institute of Archaeology at Ankara.

Holtorf, C. 1998. The Life-Histories of Megaliths in Mecklenburg-Vorpommern (Germany). *World Archaeology* 30(1): 23–8.

Holtorf, C. 2005. *From Stonehenge to Las Vegas: Archaeology as Popular Culture.* Walnut Creek, CA: AltaMira.

Holtorf, C. and T. Schadla-Hall 1999. Age as Artefact: On Archaeological Authenticity. *European Journal of Archaeology* 2(2): 229–47.

Hooper-Greenhill, E. 2000. *Museums and the Interpretation of Visual Culture.* London: Routledge.

Hubert, J. 1994. Sacred beliefs and beliefs of sacredness. In D. L. Carmichael, J. Hubert, R. Reeves and A. Schanche (eds) *Sacred Sites, Sacred Places*, 9–19. London: Routledge.

Hutton, R. 1996. 'Introduction: Who Possesses the Past?', In P. Carr-Gomm (ed.) *The Druid Renaissance: The Voice of Druidry Today*, 17–34. London: Thorsons.

Hutton, R. 1999. *The Triumph of the Moon: A History of Modern Pagan Witchcraft.* Oxford: Oxford University Press.

Ingerman, S. 1991. *Soul Retrieval: Mending the Fragmented Self.* San Francisco: HarperSanFrancisco.

Ingold, T. 2000. *The Perception of the Environment: Essays in Livelihood, Dwelling and Skill.* London: Routledge.

Ingold, T. 2006. Rethinking the Animate, Re-Animating Thought. *Ethnos* 71(1): 9–20.

Irwin, A. 2001. *Sociology and the Environment.* Cambridge: Polity.

Ivakhiv, A. J. 2001. *Claiming Sacred Ground: Pilgrims and Politics at Glastonbury and Sedona.* Bloomington and Indianapolis: Indiana University Press.

Jakobsen, M. D. 1999. *Shamanism: Traditional and Contemporary Approaches to the Mastery of Spirits and Healing.* Oxford: Berghahn Books.

Jenkins, T. 2003. Burying the evidence: A report by the UK government's 'Human Remains Working Group' shrouds history in mystery, to the detriment of science. *Spiked Culture*. Available online: <http://www.spiked-online.com/Articles/00000006DFDE.htm>.

Johnson, N. and R. J. Wallis 2005. *Galdrbok: Practical Heathen Runecraft, Shamanism and Magic.* London: The Wykeham Press.

Johnson, P. C. 1995. Shamanism from Ecuador to Chicago: A Case Study in Ritual Appropriation. *Religion* 25: 163–178.

Kennedy, M. 2006. Radical solution proposed for Stonehenge. *The Guardian*, Saturday 7 October 2006. Available online: <http://arts.guardian.co.uk/news/story/0,,1889436,00.html>.

Kennet District Council, n.d. Kennet Tourism: Avebury World Heritage Site. Available online: <http://www.visitkennet.co.uk/avebury/tourwhs/index.htm>.

Kilmartin House 1998. Shiver me timbers. *Kilmartin House Newsletter* 3: 7.

Available online: <http://www.kilmartin.org/latest-news/newsletter-issue3-pg1.html>.

Kreps, C.F. 2003. *Liberating Culture: Cross-cultural Perspectives on Museums, Curation and Heritage Preservation*. London: Routledge.

Lambrick, G. 1988. *The Rollright Stones: Megaliths, Monuments and Megaliths in the Prehistoric Landscape*. English Heritage Archaeological Report, no. 6. London: English Heritage.

Lambrick G. 2001. *The Rollright Stones: Conservation and Management Plan 2001–2005*. Banbury, Oxfordshire: The Rollright Trust.

Layton, R. (ed.) 1989a. *Who Needs the Past?: Indigenous Values and Archaeology*. London: Routledge.

Layton, R. (ed.) 1989b. *Conflict in the Archaeology of Living Traditions*. London: Routledge.

Letcher, A. 2001a. *The Role of the Bard in Contemporary Pagan Movements*. Unpublished PhD Thesis, King Alfred's College, Winchester.

Letcher, A. 2001b. The Scouring of the Shire: Fairies, Trolls and Pixies in Eco-Protest Culture, *Folklore* 112: 147–61.

Letcher, A., J. Blain and R. J. Wallis. forthcoming. Re-Viewing the Past: Discourse and Power in Images of Prehistory. *Tourism and Photography*, in press.

Lewis, J. (ed.) 1996. *Magical Religion and Modern Witchcraft*. State University of New York Press.

Liddle, R. 2002. Hooray for Badger, his Missus, and the Stonehenge Hippies. *The Guardian*, Wednesday 30 June 2002. Available online: <http://www.guardian.co.uk/g2/story/0,3604,743915,00.html>.

Lindauer, M. 2006. The Critical Museum Visitor. In J. Marstine (ed.) *New Museum Theory and Practice: An Introduction*, 203–25. London: Routledge.

Lucas, G. 2001. *Critical Approaches to Fieldwork: Contemporary and Historical Archaeological Practice*. London: Routledge.

Lucas, G. 2004. Modern Disturbances: On the Ambiguities of Archaeology. *Modernism/modernity* 11: 109–20.

MacEowen, F. H. 1998. Rekindling the Gaelic Hearthways of Oran Mor. *Shaman's Drum* 49 (Summer): 32–9.

MacLellan, G. 1995. Dancing on the Edge: Shamanism in Modern Britain. In G. Harvey and C. Hardman (eds) *Paganism Today: Wiccans, Druids, the Goddess and Ancient Earth Traditions for the Twenty-First Century*, 138–48. London: Thorsons.

MacLellan, G. 1998. A Sense of Wonder. *Performance Research* 3(3) ('On Ritual'): 60–3.

Maffesoli, M. 1996. *The Time of the Tribes: The Decline of Individualism in Mass Society*. London: Sage.

Maingueneau, D. 2006. Is Discourse Analysis Critical? *Critical Discourse Studies* 3(2): 229–30.

Marcus, G. 1998. *Ethnography through Thick and Thin*. Princeton, NJ: Princeton University Press.

MARS: Darvill, T. and Fulton, A. 1998. *MARS: The Monuments at Risk Survey of England, 1995: Main Report*. Bournemouth University and English Heritage.

Martin, G. 2002. New Age Travellers: Uproarious or Uprooted? *Sociology* 36 (3): 723–35.

Matthews, C. 1995. *Singing the Soul Back Home: Shamanism in Daily Life*. Shaftesbury, Dorset: Element Books.

Matthews, J. 1991a. *Taliesin: Shamanism and the Bardic Mysteries in Britain and Ireland*. London: Aquarian.

Matthews, J. 1991b. *The Celtic Shaman: A Handbook*. Shaftesbury, Dorset: Element Books.

Matthews, J. 1991c. *The Song of Taliesin: Stories and Poems from the Books of Broceliande*. London: Aquarian.

Mayell, H. 2002. Pagans Get Support in Battle Over Stonehenge. *National Geographic News* 21 October 2002. Available online: <http://news.national-geographic.com/news/2002/10/1031_021031_Stonehenge.html>.

McKay, G. 1996. *Senseless Acts of Beauty: Cultures of Resistance since the Sixties*. London: Verso.

McKinley, J. 2003. A Wiltshire Bog Body?: Discussion of a Fifth/Sixth Century AD Burial in the Woodford Valley. *Wiltshire Studies* 96: 7–18.

Merrill, W. L., E. J. Ladd, and T. J. Ferguson 1993. The Return of Ahayu:da: Lessons for Repatriation from Zuni Pueblo and the Smithsonian Institution. *Current Anthropology* 34(5): 523–67.

Meskell, L. 1995. Goddesses, Gimbutas and 'New Age' Archaeology. *Antiquity* 69: 74–86.

Meskell, L. 1998. Oh My Goddess! Archaeology, Sexuality and Ecofeminism. *Archaeological Dialogues* 5(2): 126–43.

Meskell, L. 1999. Feminism, Paganism, Pluralism. In C. Holtorf and A. Gazin-Schwartz (eds) *Archaeology and Folklore*, 83–9. London: Routledge.

Messenger, P. M. (ed.) 1989. *The Ethics of Collecting Cultural Property: Whose Culture? Whose Property?* Albuquerque, New Mexico: University of New Mexico Press.

Mihesuah, D. A. (ed.) 2000. *Repatriation Reader: Who Owns American Indian Remains?* Lincoln: University of Nebraska Press.

Millson, R. 1998. *Ancient Voices: Stonehenge*. Manchester: BBC BSS (Broadcasting Support Services).

Morgan, P. and V. Morgan 2001. *Rock Around the Peak: Megalithic Monuments of the Peak District*. Wilmslow, Cheshire: Sigma Press.

Morris, R. 1998. Measuring the Destruction of Monuments. *British Archaeology* (June): 15.

Murray, T. 1996. Coming to Terms with the Living: Some Aspects of Repatriation for the Archaeologist. *Antiquity* 70: 217–20.

Myers, F. 1988. Locating Ethnographic Practice: Romance, Reality, and Politics in the Outback. *American Ethnologist* 15(4): 609–24.

Naddair, K. 1990. Pictish and Keltic Shamanism. In P. Jones and C. Matthews (eds) *Voices from the Circle: The Heritage of Western Paganism*, 93–108. Northampton: Aquarian.

National Trust 1997. *Avebury Management Plan*. The National Trust.

National Trust n.d. The Avebury Sacred Sites Forum. Available online: <http://www.nationaltrust.org.uk/main/w-vh/w-visits/w-findaplace/w-avebury/w-avebury-guardians.htm>.

NCCL (National Council for Civil Liberties). 1986. *Stonehenge: A report into the civil liberties implications of the events relating to the convoys of summer 1985 and 1986*. London: Yale Press.

Newall, R.S. 1981[1959]. *Stonehenge. Department of the Environment Official Handbook*. London: Her Majesty's Stationery Office.

North-Bates, S. 2006. *The Influence of Complememtary Practices and Spirituality on British Design 1930–2005.* Unpublished PhD Thesis, Sheffield Hallam University. Submitted June 2006.

North, J. 1996. *Stonehenge: A New Interpretation of Prehistoric Man and the Cosmos.* New York: Free Press.

North Yorkshire County Council, English Heritage and Tarmac Northern Ltd. 2006. *Thornborough Henges Conservation Plan: Public Consultation Draft.* Prepared by Atkins Heritage. Available online: <http://www.northyorks. gov.uk/files/NYCC/Environment/Heritage/Thornborough%20henges%20-%201030/ThornboroughHengesConsPlanLR_v3.pdf>.

Oakley, C. 1997. National Trust Guardianship Scheme. *Pagan Dawn* 126 (Lammas): 9.

'Obbyoss' 2006. A Response to COBDO 'Request' for Reburial. Available online: <http://obbyoss.livejournal.com/869.html>.

Olding, F. 2004. Letter. British Archaeology 79, November 2004. Available online: <http://www.britarch.ac.uk/ba/ba79/letters.shtml>.

Olivier, A. n.d. *Frameworks for our Past: A Review of Research Frameworks, Strategies and Perceptions.* London: English Heritage.

Parker-Pearson, M. 1999. *The Archaeology of Death and Burial.* Stroud: Sutton Publishing.

Parker-Pearson, M. and Ramilisonina, 1998. Stonehenge for the ancestors: the stones pass on the message'. *Antiquity* 72: 308–26.

Peak District National Park Authority (PDNPA) n.d. *Peak District National Park Authority Website.* <http://www.peakdistrict-npa.gov.uk/>.

Peak District National Park Authority (PDNPA) 2000. *Peak District Park Management Plan 2000–2005.* <http://www.peakdistrict-npa.gov.uk/pubs/manplan.pdf>.

PDNPA report 2005. Planning Committee – Development Control Items, 17 June 2005. Head of Development Control, Item 6.1 'Progress Report on Planning Issues at Lees Cross/Endcliffe Quarries, Stanton Moor (P5695/JWD)'. Available online: <http://peakdistrict.vianw.co.uk/ctte/planning/reports/2005/050617Item6-1.pdf>.

Pearson, J. 1998. Assumed Affinities: Wicca and the New Age. In J. Pearson, R. H. Roberts and G. Samuel (eds) *Nature Religion Today: Paganism in the Modern World,* 45–56. Edinburgh: Edinburgh University Press.

Pearson, J. 2003. *Wicca: Magic, Spirituality and 'the Mystic Other'.* London: Routledge.

Peers, L. and A. K. Brown (eds) 2003. *Museums and Source Communities: A Routledge Reader.* London: Routledge.

Pendragon, A. 2000/01. Sacred Sites. *Druid Lore* 3: 20–21.

Pendragon, A. and C. J. Stone 2003. *The Trials of Arthur: The Life and Times of a Modern-Day King.* London: Element.

Piggott, S. 1968. *The Druids.* London: Thames and Hudson.

Pitts, M. 2000. *Hengeworld.* London: Century.

Planning Inspectorate 2004. *Stonehenge Improvement Inquiry.* Available online: <http://www.planning-inspectorate.gov.uk/stonehenge/>.

Pollard, J. and A. Reynolds 2002. *Avebury: The Biography of a Landscape.* Stroud: Tempus.

Pollington, S. 2000. *Leechcraft: Early English Charms, Plantlore, and Healing.* Norfolk: Anglo-Saxon Books.

Pomeroy, M. 1998. *Avebury World Heritage Site Management Plan*. London: English Heritage.

Pomeroy-Kellinger, M. 2005. *Avebury World Heritage Site Management Plan 2005–11*. English Heritage. Online: available <http://www.kennet.gov.uk/avebury/archaelogical/managementplan/index.htm>.

Pomeroy-Kellinger, M. n.d. Avebury WHS Management Plan (summary). English Heritage. Available online: <http://www.eng-h.gov.uk/archcom/projects/summarys/html98_9/2257aveb.htm>.

Possamai, A. 2003. Alternative Spiritualities and the Cultural Logic of Late Capitalism. *Culture and Religion* 4(1): 31–45.

Pounds, N. J. G. 2000. A History of the English Parish: The Culture of Religion from *Augustine to Victoria*. Cambridge: Cambridge University Press.

Powell, E. A. 2003. Solstice at the Stones. *Archaeology* 56(5): 36–41.

Prendergast, K. 2002. Neolithic Solar Ritual at Stonehenge: Mad Midsummer or Bleak Midwinter? *3rd Stone* 45: 38–43.

Prout, C. 1998. Saving Sacred Sites. *The Right Times* 2 (Summer Solstice): 6–7.

Pryor, F. 2001. *Seahenge: New Discoveries in Prehistoric Britain*. London: HarperCollins.

Radford, T. 1998. *Equinox: Homicide in Kennewick*. London: Channel Four Television.

Reed-Danahay, D. E. (ed.) 1997. *Auto/Ethnography: Rewriting the Self and the Social*. Oxford: Berg.

Restall Orr, E. 1998. Not my Faith. *The Druid's Voice* 9: 23.

Richards, J. 2004. *Stonehenge: A History in Photographs*. London: English Heritage.

Richardson, A. 2001. *Spirits of the Stones: Visions of Sacred Britain*. London: Virgin Publishing.

Robins, D. 1985. *Circles of Silence*. Souvenir Press, London.

Roe, N. 1991. Rollright's keeper of the stones. *Independent,* 5 Jun 1991 p. 16.

Ronayne, M. 2001. The Political Economy of Landscape: Conflict and Value in a Prehistoric Landscape in the Republic of Ireland – Ways of Telling. In B. Bender and M. Winer (eds) 2001. *Contested Landscapes: Movement, Exile and Place*, 149–64. Oxford: Berg.

Rose, W. 1992. The Great Pretenders: Further reflections on Whiteshamanism. In M. A. Jaimes and M. Annette (ed.) *The State of Native America: Genocide, Colonization, and Resistance*, 403–22. Boston: South End Press.

Ross, C. 2006. Stones are a Wonder: Giant airship marks Stonehenge's bid to become recognised throughout the world. *This is Wiltshire*, 20 October 2006. Available online: <http://www.thisiswiltshire.co.uk/display.var.978185.0.stones_are_a_wonder_in_the_making.php>.

Rountree, K. 2002. Re-inventing Malta's Neolithic Temples: Contemporary Interpretations and Agendas. *History and Anthropology* 13(1): 31–51.

Rountree, K. 2003a. Reflexivity in Practice. Çatalhöyük Archive Reports 2003. Available online: <http://www.catalhoyuk.com/archive_reports/2003/ar03_20.html>.

Rountree, K. 2003b. The Case of the Missing Goddess: Plurality, Power and Prejudice in Reconstructions of Malta's Neolithic Past. *Journal of Feminist Studies in Religion* 19(2): 25–44.

Rountree, K. 2006. Journeys to the Goddess: Pilgrimage and Tourism in the

New Age. In W. Swatos (ed.) *On the Road to Being There: Pilgrimage and Religious Tourism in Late Modernity*, 33–60. Boston: Brill.

Ruggles, C. 1999. *Astronomy in Prehistoric Britain and Ireland*. Yale, Yale University Press.

Ruickbie, L. 2006. Weber and the Witches: Sociological Theory and Modern Witchcraft. *Journal of Alternative Spiritualities and New Age Studies*, 2: 116–30. Available online: <http://www.asanas.org.uk/files/002ruickbie.pdf>.

Russell, I.A. (ed.) 2006. *Images, representations and Heritage: Moving beyond Modern Approaches to Archaeology*. London and New York: Springer.

Said, E. 1978. *Orientalism: Western Constructions of the Orient*. Harmondsworth: Penguin.

Sardar, Z. 2002. *The A to Z of Postmodern Life*. London: Vision.

Schieffelin, E. 1996. On failure in performance: throwing the medium out of the séance. In C. Laderman and M. Roseman (eds), *The Performance of Healing*, 59–90. London: Routledge.

Schieffelin, E. 1998. Problematising performance. In F. Hughes-Freeland (ed.) *Ritual, Performance, Media*, 194–207. London: Routledge.

Sebastion, T. 2001. Alternative archaeology: has it happened? In R. J. Wallis and K. J. Lymer (eds) *A permeability of boundaries: new approaches to the archaeology of art, religion and folklore*, 125–35. Oxford: British Archaeological Reports.

Semple, S. 1998. A Fear of the Past: the Place of the Prehistoric Burial Mound in the Ideology of Middle and Later Anglo-Saxon England. *World Archaeology* 30 (1): 109–26.

Shallcrass, P. 1995. Druidry Today. In G. Harvey and C. Hardman (eds) *Paganism Today: Wiccans, Druids, the Goddess and Ancient Earth Traditions for the Twenty-First Century*, 65–80. London: Thorsons.

Shallcrass, P. 1997. *The Story of Taliesin*. St. Leonard's on Sea, Sussex: British Druid Order.

Shallcrass, P. 1998. A Priest of the Goddess. In J. Pearson, R. H. Roberts and G. Samuel (eds) *Nature Religion Today: Paganism in the Modern World*, 157–69. Edinburgh: Edinburgh University Press.

Shallcrass, P. 2000. *Druidry*. London: Piatkus.

Shallcrass, P. 2003. Respect and Reburial in Action. *The Druid's Voice* 2(2): 26–8.

Simpson, J. and S. Roud, 2000. Rollright Stones. In *A Dictionary of English Folklore*, Oxford: Oxford University Press, 2000. Available Oxford Reference Online. <http://www.oxfordreference.com/views/ENTRY.html?subview= Main&entry=t71.e872>.

Smiles, S. and S. Moser (eds) 2005. *Envisioning the Past: Archaeology and the Image*. Oxford: Blackwell Publishing.

Smith, A. 1994. For All Those Who Were Indian in a Former life. In C. Adams (ed.) *Ecofeminism and the Sacred*, 168–71. New York: Continuum.

Smith, C. C. 1878. Fairies at Ilkley Wells. *Folk-Lore Record* 1: 229–31.

Smith, D. E. 1987 *The Everyday World as Problematic: a Feminist Sociology*. Toronto: University of Toronto Press.

Smith, D. E. 1990. *The Conceptual Practices of Power: A Feminist Sociology of Knowledge*. Toronto: University of Toronto Press.

Smith, D. E. 1993. *Texts, Facts and Femininity*. London: Routledge.

Smith, L. T. 1999. *Decolonizing Methodologies: Research and Indigenous Peoples*. London, New York and Dunedin, New Zealand: Zed Books/University of Otago Press.

Soja, E. 1996. *Thirdspace*. Oxford: Blackwell.

Steele, J. n.d. British Association for Biological Anthropology and Osteoarchaeology (BABAO): Response to the DCMS Consultation Document 'Care of Historic Human Remains'. Prepared on behalf of the Association by James Steele (BABAO Chair), University of Southampton. Available online: <http://www.babaotemp.bham.ac.uk/BABAOFinal VersionDCMSConsultationResponse.pdf>.

Stone, C. J. 1996. *Fierce Dancing: Adventures in the Underground*. London: Faber and Faber.

Stone, P. 1999. The Stonehenge we deserve? *Minerva: The International Review of Ancient Art and Archaeology* 10(3) (May/June): 22–25.

Strathern, M. 1998. Comment on M. F. Brown, 'Can Culture be Copyrighted?' *Current Anthropology* 39(2): 193–222.

Stukeley, W. 1740. *Stonehenge, a Temple Restor'd to the British Druids*. London: W. Innis & R. Manby.

Swidler, N., K. E. Dongoske, R. Anyon and A. S. Downer (eds) 1997. *Native Americans and Archaeologists: Stepping Stones to Common Ground*. Walnut Creek, CA: AltaMira Press.

Taussig, M. 1987. *Shamanism, Colonialism and the Wild Man: A Study in Terror and Healing*. Chicago: The University of Chicago Press.

The Stonehenge Project n.d. Available online: <http://www.thestonehenge-project.org/>.

Thomas, J. 1993. The Politics of Vision and the Archaeologies of Landscape. In B. Bender (ed.) *Landscape: Politics and Perspectives*, 19–48. Oxford: Berg.

Thomas, J. 1999. *Understanding the Neolithic*. London: Routledge.

Thomas, J. 2000. Death, identity and the body in Neolithic Britain. *The Journal of the Royal Anthropological Institute* 6 (4): 653–68.

Thomas, J. 2001. Comments on Part I: Intersecting Landscapes. In B. Bender and M. Winer (eds) 2001. *Contested landscapes: Movement, Exile and Place*, 181–7. Oxford: Berg.

Thorpe, N. 2000/2001. Science vs. Culture: The Reburial Conflict in the USA. *3rd Stone: Archaeology, Folklore and Myth* 39: 43–51.

Tilley, C. (ed.) 2004. *The Materiality of Stone: Explorations in Landscape Phenomenology*. Oxford: Berg.

Timms, S. and A. Dickson 2005. *Ladybridge Farm, Nosterfield. Report on an Archaeological Investigation*. For Mike Griffiths and Associates, on behalf of Tarmac Northern Ltd. Available online: <http://www.archaeological planningconsultancy.co.uk/mga/projects/noster/pdf/ladybridge_ additional.pdf>, summary at <http://www.archaeologicalplanning consultancy.co.uk/mga/projects/noster/pages/ladyrep.html>.

Tuan, Yi-Fu 1974. *Topophilia. A Study of Environmental Perception, Attitudes and Values*. Englewood Cliffs, NJ: Prentice-Hall.

Ucko, P. J. 1990. Foreword. In P. Gathercole and D. Lowenthal (eds) *The Politics of the Past*, ix–xxi. London: Unwin Hyman.

Ucko, P. J., M. Hunter, A. J. Clark and A. David 1991. *Avebury Reconsidered: from the 1660s to the 1990s*. London: Unwin Hyman.

Urry, J. 1990. *The Tourist Gaze: Leisure and Travel in Contemporary Societies.* London: Sage Publications.

Wainwright, G. 2000. The Stonehenge we deserve. *Antiquity* 74: 334–42.

Wallis, R. J. 1998. Journeying the Politics of Ecstasy: Anthropological Perspectives on Neo-shamanism. *The Pomegranate: A Journal of Neo-Pagan Thought* 6: 20–8.

Wallis, R. J. 1999a. Altered States, Conflicting Cultures: Shamans, Neo-shamans and Academics. *Anthropology of Consciousness* 10 (2–3): 41–9.

Wallis, R. J. 1999b. *The Socio-Politics of Ecstasy: Autoarchaeology and Neo-shamanism.* PhD Thesis, Department of Archaeology, University of Southampton.

Wallis, R. J. 2000. Queer Shamans: Autoarchaeology and Neo-shamanism. *World Archaeology* 32(2): 251–61.

Wallis, R. J. 2001. Waking the Ancestors: Neo-shamanism and Archaeology. In N. Price (ed.) *The Archaeology of Shamanism*: 213–330. London: Routledge. (Reprinted in G. Harvey (ed.) 2002. *Shamanism: A Reader*: 402–23. Routledge.)

Wallis, R. J. 2002a. Sacred Sites? Neo-Shamans and prehistoric monuments. *Hagia Chora* 12–13 (Summer): 50–4 (in German).

Wallis, R. J. 2002b. Taliesin's Trip – Celtic Shamanisms? *The Druid's Voice* 1 (10): 38–48.

Wallis, R. J. 2003. *Shamans / neo-Shamans: Ecstasy, Alternative Archaeologies and Contemporary Pagans.* London: Routledge.

Wallis, R. J. 2004. Between the Worlds: Autoarchaeology and neo-Shamans. In J. Blain, D. Ezzy and G. Harvey (eds) *Researching Paganisms*, 191–215. Walnut Creek, CA: Altamira.

Wallis, R. J. 2006. Shimmering Steel / Standing Stones: Reflections on the Intervention of Anish Kapoor at the Rollright Stones. In T. A. Dowson (ed.) *Object-Excavation-Intervention: Dialogues between Sculpture and Archaeology*: in press. Subject/Object: New Studies in Sculpture Series. Ashgate, Oxford / Henry Moore Institute, Leeds.

Wallis, R. J. In preparation. *Re-enchanting Cup-and-Ring: Animism, Shamanism and Rock Art Landscapes.*

Wallis, R. J. and J. Blain 2001. Sacred Sites, Contested Rites/Rights: Contemporary Pagan Engagements with the Past. Six-Month Pilot Project 2001. Available online: <http://www.sacredsites.org.uk/discussions/discussion2002-1.pdf>.

Wallis, R. J. and J. Blain 2003. Sites, sacredness, and stories: interactions of archaeology and contemporary Paganism. *Folklore* 114(3): 307–21.

Wallis, R. J. and J. Blain 2004. 'No One Voice: Ancestors, Pagan Identity and the 'Reburial Issue' in Britain. *British Archaeology* 78: 10–13.

Wallis, R. J. and J. Blain 2005. Sacred Sites in England. In B. Taylor and J. Kaplan (eds) *Encyclopedia of Religion and Nature*, 1460–2. New York and London: Continuum.

Wallis, R. J. and K. J. Lymer (eds) 2001. *A Permeability of Boundaries: New Approaches to the Archaeology of Art, Religion and Folklore.* BAR International Series 936. Oxford: BAR.

Watkins, J. 2000. *Indigenous Archaeology: American Indian Values and Scientific Practice.* Walnut Creek, CA: AltaMira Press.

Weller, P, 1997. *Religions in the UK: directory 1997–2000*. Mickleover, Derby: University of Derby.

Wessex Archaeology 2003. Stonehenge Laser Scans. An Application of Laser Scanners in Archaeology. On-line press release: <http://stonehenge. archaeoptics.co.uk/press.html>.

Western Daily Press 2004. Druid community calls for a new shrine at Stonehenge. *This is Bristol, Western Daily Press*: 2 March 2004.

Whittle, A. 1997. *Sacred Mound, Holy Rings*. Oxford: Oxbow.

Whittle, A. 1990. A Model for the Mesolithic–Neolithic Transition in the Upper Kennet Valley, North Wiltshire. *Proceedings of the Prehistoric Society* 56: 101–10.

Williams, H. 1998. Monuments and the Past in Early Anglo-Saxon England. *World Archaeology* 30 (1): 90–108.

Wilson, R. C. 1994. Seeing they see not. In D. E. Young and J.-G. Goulet (eds) *Being Changed by Cross-Cultural Encounters: the Anthropology of Extraordinary Experience*, 197–209. Peterborough, Ontario: Broadview Press.

Wodak, R. and M. Meyer 2001. *Methods in Critical Discourse Analysis*. London: Sage.

Wood, C. 2002. The Meaning of Stonehenge. *3rd Stone: Archaeology, Folklore and Myth* 43 (Summer): 49–54.

Worthington, A. 2004. *Stonehenge: Celebration and Subversion*. Loughborough: Heart of Albion Press.

Worthington, A. 2005 (ed.) *The Battle of the Beanfield*. Teignmouth: Enabler Publications.

York, M. 2005. Wanting to Have Your New Age Cake and Eat It Too. *Journal of Alternative Spiritualities and New Age Studies* 1. Available online: <http:// www.open.ac.uk/Arts/jasanas/>.

Index

3rd Stone magazine, 91

Achnabreck, 157, 160, *161*
Aggregate Levy Sustainability
    Fund, 144
Alexander Keiller Museum, 48
Alexander, M., 203
All Party Parliamentary
    Archaeology Group
    (APPAG), xvii, 33
alternative archaeology, 4, 22,
    45, 53, 113
Alternative Spiritualities and
    New Age Studies (ASANAS),
    xvii
Alves, L.B., 224*n*
Alvesson, M., 13
Amesbury, 83
ancestors
    Avebury, 48, 64, 65, 75
    Druidry/Druids, 41, 64
    Heathenry/Heathens, 65, 191
    Ilkley Moor, 152
    Kilmartin Valley, 152, 155–60
    Nine Ladies Circle, 138
    paganism/pagans, 41,
        189–201, 202
    Stonehenge, 79, 80, 95, 97,
        113, 121
    see also reburial issue
Ancient Order of Druids, 83
*Ancient Sacred Landscapes
    Network* (ASLAN)
    founding of, 59
    preservation ethos, 38–9, 42,
        97
    Rollright Stones, 42, 178
    Sacred Sites Charter, 42, *43*,
        58
    Stonehenge proposals, 111,
        117
Ancient Voices: Stonehenge, 96
Angkor Watt, xviii
animism
    engagement with landscape,
        7, 31, 184, 209
    new indigenes, 10
    reburial issue, 206
    and shamanism, 217*n*
    Stonehenge, 121–3
anthropologists, 3
    reburial issue, 19, 189, 190
    Sacred Sites project, xvii
Antiquity, xv, 55, 180
Antrobus, Sir Edmund, 83
Anyon, R., 190
APPAG (All Party Parliamentary
    Archaeology Group), xvii,
    33
APT (Association of Polytheist
    Traditions), xvii, 197

Arbor Law Henge, 103, 132–3,
    132
Arch-Druid's barrow, 175
Archaeological Institute of
    America, xiv
archaeologists
    condition of heritage, 1
    contemporary ritual activity,
        36
    dismissive attitude, 74
    Druidry/Druids, 212
    paganism/pagans, 1–3, 39,
        74–6, 173–4, 209–14
    and personal-growth druids,
        39
    preservation ethos, 33, 36,
        107–8
    reburial issue, 19, 189, 190,
        198, 200, 202–4, 223*n*
    sacred sites, xvi, 31, 209
    Sacred Sites project, xvii
    and Stonehenge, 79, 107–8,
        118
    suspicion of alternative
        archaeology, 113
    visual engagement, 106–7
archaeology
    on television, xiii, xvii, 21
    see also alternative
        archaeology
artefacts, repatriation of, 28,
    190, 192, 207–8, 210
ASANAS (Alternative
    Spiritualities and New Age
    Studies), xvii
Asatru Folk Assembly, 192
ASLAN *see Ancient Sacred
    Landscapes Network*
    (ASLAN)
Asphodel, 181
ASSF *see* Avebury Sacred Sites
    Forum (ASSF)
Association of Polytheist
    Traditions (APT), xvii, 197
Association of Social
    Anthropologists
    conference, xvii
astronomical celebrations, 28
Atkinson, Richard, 70
Attwood, Karin, 176–7, 178,
    181
Aubrey, John, 47, 48, 49, 50,
    174
Australia, reburial issue, 190
authenticity
    Avebury, 54
    Druidry/Druids, 11, 26, 211,
        212
    paganism/pagans, 11, 25–6
    shamanism, 157
autoethnography, 14

Avebury, 47–76
    ancestors, 48, 64, 65, 75
    archaeological interpretation,
        48, 50, 53
    authenticity, 54
    autumn equinox, 65–6
    the Avenue, 47, 66
    child blessing, 64
    collaborative dialogue, 212
    damage, 17, 49, 50, 55, 56–9,
        72–3, 124
    Druidry/Druids, 8, *25*, 41,
        48–9, 54, 55, 64–5, 67,
        192
    English Heritage
        Management Plan, 1, 4,
        30, 47–8, 49, 51, 70–1
    excavations, 50, 51–2, 70, 74,
        192
    Goddess Spirituality, 9
    graffiti, 47, 55
    Heathenry/Heathens, 48, 65,
        219*n*
    heritage management, 52, 54,
        70, 74, 124
    as icon of Britishness/
        Englishness, xiii, 108
    National Trust, 47, 48, 52, 55,
        59, 61, 63, 108, 201
    National Trust Management
        Plan, 4, 108
    Negotiating Avebury Project,
        52–3
    new travellers, 48, 61
    pagan hand-fasting, 59–60,
        61, 64, 66, 67
    paganism/pagans, xv, 1,
        17–18, 48–9, 52–4,
        55–69, 70–3, 124, 189,
        213–14
    Prophets Conference (2002),
        58, 187
    reburial issue, 201
    ritual fires, 56
    ritual litter, 58–9
    as sacred site, 1, 22, 30, 48,
        52–4, 67–9, 117
    sarsens, 49, 50, 56
    spring equinox, 65–6
    summer solstice, 55, 59, 61,
        62, 65–6, 67, 103
    tourists, 48, 51, 55, 108
    visitors, 48, 51, 52, 55, 61–2,
        63, 74, 108–9
    votive offerings, 56–8, *56*, 64,
        75
    Wicca/Wiccans, 48, 49, 66
    winter solstice, *56*, 65–6
    as World Heritage Site (WHS),
        47–8, 50–1
Avebury Forum, 52

Avebury Guardians, xv, 17, 59, 60, 173, 213–14
Avebury Henge and stone circles, 47, 49, 51
  acoustic properties, 75
  damage, 50, 56
  Druid rituals, 8, 64–5
Avebury Sacred Sites Forum (ASSF), 59, 61, 62
Avebury Tour CD, 50
Avebury Trusloe, 52
Avebury village, 47, 49, 51, 52
Avebury Visitor Research (1996–1998), 4
the Avenue, Avebury, 47, 66
the Avenue, Stonehenge, 77, 79, 105, 110, 114
'Awen', 43, 65, 218n
Ayer's Rock, xviii

BABAO (British Association for Biological Anthropology and Osteoarchaeology), 202
Back Hill TV, 101
Badger Stone, 170–1
Bakewell Rural District Council, 127
Bakhtin, M.M., 31, 98
Bannister, V., 39
Barbrook II circle, 221n
Barnatt, John, xv, 42, 129, 133, 170, 221n
'Barry', 40
Bauman, Z., 26, 195
Baxter, I.
  Stonehenge Management Plan, 116
  Stonehenge road proposals, 112
  Stonehenge visitor capacity, 117
  Stonehenge visitor engagement, 109, 114–15, 221n
  Stonehenge visitor facilities, 37, 107, 109, 111, 112, 113, 220–1n
BBC
  Ancient Voices: Stonehenge, 96
  Avebury, 51
  heritage management documentary, 118–19
  Restoration programmes, 34
  Silbury Hill excavations, 70
  Silbury Hole documentary, 72
  Time Fliers, 146
BBC News, 194, 200
BBC News Online, 92
BDO (British Druid Order), 64
Beckensall, S., 159
Being Changed by Cross Cultural Encounters, 75
Bender, B.
  Avebury, 49
  contemporary ritual activity, 36
  dialogues, 217n
  landscape archaeology, 209
  new traveller opinions, 194

paganism/pagans, 3–4
preservation ethos, 33
Stonehenge, 78, 79, 81, 84, 91, 93
Stonehenge as a palimpsest, 36
visual engagement, 37
Bennett, P., 170, 174
Beowulf (Heaney), 189
Bhabha, H., 4, 32
Bigger Picture, 11
Bingham, John, 92
Biolsi, T., 28, 190
Birchover, 127, 142
Blackmore, Sasha, 92
Blain, Dr Jenny
  ancestors and bloodlines, 156, 191
  at Kilmartin, 151, 162
  authenticity, 25, 54
  Avebury, 49, 54
  Castlerigg stone circle, 218n
  Celts, 156, 223n
  discourse, 12
  entheogens, 222n
  Eurocentrism, 155
  Heathen ceremonies, 191
  new-indigeneity, 54
  Nine Worlds of Seid-magic, 14
  paganism/pagans, 3, 38
  public performances of paganism, 67
  re-enchantment, 27
  reburial issue, 195, 202
  researcher status, 14, 16
  Researching Paganisms, 14
  Rollright Stones, 183
  sacred sites, 98
  Sacred Sites project, xvi, xvii, 2, 6
  shamanism, 156, 181, 221n, 222n, 223n
  Stonehenge, 86, 88
Boniface, P., 3, 22
Bowers, Paul, 169
Bowman, M., 21, 27, 54, 156, 191
Bradley, R., 28, 45, 209, 218n
Britannia (Camden), 173
Britarch, 149, 211, 212, 223n
British Archaeology, 44, 145, 193, 194, 202–3
British Association for Biological Anthropology and Osteoarchaeology (BABAO), 202
British Druid Order (BDO), 64
British Museum, 204, 208
British Polytheist, 197
British Sociology Association Study Group on Religion, xvii
Britishness, xiii, xiv
Brown, A.K., 28, 190
Buffalo Bill, 192
bureaucratic rationalism, 26
Burl, A., 49, 145, 174, 181, 223n
Butterfield, William, 164

CADW (Welsh National Heritage), 1
calendrical celebrations, 28
Callanish, xiii–xiv
Calver, S., xv, 4
'Cam', 133
Cambridge Heritage Seminars, xvii
Camden, William, 173, 174, 175
Cameron, Geo, 160, 222n
Cana Barn Henges, 145
Canada, reburial issue, 189–90
'cardiac celts', 191
Cardigan, Lord, 84
Carmichael, D.L., 3, 28
Carnac, 2
Carnasserie castle, 160
Carpenter, D., 38, 55
Carroll, Peter, 170
Castlerigg stone circle, 17, 103, 218n
Çatalhöyük, 5
cellular memory, 157, 158
Celtic shamanism, 154, 157, 158, 160, 222n
Celticity, 54, 191
Centre for Tourism and Cultural Change, xvii, 3
Cernunnos, 167
Chaco Canyon, xviii, 4, 15
Chadburn, A., 70
Champion, M., 43
Chandler, J., 52
change, 21–2, 34
Channel 4, 21
Chaos Magickians, 170
Chaplin, George, 146, 147
character assessment, 34
Chartered Institution of Water and Environmental Management, 147
Chatters, J.C., 190, 192
Cherhill, 218n
child blessing, xvi, 28
  Avebury, 64
  Rollright Stones, 179
  Stonehenge, 116, 121
Chippindale, C.
  contemporary ritual activity, 36
  paganism/pagans, 3–4
  preservation ethos, 33
  Stonehenge, xiii
  Stonehenge free festival, 84
  Stonehenge as a palimpsest, 36, 81
  Stonehenge road proposals, 112
  Stonehenge visitor capacity, 117
  Stonehenge visitor engagement, 109, 114–15, 221n
  Stonehenge visitor numbers, 106
  Stonehenge visual engagement, 37
  Stonehenge visitor facilities, 107, 109, 111, 112, 113, 220–1n

Christians, sacred sites, 31
Church of England, 177, 193, 205, 206
Church of the Universal Bond, 83
City of Bradford Metropolitan District Council, 164
Clandon Park, 219*n*
Cleere, H.F., 1, 22
Clifton, C., 3
Cohen, M., 12
Coleman, S., 54
College of Druidism, 154
Community Archaeology Project, 5, 214
community vibrancy, 34
Coneybury Henge, 79
Constable, John, xiv
Cooney, G., 32
Cope, Julian, 17, 42, 73
Copp, A., 148
Core Shamanism, 160
Cork Stone, 129
Cork, T., 63
Cornwell, B., 96
Cotswold Order of Druids, 188
Cottingley Fairy phenomena, 166
Cottingley Woods, 166
Coughlan, S., 40
Council for British Archaeology, 148, 149
Council of British Druid Orders, 201
Council for the Protection of Rural England (CPRE)
    Stanton Moor, 125, 127, 143, 144
    Stonehenge, 111, 117, 200
Council on Spiritual Practices, 220*n*
counter-cultural druids, 18, 38, 39–40, 54
counter-cultural pagans, 105
Countess East farm site, 111
Cowan, Tom, 160, 223*n*
CPRE *see* Council for the Protection of Rural England (CPRE)
Craig, S., 93
Crook, S., 165, 166
crop circle community, 72–3
Cruithni, 42, 97
cultural appropriations, 157
cultural consumption, 159
cultural theft, 25

The Daily Express, 92
The Daily Mail, 91
Daily Mirror, 92
The Daily Telegraph, 91, 134
Dale View quarry, 128, 130, 143–4
Dames, Michael, 42, 70
Davies, P., 194–5, 200–1
Davison, B., 106
Davison, J., 91
De Bruxelles, Simon, 91, 92
de-traditionalisation, 24
Dead to Rights, 200

decolonizing methodologies, 29, 190
Denison, Simon, 44
Denning, K., 4
Denton, N.R., 144
Department of Constitutional Affairs, 193
Department of Culture, Media and Sport, 192, 201–2, 205–6
Descartes, R., 31
Devereux, Paul, 42, 70, 180
Devil's Arrows standing stones, 145
Devizes Museum, 201
Dickson, A., 148
'dirt' archaeologists, 34
discourse, and power, 12, 123
discourse analysis, 11–13
disenchantment, 26
disillusionment, 21–2
Dísir, 68
Dobney, Terry, 66
Doll Tor circle, xv, 170, 221*n*
    votive offerings, *10*, 140
Dongoske, K.E., 190
Dove Holes Henge, 132
Dowson, T.A., 33
Draft Code of Practice for The Care of Human Remains in Museums, 205–6
Dragon bind-rune, 140
Dragon Network, 140
Dragon Project, 180, 223*n*
Drax, Colonel, 70
DreamFlesh journal, 170
Druid Network, 64, 117
Druid Prayer, 64
The Druid Renaissance, 25–6
Druid Vow, 64, 65
Druidry/Druids, xiv
    and ancestors, 41, 64
    and archaeologists, 212
    authenticity, 11, 26, 211, 212
    Avebury, *8*, *25*, 41, 48–9, 54, 55, 64–5, 67, 192
    Kilmartin Valley, 153
    leadership, 63
    Nine Ladies Stone circle, 131, 140
    preservation ethos, 38–40
    reburial issue, 194–201, 205
    Rollright Stones, 177, 178
    sacred sites, 30–1
    Seahenge timber circle, 44, 211
    shamanism, 154, 217*n*
    Stonehenge, 8, 39–40, 41, 83, 91, 93, 96–7, 98, 113, 117, 121
    Thornborough Henges, 146, 149
    see also counter-cultural druids; personal-growth druids
The Druid's Voice, 38, 194, 199, *199*
dualism, 31
Dunadd, 160
Durkheim, E., 31

Durrington Walls, 79

EAA (European Association of Archaeologists), 223*n*
Earl Grey Tower, 134
earth mystics, xv, 8–9
    Avebury, 48
    preservation ethos, 2
    Rollright Stones, 179, 180
    Stonehenge, 113
    Temple Wood circles, 153, *153*
    understandings of pasts, 22
Eco-Warriors, 125
Economic and Social Research Council (ESRC), xvii
Eden Millennium Project, 31
Edmonds, M.
    contemporary ritual activity, 36
    dialogue, 209
    Nine Ladies Stone circle, 124, 130
    Peak District, 126, 133
Edwards, B., 52
The Elementary Forms of Religious Life (Durkheim), 31
Eliade, M., 221*n*
Elliott, R.W.V., 219*n*
Elsner, J., 54
enchantment *see* re-enchantment
Endcliffe quarry, 127–8, 130, 133, 136, 143
English Heritage
    alternative discourses, 179
    alternative visitors at Stonehenge, 113
    Avebury Management Plan, 1, 4, 30, 47–8, 49, 51, 70–1
    BBC documentary series, 118–19
    change in the past, 34
    character assessment, 34
    elitist tendencies, 105
    environmental capacity, 35
    historic capital, 34
    historic environment, 34–5
    Monuments at Risk Survey (MARS), 34
    Nine Ladies Stone circle, 137
    Power of Place, 35
    preservation ethos, 34–5, 97, 182
    reburial issue, 193, 197–8, 200
    Rollright Stones, 176, 178
    sacred sites, 1
    Sacred Sites project, xvii
    Seahenge, 43–4, 214
    Silbury Hill, 17, 70, 71–2, 73
    Stanton Moor, 144
    State of the Historic Environment, 35
    Stonehenge control barriers, 104
    Stonehenge Inquiry (2004), 117

English Heritage – *continued*
  Stonehenge managed open access, xv, 82, 85, 100, 105, 117–18
  Stonehenge as 'must see' attraction, 108
  Stonehenge partying, 97, 99
  The Stonehenge Project, xiv, 77, 78–9, 220*n*
  Stonehenge summer solstice, xv, xvi, 82, 84, 85, 89, 90, 105
  Stonehenge visitor facilities, xiv
  Stonehenge visual engagement, 37, 38, 106–7
  Stonehenge winter solstice, 96
  Thornborough Henges, 18, 144, 147, 148
Englishness, xiii, 108
entheogens, 83, 154, 171, 219–20*n*, 222*n*
Environment Act (1995), 127, 129
environmental capacity, 35
ESRC (Economic and Social Research Council), xvii
European Association of Archaeologists (EAA), 223*n*
Evans, A.J., 173
Everard, Clews, 1–2, 30, 96, 97, 119
Ezzy, D., xvii, 3

Fabian, J., 45
Fairclough, N., 12
Fellowship of Isis, 177
Festival Eye, 39
Fielden, K., 106
Financial Times, 92
Finn, C., 4
Firsoff, George, 86–7, 93, 114
Flaherty, G., 221*n*
Fleet, M., 91
Fleming, Sam, 6, 38, 41, 182, 183
Flick, Pauline, 176
Folklore Record, 164–5
Forbes, Patrick, 121
Forte, R., 219*n*
Foucault, M., 4, 12, 32, 33, 123
Fowler, Peter, 3, 22, 112
Freyr, 141
Fridman, E.J.N., 223*n*
Friends of the Earth, 200
Friends of the Stone, xv, 42
Friends of Thornborough Henges, 18, 144, 147–8
Frogatt Edge, 9
Futharks, 219*n*

Gaelic shamanism, 155
galdr, 68, 140
Gallagher, A-M., 156, 195
Gallop, A., 219*n*
Gandalf's Garden, 39
Gell, A., 45
Getty, Sarah, 92

Ghost Dance shirt, 192
Giddens, A., 24
Gillings, M., 52
Gingell, Chris, 55, 59, 61
Glastonbury, 4, 32
Glastonbury music festival, 89, 103, 220*n*
Glastonbury Order of Druids (GOD), 64
Glastonbury, Pete, 53
Glebe Cairn, *162*
Glentoal Associates, 127
GOD (Glastonbury Order of Druids), 64
Goddess Spirituality, xiv, 4
  ancient places as temples, 183
  Avebury, 9
  Çatalhöyük, 5
  Malta, 5
  sacred sites, 31, 218*n*
Goodrick, G.T., 145
Gorsedd of Bards of Caer Abiri, 48, 64, 65
graffiti, xvi, 2
  Avebury, 47, 55
  Ilkley Moor, 19, 166, 167, 169–70
  Nine Ladies Stone circle, 131
  Stonehenge, 81, 115
Gray, Harold St. George, 50
Great Wall of China, 108
Green, D., 24, 26
Green, R., 191
Green, Scott, 63
Greene, S., 24
Greenwood, S., 3, 26
Grey, Harold, 201
Greywolf *see* Shallcrass, Philip 'Greywolf'
Griffin, W., 26
Gross, D., 24
The Guardian, 59–60, 84, 92, 133, 135
Guidance for Best Practice for Treatment of Human Remains Excavated from Christian Burial Grounds in Britain, 193
'Guidance and Request for the Reburial of Druid Ancestral Remains at Avebury', 201
Gyrus, 42, 151, 170–1

HAD (Honouring the Ancient Dead), 196, 197, 205–6
Haddon Estates, 133
hand-fasting (marriage), xvi, 28
  Avebury, 59–60, 61, 64, 66, 67
  Nine Ladies Stone circle, 138
  Rollright Stones, 179
  Stonehenge, 116, 121
  Thornborough Henges, 146
Hanging Stones, 167
Hanson Environment Fund, 177
Haraway, D., 13
Harding, J., 144, 145, 148, 149, 150

Hardman, C., 3
Harner, M., 160
Harris, Adrian, 7
Harrop, Andrew, 137
Harvey, G.
  animism, 217*n*
  Druidry/Druids, 64
  entheogens, 220*n*, 222*n*
  new agers, 6
  new animists, 122
  paganism/pagans, xvii, 3
  shamanism, 217*n*, 221*n*, 222*n*
  Stonehenge, 96, 98, 122
  third position, 14
Hassan, F.A., 5
Hattersley, Roy, 128–9
Hawkes, J., 77
Hawkwind, 39
Haystack Stone, 169, 172
Heaney, Seamus, 189
Heathenry/Heathens, xiv
  and ancestors, 65, 191
  Avebury, 48, 65, 219*n*
  Kilmartin Valley, 153
  Nine Ladies Stone circle, 140, 141
  Rollright Stones, 178
  sacred sites, 30–1
  seidr-shamanism, 14
  Stonehenge, 96
  Thornborough Henges, 146
  Thor's hammer, 8
'hedglings' of Green Street, 61
Heelas, P., 22, 24
Hegel, G.W.F, 300
The Henge Shop, Avebury, 48, 55
Hengeworld, 52
Heritage Action organisation, 146
  Avebury, 49
  Silbury Hill, 73
  Stonehenge, 112
  Thornborough Henges, 144
heritage managers
  Avebury, 52, 54, 70, 74, 124
  condition of heritage, 1
  dismissive attitude, 74
  ideas of rationality, 75
  and indigenous communities, 210
  paganism/pagans, 1–3, 39, 63, 172, 173, 189, 191, 204–5, 209–14
  preservation ethos, 33, 34–5, 97, 107, 108, 113, 182, 183
  Rollright Stones, 204
  sacred sites, xvi, 1–3, 30, 31
  Sacred Sites project, xvii
  Silbury Hole, 70
  Stanton Moor, 18, 125, 204
  Stonehenge, 18, 78–9, 107, 108, 124, 204
  threat of alternative visitors, 113
  see also English Heritage; Historic Scotland; National Trust
Heritage Today, 44

heritage tourism, xiii, 3, 48
 Avebury, 48, 51, 55, 108
 Kilmartin Valley, 152
 Stonehenge, 79, 108–9,
  114–15
 Thornborough Henges, 147
Heselton, P., 11
Hetherington, K., 4, 5, 32, 38,
 83
Heyworth, Mike, 149
Highways Agency, 117, 200
Hill, J.D., 209
Hill, R., 99
Hine, Phil, 170
Hinemihi, 219n
historic capital, 34
Historic Environment Enabling
 Programme, 35
Historic Scotland, 1, 152, 190
history, on television, xiii, 21
History of Britain, 21
Hobsbawm, E., 21, 24
Hodder, Ian, 5, 218n
Holland, P., 173
Holtorf, C., 33, 157
Home Office, 199
Honouring the Ancient Dead
 (HAD), 196, 197, 205–6
Hooper-Greenhill, Eileen, 223n
Hope, Wally, 39, 84
Horton, Mike, 146
Hotton Moor Henges, 145
Hubert, J., 3, 29, 31, 32
Human Remains Report, 192,
 201–2, 205, 207
Hutton, R., 3, 7, 11, 25–6, 121,
 212

ICOMOS, 111
Idle Rock, 169
Ilkley Moor, 164–72
 and ancestors, 152
 Badger Stone, 170–1
 damage, 19, 166, 169–70, 172
 fairy sightings, 164–6
 graffiti, 19, 166, 167, 169–70
 Hanging Stones, 167
 Haystack Stone, 169, 172
 Idle Rock, 169
 paganism/pagans, 19, 152,
  164, 166–7, 170, 171–2
 rock art, 19, 151–2, 164,
  166–7, 168, 169–71
 Twelve Apostles circle, xv, 19,
  169, 170
 Willy Hall's Wood Stone, xv,
  166, 168, 169
Ilkley Moor Management Plan,
 164, 172
The Independent, 91, 92, 176
indigenous communities
 British context, 190–1
 and heritage managers, 210
 irrational views, 75, 155
 and museum curators, 204
 and paganism/pagans, 6, 28
 reburial issue, 28, 190, 192,
  204
 sacred sites, 28, 31
Ingerman, S., 160

Ingold, T., 122
International Times, 39
Inuit culture, 158
irony, 54
Irwin, A., 35
Itinerary (Leland), 49
Ivahkiv, A.J., 4, 5, 26, 32

Jahn, R.G., 180
Jakobsen, M.D., 222n
Jenkins, T., 201–2
Jenny, 67, 68, 69
'Jo', 137
Johnson, B., 145
Johnson, N., 16
Johnson, P.C., 222n
Jones, 222n

Kapoor, Anish, 186, 188
Keiller, Alexander, 50, 51–2
Keltic Druids, 154
Keltic shamanism, 154, 157,
 158, 160, 222n
Kelvingrove Museum, Glasgow,
 192
Kennedy, Maev, 92, 112
Kennet District Council, 48, 63
Kennewick Man, 192
Kernow, 215
'Kevin', 55
Kilmartin castle, 160
Kilmartin hamlet, 161
Kilmartin House Museum, 152,
 159, 160, 161, 162
Kilmartin Valley, 2, 152–63
 and ancestors, 152, 155–60
 appropriateness of behaviour,
  103
 Druidry/Druids, 153
 excavations, 163
 Heathenry/Heathens, 153
 paganism/pagans, 19, 152–3,
  160
 re-enchantment, 157, 160
 rock art, 19, 152, 153, 154,
  157–8, 159
 shamanism, 153, 155–60
 tourists, 152
King Stone
 Rollright Stones, 174–5, 176,
  180, 182
 Stanton Moor, 131
King's Men, Rollright Stones,
 174, 175–6, 178–9, 181,
 182, 185, 188
Kreps, C.F., 28, 190

Ladybridge Farm, 146, 147, 148
Ladyman, Stephen, 112
Lambrick, George
 needs of pagans, 39
 Rollright Stones, 2, 4, 174,
  175, 181
 sensitivity of ancestors, 22
 Stonehenge, 115
Lammy, David, 112
landscape
 Avebury, 48, 49, 50, 53
 as having agency, 209
 Kilmartin Valley, 157, 160

pagan attachments, 26–7, 32,
 45, 184, 191
sacredness, 31–2
Stanton Moor, 125, 133,
 140–1, 149
Stonehenge, 37, 79, 80, 99,
 106–7, 110, 114, 121–3
Thornborough Henges, 145,
 147–50
tourism research, 3
landscape archaeology, 209
Lark Hill, 111
Larkhill Camp, 83
LAW (Loyal Arthurian
 Warband), 64
Lawson, Andrew, 115
Layton, R., 3, 28, 190
Lees Cross quarry, 127–8, 130,
 133, 136, 143
Leicester Museums, 197
Leland, John, 49
Leskernick Project, 5
Letcher, Dr Andy
 countercultural identity, 38,
  39, 54
 Druidry/Druids, 38, 54
 neo-tribes, 9
 personal-growth druids, 38
 protester experiences, 142
 Rollright Stones, 186
 Sacred Sites project, xvii, 6
 Stonehenge visual
  engagement, 38
Lewis Chess Pieces, 208
Lewis, J., 7
leys
 Rollright Stones, 179–80
 Stonehenge, 79
 Temple Wood circle, 153
Liddle, Rod, 59–60
Lindauer, M., 220n
liquid modernity, 26
Lister, Jeremiah, 165
Living Wetlands Award, 147
Lockyer, Sir Norman, 174
Lodge, Alan, 83
Longstone Edge, 126, 129
Longstones, 74
Louise, Anita, 218n
Lower Ure Conservation Trust,
 147
Loyal Arthurian Warband
 (LAW), 64
Lucas, G., 5, 21
lunar festivals, 66
Lymer, K. J., 1, 6, 30, 45

Mabinogi, 8
MacEowen, F.H., 155, 156–7,
 158–9, 162, 191
Machu Piccu, xviii
McKay, G., 40, 84
McKinley, J., 199
MacLellan, Gordon 'the toad',
 40, 217n, 222n
Maffesoli, M., 9, 10, 195
Maingueneau, D., 12–13
'Malcolm', 222n
Manchester Museum, 197
Manners, Lord Edward, 133

Maori marae, 219*n*
Marcus, G., 13, 81–2
'Mark', 119
MARS (Monuments at Risk Survey), 34
Marshalls PLC, 126, 127
Martin, G., 32
'Matt', 72
Matthews, Caitlin, 222*n*
Matthews, John, 222*n*
Mayan Elders, 187
Mayburgh henge, 31
Mayell, H., xiv
The Megalithic European (Cope), 17
Megalithic portal, 132, 166
megalithic tombs, 191
Men-an-Tol, xv, 42
Merrill, W.L., 28
Meskell, L., 4
Messenger, P.M., 28
Meyer, M., 12
Mihesuah, D.A., 28, 190
Mike Griffiths and Associates, 148
Miles, David, 1, 30, 144
Millson, R., 96
MMC Mineral Processing Ltd, 126
Modern Antiquarian group, 73, 132, 142–3
Montelius, Oscar, 219*n*
Monumenta Britannica - Templa Druidum (Aubrey), 47
Monuments at Risk Survey (MARS), 34
Morgan, P., 126
Morgan, V., 126
Morris, Nora, 87, *87*
Morris, R., 1
Moser, S., xiii
Mother Shipton, 175–6, 223*n*
Murray, T., 28
Museum of Archaeology and Anthropology, 204
Museum of London, 208
Museum of Scotland, 208
Museums Association, 197
Myers, F., 13

Naddair, Kaledon, 154–5, 156, 222*n*
NAGPRA (Native American Graves Protection and Repatriation Act 1990), 190
National Council for Civil Liberties (NCCL), 220*n*
National Geographic, xiv
National Trust
alternative discourses, 179
Avebury, 47, 48, 52, 55, 59, 61, 63, 108, 201
Avebury Visitor Research (1996-1998), 4
BBC documentary series, 118–19
Clandon Park, 219*n*
elitist tendencies, 105
preservation ethos, 182

reburial issue, 197–8, 200, 201
Rollright Stones, 176
sacred sites, 1
Stonehenge, 111, 112, 117
Native American Graves Protection and Repatriation Act 1990 (NAGPRA), 190
Native American practices, 25, 155, 157
Native Americans, reburial issue, 192
NCCL (National Council for Civil Liberties), 220*n*
Negotiating Avebury Project, 52–3
neo-shamanism, 14, 69, 194
neo-tribes, 9–11
Nether Largie South cairn, 154, 156, 160, *207*
new age travellers, 6, 32, 91, 217*n*
new travellers, xv, 7, 8–9
on archaeologists, 194
Avebury, 48, 61
heterotopias, 4
sacred sites, 32
Stonehenge, 4, 9–10, 80, 81, 91, 93, 105, 113, 115, 116, 118, 121
new-indigeneity
ancestors, 194, 195
Avebury, 54
re-enchantment, 10
Stonehenge, 121–2
Newall, R.S., 78
Ngati Ranana, 204, 219*n*
Nine Herbs Charm, 222*n*
Nine Ladies Anti-Quarry Campaign, 135
Nine Ladies Stone circle, 124, 129, 130–1, *139*
and ancestors, 138
archaeologists, 130
damage, 135, 137
Dragon bind-rune, 140
Druidry/Druids, 131, 140
excavations, 130
graffiti, 131
hand-fasting, 138
Heathenry/Heathens, 140, 141
paganism/pagans, 125, 130, 131, 138–41
rock art, *131*
as sacred site, 125, 130
signage, 137–8
visitors, 130
votive offerings, 9, 138–41
Wicca/Wiccans, 138, 140
Nine Worlds of Seid-magic (Blain), 14
Norfolk, Andy, *43*, 115–16, 177
Norfolk Archaeological unit, 44
Norse myths/sagas, 8
North, J., 96
North Yorkshire County Council (NYCC), 148, 149
North-Bates, S., 27
Northern Echo, 169

Northumberland, Duke of, 70
Norton, Graham, 11
Nosterfield quarry, 146, 147, 148, 150
Nunwick Henges, 145

Oakley, C., 59
'Obbyoss', 201
objectivity, 13, 35
The Observer, 128–9
Odin, 8
Odinshof, 177
Olding, F., 203
Olivier, A., 34
Operation Solstice, 84
Oran Mor, 157
Orr, D., 91
osteoarchaeologists, 190, 198, 202
the other, 21

Pacific art, 204
Pagan Dawn, 38, 42, 59
Pagan Federation, xvii, 87
numbers of pagans, 7
Rollright Stones, 177, 188
"Sacred Sites Charter", 43
Stonehenge, 117, 200
Thornborough Henges, 146
Pagan Warriors email list, 125
paganism/pagans, xiv–xvii, 6–9
and ancestors, 41, 189–201, 202
and archaeologists, 1–3, 39, 74–6, 173–4, 209–14
at Silbury Hill, 70–3
attachment to place and landscape, 26–7, 32, 45, 184, 191
authenticity, 11, 25–6
Avebury, xv, 1, 17–18, 48–9, 52–4, 55–69, 70–3, 124, 189, 213–14
as bricoleurs, 26
condition of heritage, 1
defined, 6–7
discourses, 38–40
diversity of, 4, 7, 22, 26, 197, 210, 213
and excavations, 30, 74, 189
as guardians, xv, 38, 42, 59, 213–14
heritage management, 1–3, 39, 63, 172, 173, 189, 191, 204–5, 209–14
Ilkley Moor, 19, 152, 164, 166–7, 170, 171–2
and indigenous communities, 6, 28
indigenous spiritual practices, 194
Kilmartin Valley, 19, 152–3, 160
leadership, 62–3, 213
and new agers, 6, 217*n*
as new indigenes, 29, 121–2
Nine Ladies Stone circle, 125, 130, 131, 138–41
numbers of, 7
pre-modern, 23

paganism/pagans – *continued*
    preservation ethos, 2
    re-enchantment, 10, 22, 26–8
    reburial issue, 189–201,
        202–7
    ritual litter, 2, 42
    and rock art, 157, 171
    Rollright Stones, 2, 4, 19,
        173–4, 176, 178–87, 189,
        213
    sacred sites, xvi–xvii, 1–6,
        27–8, 40–6, 191–2
    Seahenge, 43–4, 46, 189
    Stanton Moor, 18, 125,
        132–3, 137–41, 192
    Stonehenge, xiv, 18, 80, 89,
        91, 93, 96–100, 105,
        113–23, 124
    Thornborough Henges, 146,
        192
    tradition, 24–5
    understandings of pasts, 22–4
    see also Druidry/Druids;
        Goddess Spirituality;
        Heathenry/Heathens;
        Wicca/Wiccans
Parker-Pearson, Mike, 74–5, 200
Pasifska Styles exhibition, 204
Paxson, Diana, 181
PBLCBP (Public Bodies Liaison
    Committee for British
    Paganism), 197
Peachey, Paul, 92
Peak District National Park, 126
Peak District National Park
    Authority (PDNPA), xvii
    community vibrancy, 34
    Stanton Moor, 125–6, 127,
        128, 129, 135–6, 144
Pearson, J., 3, 6
PEBBLE (Public Bodies Liaison
    Committee for British
    Paganism), 197
Peers, L., 28, 190
Pender, Robin, 101
Pendragon, Arthur
    Avebury, 60, 62, 73
    Nine Ladies Stone circle, 131
    Stonehenge, 86, 90, 98
Pentre Ifan, xiii
Peoples Free Festival, 83
A Permeability of Boundaries?
    Conference, 45
personal-growth druids, 38–9,
    54
personal-growth pagans, 105
Pictish Druids, 154
Pictish shamanism, 154, 155
Piggott, S., 21
Pitts, Mike, 50, 145, 150
place, pagan attachments, 26–7,
    32, 45, 184, 191
Planning Inspectorate, 117
Plutarch, 77
Pollard, J., 48, 49, 218n
Pollington, S., 222n
Poltalloch, 151
Poltalloch House, 161
Pomeroy-Kellinger, M., 1, 4, 30,
    48, 49, 70

Possamai, A., 159
postmodernity, 9
Pounds, N.J.G., 99
Powell, E.A., xiv
power, and discourse, 12, 123
Power of Place, 35
Power and Taboo exhibition, 204
Prendergast, K., 96
preservation ethos, 2, 32–8
    alternative discourses, 113
    *Ancient Sacred Landscapes
        Network* (ASLAN), 38–9,
        42, 97
    archaeologists, 33, 36, 107–8
    and counter-cultural Druids,
        39–40
    heritage management, 33,
        34–5, 97, 107, 108, 113,
        182, 183
    and personal-growth Druids,
        38–9
    Rollright Stones, 179, 182,
        183
    Stanton Moor, 138
    Stonehenge, 36–7, 81, 97,
        105, 106, 113
Prior, Francis, 1
Prittlewell cemetery, 125, 196
Private Eye, 134–5
progress, 33–4
Prophets Conference (2002),
    58, 187
Prout (Slaney), Claire, 38, 43–4,
    72, 182
Pryor, F., 43, 44
psychic vandalism, 41, 183
Public Bodies Liaison
    Committee for British
    Paganism (PBLCBP), 197

Quseir al-Qadim, 5, 214

Radford, T., 190, 192
Radio 4, 133
Ramblers Association, 200
Ramilisonina, 75
Ranger, T., 21
rationalism, 26, 75, 155, 213
Rawle, Sid, 40
re-enchantment
    Kilmartin Valley, 157, 160
    neo-tribes, 10
    paganism/pagans, 10, 22,
        26–8
    shamanism, 157
    Stonehenge, 83
re-traditionalisation, 24
reburial issue, 189–208, 213
    anthropologists, 19, 189, 190
    archaeologists, 19, 189, 190,
        198, 200, 202–4, 223n
    Druidry/Druids, 194–201, 205
    English Heritage, 193, 197–8,
        200
    indigenous communities, 28,
        190, 192, 204
    National Trust, 197–8, 200,
        201
    paganism/pagans, 189–201,
        202–7

Stonehenge, 117, 196, 197–8,
    200
Red Lady of Paviland, 200
Red Lion pub, Avebury, 48, 55,
    59, *62*
Reed-Danahay, D.E., 14
repatriation issue, 28, 190, 192,
    207–8, 210, 213
research frameworks, 34
Researching Paganisms (Blain),
    14
Restall Orr, Emma, 38, 196,
    197, 202
Restoration programmes, 34
Reuters, 92
Reynolds, A., 48, 49, 218n
Richards, J., 78, 83, 91
Richardson, A., 48
Ridgeway, 191, 219n
The Right Times, 42, 182
Ring Stone, Avebury, 64
ritual fires, 2, 42, 212
    Avebury, 56
    Castlerigg stone circle, 218n
    Nine Ladies Stone circle, 124,
        131, 135
    Rollright Stones, 181, 182,
        187
    Twelve Apostles circle, 170
ritual litter, 2, 42, 212
    Avebury, 58–9
    Nine Ladies Stone circle, 141
    Rollright Stones, 182–3
    Stonehenge, 88, 90
'Robert', 68
Robins, D., 223n
rock art
    Achnabreck, 157, 160, *161*
    dating of, 218n
    Ilkley Moor, 19, 151–2, 164,
        166–7, *168*, 169–71
    Kilmartin Valley, 19, 152,
        153, 154, 157–8, 159
    Nine Ladies Stone circle, *131*
    paganism/pagans, 157, 171
    as Pictish, 222n
    shamanism, 153, 154–5, 157
Roe, N., 176
Rollo the Dane, 223n
Rollright Stones, 173–88
    *Ancient Sacred Landscapes
        Network* (ASLAN), 42, 178
    and archaeologists, 173–4
    child blessing, 179
    collaborative dialogue, 212
    damage, xv, 181–4, 187
    Druidry/Druids, 177, 178
    earth mystics, 179, 180
    English Heritage, 176, 178
    excavations, 175, 182
    folklore, 175–6, 179, 180
    Friends of the Stones, 179
    hand-fasting, 179
    Heathenry/Heathens, 178
    heritage management, 204
    King Stone, 174–5, 176, 180,
        182
    King's Men, 174, 175–6,
        178–9, 181, 182, *185*,
        188

Rollright Stones – *continued*
  Ley Hunters, 179–80
  management plan, 2, 4, 19
  multivocality, 179–81
  National Trust, 176
  paganism/pagans, 2, 4, 19,
    173–4, 176, 178–87, 189,
    213
  plurality, 179–81
  preservation ethos, 179, 182,
    183
  Prophets Conference (2002),
    58, 187
  ritual fires, 181, 182, 187
  ritual litter, 182–3
  as sacred site, 179
  summer solstice, 180
  visitors, 178–9
  votive offerings, 182
  Whispering Knights, 174,
    175, 179, 180, 182, *186*
  Wicca/Wiccans, 178
The Rollright Trust, 19, 42,
    176–9, 180, 181–2, 183,
    185, 187, 188, 214
romanticism, 7, 155, 157
Rombalds Moor, 164
Ronayne, M., 32
Rose, W., 25
Ross, C., 219*n*
Roud, S., 176
Rountree, K., 5
Royal Artillery, 83
Royal College of Surgeons, 192
Royal Flying Corps, 83
Royal Society for the Protection
  of Birds (RSPB), 147
Ruggles, C., 96
Ruickbie, L., 26
Rune-rows, 65, 219*n*
Russell, Phil *see* Hope, Wally

Sacred Brigantia, 146, 149
sacred sites, 28–32
  archaeologists, xvi, 31, 209
  Avebury, 1, 22, 30, 48, 52–4,
    67–9, 117
  Druidry/Druids, 30–1
  Goddess Spirituality, 31, 218*n*
  Heathenry/Heathens, 30–1
  heritage management, xvi,
    1–3, 30, 31
  as heterotopic, 4, 32
  indigenous communities, 28,
    31
  Nine Ladies Stone circle,
    125–30
  paganism/pagans, xvi–xvii,
    1–6, 27–8, 40–6, 191–2
  re-enchantment, 27–8
  and reburial issue, 205–6
  Stanton Moor, 125, 130, 138
  Stonehenge, 22, 97–100,
    113–23
  Thornborough Henges,
    149–50
  Wicca/Wiccans, 31
'Sacred Sites Charter', 42, *43*, 58
Sacred Sites project, xvi–xviii, 6,
    10

sacredness, constituted within
  discourse, 209–10
Said, E., 21
Salisbury Cathedral, 97, 98–9
Salisbury District Council, 106,
    112
Salisbury Journal, 91, 92
the Sanctuary, 47, 51
Sardar, Z., 22
sarsens
  Avebury, 49, 50, 56
  Stonehenge, 83, 100, 101
Satanism, 217–18*n*
Save Our Sacred Sites, 38–9, 42,
    97
Schadla-Hall, T., 33
Schama, Simon, 21
Schieffelin, E., 156
Scottishness, xiii, xiv
Seabourne, T.
  contemporary ritual activity,
    36
  dialogue, 209
  Nine Ladies Stone circle, 124,
    130
  Peak District, 126, 133
Seahenge
  Druidry/Druids, 44, 211
  English Heritage, 43–4, 214
  excavations, 43–4, 189, 214
  paganism/pagans, 43–4, 46,
    189
  as sacred site, 1
  Time Team, 1, 44, 211
Sebastion, Tim, 11, 67, 93, 96,
    102, 221*n*
Secular Order of Druids (SOD),
    38, 64, 93
Sedona, 4, 32
seidr-shamanism, 14, 181
Semple, S., 33
Shallcrass, Philip "Greywolf"
  Avebury, 47
  'Awen', 218*n*
  Celtic shamanism, 222*n*
  Druid rituals, 41
  new agers, 6
  reburial issue, 194, 197–8,
    199–200, *199*
shamanic tourism, 157–62
shamanism, 10, 154–60, 221–3*n*
  and animism, 217*n*
  authenticity, 157
  Celtic, 154, 157, 158, 160,
    222*n*
  Druidry/Druids, 154, 217*n*
  fluidity of practices, 24
  indigenous spiritual practices,
    194
  Kilmartin Valley, 153, 155–60
  Pictish, 154, 155
  rock art, 153, 154–5, 157
  seidr, 14, 181
Shaman's Drum, 155, 156, 158
Shamans/neoShamans (Wallis),
    14
Sheffield Hallam Human Rights
  Centre, xvii, 6
Shipton, Mother, 175–6, 223*n*
Silbaby, 53

Silbury Glory, 219*n*
Silbury Hill, 17, 47, 49, 51,
    70–3, 213, 219*n*
Silbury Hole, 17, 70–3, 213
Simpson, J., 176
Site of Special Scientific Interest
  (SSSI), 71, 164
Sköldberg, K., 13
Slaney (Prout), Claire, 38, 43–4,
    72, 182
Smiles, S., xiii
Smith, A., 25
Smith, C.C., 164–5
Smith, D.E., 12
Smith, K., 133
Smith, L.T., 3, 29, 190
Smith, Richard, 92
social change, 21–2
Social Sciences and Humanities
  Research Council of
  Canada, 6
SOD (Secular Order of Druids),
    38, 64, 93
Soja, E., 4, 32
solar festivals, 66
  see also Stonehenge
South Australian Aboriginal
  Heritage Act, 190
'Sparky', 138
Stancliffe Stone, 127, 128
Stanton Lees Action Group,
    127, 143
Stanton Moor, 125–44, 173
  Arbor Law Henge, 132–3, *132*
  and archaeologists, 214–15
  CPRE, 125, 127, 143, 144
  Dove Holes Henge, 132
  excavations, 214–15
  heritage management, 18,
    125, 204
  King Stone, 131
  paganism/pagans, 18, 125,
    132–3, 137–41, 192
  PDNPA, 125–6, 127, 128,
    129, 135–6, 144
  preservation ethos, 138
  protesters, 130, 133–7, 141–4
  as sacred site, 125, 130, 138
  threat of quarrying, 18, 123,
    125–9, 133–7, 143–4,
    151
  visitors, 130
  votive offerings, 9, 132,
    138–41
Stanton Quarries Ltd., 127
Star newspaper, 83
Starhawk, 187
State of the Historic Environment,
    35
Steele, J., 202
Stone, C.J., 62, 84, 86
Stone e-list, 132
Stone, P., 79
Stonehenge, 77–123
  alternative archaeologists,
    113
  alternative discourses, 79–80,
    113–21
  as an English experience,
    108–9

Stonehenge – *continued*
and ancestors, 79, 80, 95, 97, 113, 121
animism, 121–3
appeal to contemporary culture, 108
archaeological evidence, 81
and archaeologists, 79, 107–8, 118
autumn equinox, 62, 82
the Avenue, 77, 79, 105, 110, 114
'battle of the beanfield', xv, 39, 84, 91
carrying capacity, 35
child blessing, 116, 121
collaborative dialogue, 212
and counter-cultural druids, 39–40
CPRE, 111, 117, 200
the Cursus, 79, 106
damage, xvi, 36–7, 81, 90, 97, 100, 104, 105
discourses, 77–82, 113–21
Druidry/Druids, 8, 39–40, 41, 83, 91, 93, 96–7, 98, 113, 117, 121
earth mystics, 113
excavations, 36, 81, 100, 105
free-festivalers, 80, 113, 114
future proposals, 110–12, 113–17, 220–1*n*
graffiti, 81, 115
Grand Eisteddfod suggestion, 221*n*
Heathenry/Heathens, 96
heritage management, 18, 78–9, 107, 108, 124, 204
as icon of Britishness/ Englishness, xiii
as icon of hippy counterculture, 39–40
managed open access, xiv, xv, 2–3, 9, 18, 62, 82–92, 93, 96–7, 100, 103, 104, 105, 117–18, 173
media attention, 91–2
meeting place of tribes, 9–10
Mesolithic pits, 191
National Trust, 111, 112, 117
New King Barrows, 103
new travellers, 4, 9–10, 80, 81, 91, 93, 105, 113, 115, 116, 118, 121
Old King Barrow Ridge, 79
pagan hand-fasting, 116, 121
paganism/pagans, xiv, 18, 80, 89, 91, 93, 96–100, 105, 113–23, 124
as a palimpsest, 36, 81
partying, 80, 88–90, 98–100
Peace Stewards, 90
preservation ethos, 36–7, 81, 97, 105, 106, 113
Prophets Conference (2002), 58, 187
re-enchantment, 83
re-presentation of, xiv
reburial issue, 117, 196, 197–8, 200

religious significance, 29
ritual litter, 88, 90
road proposals, 110–11, 112, 117
as sacred site, 22, 97–100, 113–23
sarsens, 83, 100, 101
spirituality, 88–90
spring equinox, 62, 82
Stone circle access visits, 104, 113
stone standing, 100–4
summer solstice, xiv, xv, xvi, 9, 39, 62, 82, 84–92, 93–5, 99, 102–3, 105, 113–14, 173, 214
tourists, 79, 108–9, 114–15
visitor facilities, xiv, 37, 106–7, 110, 111, 112, 117, 220*n*
visitors, 79, 104–7, 108–10, 114–16, 220–1*n*
visual engagement, 37–8, 106–7
Wicca/Wiccans, 117
winter solstice, 62, 82, 96–7, 98
as World Heritage Site (WHS), 47, 78, 108, 112
Stonehenge Alliance, 117
Stonehenge Free Festival, 40, 83–4, 89, 90, 93, 99, 116
Stonehenge Inquiry (2004), 117
Stonehenge Peace Process, 30, 86, 100
Stonehenge Project, xiv, 77, 78–9, 107, 110, 196, 198, 220*n*
Stonehenge Round Table, 18, 87, 103, 120–1, 213
Grand Eisteddfod, 221*n*
sacredness, 100
summer solstice managed access, 30, 173, 214
Stonehenge World Heritage Site Management Plan, 12, 79, 107, 110, 113, 116, 215
StonehengePeace email list, 18, 86, 103, 119, 120
Strathern, Marilyn, 223*n*
Stukeley, William
Avebury, 49, 50
Druidry/Druids, 11, 212
Rollright Stones, 174
Stonehenge, 77, 78, 96, 121
subjectivity, 13
The Sun, 91
sustainability, 35
Swale and Ure Washlands project, 147
Swidler, N., 3, 28, 190, 211
synaesthesia, 171

Taj Mahal, 108
taonga, 204
Tara, hill of, 17, 125
Tarmac, 18, 145, 146–7
'Tash', 83
Taussig, M., 24

television
archaeology and history programmes, xiii, xvii, 21
see also Restoration programmes; *Time Team*
Temple Wood circles, 153, *153*
Theoretical Archaeology Group, 100
Thingvellir, *29*
Thomas, J., 32, 37, 83, 197, 209
Thomsen, Christian Jürgensen, 219*n*
Thomson, Ian, 180
Thornborough Henge Advisory Group, 149, 212
Thornborough Henges, 144–50, 191
appropriateness of behaviour, 103
archaeology, 148–9
collaborative dialogue, 212
damage, 149
Druidry/Druids, 146, 149
English Heritage, 18, 144, 147, 148
excavations, 215
hand-fasting, 146
Heathenry/Heathens, 146
nature reserves, 147
paganism/pagans, 146, 192
as sacred site, 149–50
threat of quarrying, 18, 123, 125, 144–8, 151
tourism, 147
see also Friends of Thornborough Henges
Thornborough Moor, 147
Thorpe, N., 192
Tilley, C., 209
time, 45–6
Time Fliers, 146
Time Team, 1, 21, 44, 211
The Times, 91, 92, 194
Timewatch, 144, 146
Timms, S., 148
'tinsel', 142
Toop, N., 148
topophilia, 27
tourism *see* heritage tourism
tradition
continuity of, 21
paganism/pagans, 24–5
shamanism, 157
Trevarthen, Geo, 160, 222*n*
tribes, 9–11
truth claims, 157
Tuan, Yi-Fu, 27
Tungus culture, 158
Turner, J.M.W., xiv
Twelve Apostles circle, xv, 19, 169, 170
Tyr, 23

Ucko, P.J., 49, 203–4
UFOlogy, 166, 180
Uluru, xviii
UNESCO World Heritage Convention, 47–8

United States
  indigenous articulations of
    sacred site, 28
  reburial issue, 189–90, 204
Urry, J., 3, 22
vandalism, xv–xvi, 42, 209
  Avebury, 55
  Ilkley Moor, 152, 166,
    169–70, 172
  Kilmartin Valley, 163
  Rollright Stones, 181–2, 183
Vasagar, Jeevan, 92
Verbeia, 170
Viziondanz, Brian, 102, 118,
  119–21
votive offerings, 2, 8, 42
  Avebury, 56–8, 56, 64, 75
  Badger Stone, 170–1
  Doll Tor circle, 10, 140
  Nine Ladies Stone circle, 9,
    138–41
  Rollright Stones, 182
  Stanton Moor, 9, 132, 138–41

Waden Hill, 219n
Wainwright, G., 116
Wallis, Dr Robert J.
  alternative archaeology, 4
  ancestors and bloodlines, 156
  authenticity, 54
  Avebury, 49, 54
  Celtic ancestry, 223n
  contemporary ritual activity,
    36
  conversations with Gyrus,
    170
  entheogens, 220n, 222n
  Kennewick Man, 192
  neo-shamanism, 14
  new-indigeneity, 54
  paganism/pagans, 3, 38
  A Permeability of Boundaries?
    Conference, 45

public performances of
  paganism, 67
re-enchantment, 27
reburial issue, 195, 202,
  223n
researcher status, 14, 16
rock art, 159
Rollright Stones, 186, 188
sacred sites, 1, 30, 98
Sacred Sites project, xvi, 2, 6
shamanism, 156, 160, 221n,
  222n, 223n
Shamans/neoShamans, 14
Stonehenge, 84, 88
visual engagement, 37
Watkins, J., 3, 29, 190
Watson, Aaron, 75
Webb, John, 78
Weber, M., 26
Weller, P., 7
Welsh National Heritage
  (CADW), 1
Welshness, xiii
Wemyss Bay, 222n
Wessex Archaeology, 36, 81,
  199
West Kennet Avenue, xv, 51,
  55
West Kennet Long Barrow, 47,
  51
  chalk art, 57
  chanting, 74, 75
  Druidry/Druids, 66
  fire damage, 56, 223–4n
  public performances of
    paganism, 68
  reburial issue, 206–7
  vandalism, 55
  votive offerings, 56–8, 56
  Wicca/Wiccans, 66
West Yorkshire Archaeology
  Service, 169
Western Daily Press, 63, 91, 197

Whispering Knights, Rollright
  Stones, 174, 175, 179, 180,
  182, 186
White Wells' cottage, 164
Whittle, A., 48, 50, 218n
Wicca/Wiccans, xiv, 7
  adoption of pentangle, 221n
  ancient places as temples,
    183
  athame (ritual knife), 8
  authenticity, 11
  Avebury, 48, 49, 66
  hand-fasting, 66
  harm principle, 212
  Nine Ladies Stone circle, 138,
    140
  rites in private, 8
  Rollright Stones, 178
  sacred sites, 31
  Stonehenge, 117
Williams, H., 33
Willy Hall's Wood Stone, xv,
  166, 168, 169
Wilson, R.C., 75, 155
Wilson, T., 174
Windmill Hill, 47, 51
Winer, M., 49
witchcraft, 11
Wodak, R., 12
Woden, 68, 75, 181
Wood, Chris, 44
Wood and Water magazine, 181
Woodford Valley, 199, 199
Woodhenge, 79, 114
World Archaeological Council,
  192
Worthington, Andy, 83, 84, 93,
  99, 220n

York, M., 217n

Zil, King, 70
Zimmerman, L.J., 28, 190